Paul Weingartner

Nature's Teleological Order and God's Providence

Philosophische Analyse / Philosophical Analysis

Herausgegeben von/Edited by
Herbert Hochberg, Rafael Hüntelmann,
Christian Kanzian, Richard Schantz, Erwin Tegtmeier

Volume / Band 61

Paul Weingartner

Nature's Teleological Order and God's Providence

Are they compatible with chance, free will, and evil?

DE GRUYTER

ISBN 978-1-61451-891-4
e-ISBN (PDF) 978-1-61451-886-0
e-ISBN (EPUB) 978-1-61451-950-8
ISSN 2198-2066

Library of Congress Cataloging-in-Publication Data
A CIP catalog record for this book has been applied for at the Library of Congress.

Bibliographic information published by the Deutsche Nationalbibliothek
The Deutsche Nationalbibliothek lists this publication in the Deutsche Nationalbibliografie; detailed bibliographic data are available on the Internet at http://dnb.dnb.de.

Printing: CPI books GmbH, Leck
♾ Printed on acid-free paper
Printed in Germany

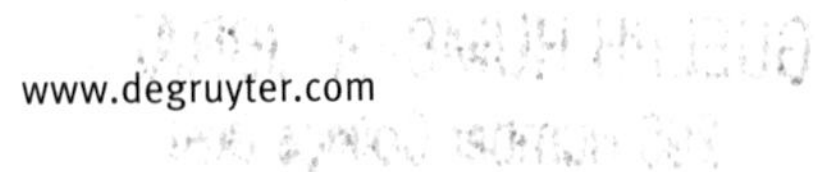

www.degruyter.com

Contents

Preface

The purpose of this book is to show that nature's order and God's providence are compatible with chance, free will and evil. In particular, it is shown in detail that there is both order and chance in nature; where order and chance come in different types, weaker ones and stronger ones. This holds for both non-living and for living systems. Moreover, it is shown that there is teleological order in both non-living and living systems.

Instead of the expression "order" one could, in principle, also use "design" and use the same definitions for different levels of design as they were used for different levels of order. But there is a strong reason for not doing so. The expression "design" is abused to such a high degree in non-scientific and scientific literature that it is rather hopeless that the respective definitions could be understood in a serious way and without prejudices. Therefore the expression "design" will not be used in this book.

It should be noted from the beginning that this book is not a book on the existence of God. For this topic, see Swinburne (1991) and Weingartner (2010c), where the five ways of Thomas Aquinas are formulated in First Order Predicate Logic. This book presupposes the existence of God as the creator of the universe and as an omniscient almighty and benevolent personal being (cf. 1.3.3 below).

The first chapter shows that providence is possible if there is order and teleological order in this universe. The latter is then shown in chapters 1–8. The second and third chapter defend that providence can be attributed to God and that it is concerned with creatures. In chapter 5, different types of order are defined, and it is established that they are present in non-living things. Moreover, it is shown that a certain type of teleological order defined by decreasing entropy is also present in non-living things. As a complementation to that, chapter 6 shows that chance and randomness are also present in non-living things; and that there is no conflict that both order and chance coexist in the same physical or chemical system. Chapter 7 deals with order in living things. Following a definition of *living system* (biosystem), it is shown that there is teleological and goal directed order in living things (biosystems); moreover, values and goals can be defined and found in living things.

In chapter 9, it is shown that both order and chance are compatible with God's providence. Chapter 10 gives a differentiated definition of God's providence by listing several necessary conditions in the definiens. The first conditions are that

God's providence includes all events and processes of the universe, be they omnitemporal or at some time interval.

This is defended in chapter 10. A further condition, dealt with in chapter 11, is that everything that comes under God's providence is known by God. Other necessary conditions for states of affairs that belong to God's providence are that he wills or permits them (ch.12), that he causes them or entrusts creatures to cause them (ch.13), that he directs them towards some goal or integrates them into a network of goals (ch. 14).

The last two chapters (15 and 16) deal with the problem of compatibility of God's providence with free will and evil. In chapter 15, definitions of free will and free will decision are given and it is shown that both human free will and free will decision are compatible with God's providence. Moreover, it is shown that certain results of neuro-science do not rule out the possibility of free will decision; and further that some of the claims of some neuro-scientists contain serious confusions concerning determinism and indeterminism. Chapter 16 deals with the problem of evil. First, different types of evil, including moral evil, are distinguished. It is stressed that there are a lot of *necessary evils* in the sense that they are necessary for achieving a higher good. Finally, it is shown that providence is compatible with necessary evil and with moral evil. The difficult problem of theodicy, especially with respect to evil uncontrollable by humans, is discussed, and three possible explanations are offered.

Acknowledgments: I want to thank Edgar Morscher, Albert Anglberger and Silvia Haring for valuable suggestions concerning improvements. Moreover, my thanks go to Nora Sümegi and Christian Feldbacher for typing and layout and to Kathryn Bishop for improving my English style.

I would like to dedicate this book to Silvia Haring. The many valuable discussions with her stimulated the chapters of this book.

Salzburg, November 3, 2012 Paul Weingartner

1 Whether there can be providence at all?

1.1 Arguments Contra

1.1.1 First argument

Providence – as it is usually understood – is God's plan by which the development of things is ordered towards their ends. But as Monod says, the development of things is not based on order but on chance and blind freedom:

> "Chance alone is the source of every innovation, of all creation in the biosphere. Pure chance, absolutely free, but blind, is at the very root of the stupendous edifice of evolution."[1]

Therefore there cannot be providence at all.

1.1.2 Second argument

If by providence things are ordered towards their ends then providence implies the existence of ends in things. But only creatures with intellect and will, i.e. human beings can have ends. Accordingly Moses Maimonides says that in contradistinction to all other corruptible things only men are subject to providence.[2]

Therefore there cannot be providence except concerning human beings.

1.1.3 Third argument

That there is chance in many domains of the universe is a brute fact. Examples are the movements of the atoms in a gas (i.e. thermodynamic processes) or the emittance of elementary particles (i.e. processes of radiation), further mutations, DNA/RNA-recombinations ... etc. But chance seems to exclude order and directedness towards an end. Now order and directedness towards an end are necessary conditions for providence.

Therefore there cannot be universal providence.

1 Monod (1972) p.110.

2 Moses Maimonides (1856–66) part 3, ch.17.

1.2 Argument Pro

If God is the creator of the world (universe) and if he is good then he will care about his creation and creatures. But to care about his creation and creatures involves a plan for guiding and helping them towards their ends.

Therefore if God is the creator of the world (universe) and if he is good then there can be providence.

1.3 Proposed Answer

1.3.1 Definition of 'providence'

By God's 'Providence' we understand God's plan together with its execution by which the change and development of things is ordered and directed towards their ends. In other words: ... by which there is order and teleological order in things. To show that providence is possible we do not need factuality of the definition above; we need to assume only its possibility. Then it follows that: possibly: if there is providence there is ordered change and development and directedness towards ends and conversely: possibly: if there is ordered change and development and directedness towards ends then there is providence. And from the latter it follows by the principles of Modal Logic: if there is ordered change and development and directedness towards ends, i.e. order and teleological order, then possibly there is providence. But it will be shown in chapters 4, 5 and 7 below that there is ordered change and development among things of this world (universe) and directedness towards their ends.

Therefore it is possible that there is providence. This argument can be formulated in a more precise way as follows:

Df 1.1. The state of affairs p belongs to God's Providence (abbreviated as $Prov(p)$) iff p belongs to God's plan ($PL(p)$) or p belongs to God's execution of his plan ($EC(p)$).
In symbols: $Prov(p) \leftrightarrow (PL(p) \vee EC(p))$

Df 1.2. The state of affairs p belongs to God's plan (abbreviated as $PL(p)$) iff p belongs to the state of affairs which describe the order in change and in the de-

velopment of things (abbreviated as $Ord(p)$ i.e. their order) and p belongs to the states of affairs which describe the directedness of the things towards their ends (abbreviated as $TO(p)$ i.e. their teleological order).
In symbols: $PL(p) \leftrightarrow (Ord(p) \wedge TO(p))$

1.3.2 Possibility of Providence

We assume the definitions now only as possible:

1. $\Diamond[Prov(p) \leftrightarrow (PL(p) \vee EC(p))]$
2. $\Diamond[PL(p) \leftrightarrow (Ord(p) \wedge TO(p))]$

From these it follows with the help of modus ponens $[\Diamond A \wedge A \Rightarrow B] \Rightarrow \Diamond B$:

3. $\Diamond[PL(p) \rightarrow Prov(p)]$ from 1.
4. $\Diamond[(Ord(p) \wedge TO(p)) \rightarrow PL(p)]$ from 2.

And from these it follows by the principles of Modal Logic $\Diamond(A \rightarrow B) \rightarrow (\Diamond A \rightarrow \Diamond B)$; $(\Diamond A \rightarrow \Diamond B) \rightarrow (A \rightarrow \Diamond B)$:

5. $\Diamond PL(p) \rightarrow \Diamond Prov(p)$ from 3.
6. $(Ord(p) \wedge TO(p)) \rightarrow \Diamond PL(p)$ from 4.

And therefore also:

7. $(Ord(p) \wedge TO(p)) \rightarrow \Diamond Prov(p)$ from 6 and 5.

From the results then it follows that it is possible that there is providence provided there is order (Ord) and teleological order (TO). This is then an answer to question 1.: Can there be providence? That there is order and teleological order in both non-living and living things will be established in chs. 4., 5. and 7. below.

1.3.3 Remark on terminology

Terminology and terminological problems should not be overestimated. However, terminology should be kept flexible to provide a maximum of transparency and unambiguous understanding. To keep arguments transparent and simple, simple terminology is preferable over a more sophisticated one if it is unambiguous and sufficiently clear. Accordingly, the proof for the possibility of providence was symbolized in a most simple way: '$Prov(p)$', '$Pl(p)$', '$EC(p)$' were used respectively for 'the state of affairs p belongs to God's providence' '… to God's plan', '… to God's execution of his plan'. Similarly with '$Ord(p)$' and '$TO(p)$'. The simple terminology used here does not affect the proof or its validity. We could instead use a more sophisticated terminology like the one used in chapter 10. In this case we would interpret 'the state of affairs p belongs to God's providence' as 'the state of affairs p is an element of the theorems (i.e. true propositions corresponding to obtaining states of affairs) of God's providence' and symbolize this as: $p \in Tg's(Prov)$ and the other propositions accordingly as: $p \in Tg's(Pl)$, $p \in Tg's(EC)$. Definitions Df 1.1 and Df 1.2 can then be written as:

Df 1.3. $p \in Tg's(Prov) \leftrightarrow p \in Tg's(Pl) \vee p \in Tg's(EC)$

Df 1.4. $p \in Tg's(Pl) \leftrightarrow p \in T(Ord) \wedge p \in T(TO)$

Here '$p \in T(Ord)$' and '$p \in T(TO)$' stand for 'p is an element of the theorems which describe the order in change and in the development of things' and 'p is an element of the theorems which describe the directedness of the things towards their end'.

There is no essential difference, i.e. no difference concerning validity, if the proof (in 1.3.2) is carried out with this more sophisticated terminology which is used in chapter 10.

One difference in the terminology used in 1.3.3 compared to that in 1.3.2 is that expressions like '$p \in Tg's(Prov)$' contain the undefined constant 'g' for 'God'. This is also the case with similar expressions used in ch.10. In order to avoid respective difficulties, we shall introduce this constant by the definition below.

We agree with Thomas Aquinas that we are not able to give a *real definition* of God in this life. According to Aristotle and Thomas Aquinas, a *real definition* is one in which the essence of something is defined. Thus Aristotle's definition of life (or living system) as possessing nutrition, growth and propagation is a *real definition*, since it tells us the three components of the essence of living things. In this sense, we cannot give a definition of God which tells us his complete essence according to Thomas Aquinas. However, we can certainly give some important characterisations even though they do not belong to the essence of God. The most important one for us, since it is the one accessible to us, is that he is the creator of the universe. This property of God does not belong to his essence, because creation is an action of his free will and does not necessarily follow from his essence and existence. On the other hand, the following properties seem to be at least partially belonging to his essence: being a person, being omniscient, omnipotent and all-good. Therefore we might formulate the following definition, while being aware that it is not a definition of his complete essence:

$$x = g \leftrightarrow x \text{ is the creator of the universe and } x \text{ is a person and } x \text{ is omniscient and } x \text{ is omnipotent and } x \text{ is allgood}$$

That this definition is not contradictory concerning the concept of omniscience I tried to show in my Weingartner (2008a).

1.3.4 Result of chapter 1

The result of chapter 1 can be formulated in the following theorem:

T 1.1. *It is possible that there is providence, provided that there is order and teleological order in non-living and in living things.*

It should be added that the above definitions Df 1.1 and Df 1.2 are still incomplete, since they should include several additional components concerning God's knowledge and God's will: If p belongs to God's providence then p is known by God (i.e. God knows that p is the case or that p will be the case) and p is either willed or is permitted by God (i.e. it is not the case that God wills that $not\text{-}p$) and p is caused by God or by his creatures. Cf. ch. 10. The further point whether p then belongs just to God's creation will be dealt with in ch. 3.

1.4 Answer to the Objections

1.4.1 (to 1.1.1)

The passage of Monod contains two claims:

1. The first is that there is such a "thing" as "chance alone", "pure chance", "absolute and free chance" and "blind chance". Little experience with scientific concepts suspects here a rather naive exaggerated and popularized use of terminology. As the definitions of different kinds of chance and randomness show, chance and randomness can only be defined relative to a certain

type of order or structure or law.[3] Thus a state of affairs may be called chance-like or random if it can change without changing a dynamical or a statistical law. Or a series may be called random if there is no law-like code, which can produce the series.[4] And a biological system may be called chance-like or random if it does not have a certain structure or order. Therefore expressions like "chance alone", "pure chance", "absolutely free chance", "blind chance" are scientifically rather useless.

2. The second claim involved in the passage of Monod is what has been called the "chance hypothesis".[5] It says that life or more specifically the DNA-molecule of the first organism emerged by a purely random process. That such a claim cannot be correct has been shown by different authors[6] and will be discussed in more detail in section 8.3.2 below. Since Monod's claim as a premise in 1.1.1 is either useless or wrong the conclusion of this argument is not proved.

1.4.2 (to 1.1.2)

End or *goal* can be understood in a twofold way. They can, in the first sense, belong to the intellect and will of a rational being. And in this sense it is correct to say that only human beings (or more generally: rational beings) can have ends and goals. However in a second sense an end or goal can be understood as the final state of a developing thing or process. Thus for example the final state of a school-house with all its functions can be viewed as the end or goal with respect to its earlier carcass. And although this end or goal belongs to the plan in the intellect and will of the master builder according to the first sense, it is caused by the final work of the execution of his plan to become the end or goal of the school-house (according to the second sense). In this second sense already Aristotle understood the final crystal-structure as being the goal (end) of the crystalline growth or the full-grown frog as the goal w.r.t. earlier stages like that of a tadpole. In this sec-

3 See Weingartner (2009a) where 15 definitions of different kinds of chance are given beginning from the domains of arithmetic and geometry to those of biology. See also Weingartner (2010b) and chs. 5. and 6. below.

4 According to Kolmogorov and Chaitin.

5 See for example Küppers (1990) ch.6.

6 See for example Stegmüller (1975) p.407ff., Yockey (1977), Ayala (1978), Ayala (2010), Küppers (1990) ch.6, Weingartner (2010b).

ond sense – opposite to Maimonides – corruptible things can have ends or goals. A detailed elaboration of this second sense is contained in ch. 5 below. Just as there is no hindrance that the master builder has a plan containing the goal of the school-house there is no hindrance that God has a plan containing the goal of his creatures; even if his plan may be different concerning creatures endowed with intellect and free will on the one hand and those not endowed with it on the other (see below ch. 7). From these considerations it follows that the conclusion of the argument 1.1.2 is not correct.

1.4.3 (to 1.1.3)

It is correct that there is chance in many domains (see below ch. 6). But as will become clear there, both chance and randomness on the one hand and law and order on the other coexist in the same physical, chemical or biological system; and this is not an exception but it is the normal case.

Moreover, chance and randomness can only be defined relative to law and order. Thus although a sequence like the DNA or the RNA cannot be random and law-like w.r.t. the same property or aspect it can be random w.r.t. property $P1$ and not random (or law-like) w.r.t. property $P2$. Thus a recombination mistake (a single exchange of a letter of the DNA) is not random concerning the place where it occurs in the DNA-sequence, nor is it random w.r.t. its physico-chemical emergence (ruled by laws); but it is random w.r.t. a benefit for the living system.

Therefore the conclusion of the argument 1.1.3 is not proved and there is no hindrance for a universal providence.

2 Whether providence can be attributed to God?

2.1 Arguments Contra

2.1.1 First argument

If time is time of this world (universe) and God is outside time, then God is not time-dependent. But providence is usually understood as the plan for the timely development of things ordered towards an end. Now it can be strongly defended that time is time of this world and that God is outside time[1].

Therefore it does not seem that providence can be attributed to God.

2.1.2 Second argument

The rule, which orders the changeable things towards an end, is called providence. But God is not changeable.

Therefore providence cannot be attributed to God.

2.2 Argument Pro

Every rational being plans his (her) free actions. Since God is a rational being in a most perfect sense and since his creation of the universe is a free action, we have to assume that he possesses a plan for his creation. But such a plan for his creation is called providence.

Therefore providence can be attributed to God.

1 That time is time of this world is the view of the Special and the General Theory of Relativity which are both very well confirmed. For a defence that God is "outside" the time of this world cf. Weingartner (2008a) ch. 3 and ch. 8.

2.3 Proposed Answer

It is here assumed that God is the creator of this world (of this universe). As has been pointed out in the introduction, this investigation is not devoted to a discussion of the many reasons for this assumption.. However several consequences of this assumption will be carefully investigated in this study.

One consequence is the one concerning us here: If God is the creator of the universe then providence must be attributed to God. Why this follows can be substantiated thus:

If God is the creator of the universe he must have knowledge about the universe. And moreover if he is omniscient[2] he must have complete knowledge about the universe. If God is the creator of the universe he must have will concerning the universe; not only his free will to create it but also the will concerning the many different details and properties of the universe. And since every action of willing has an intention towards some goal, God's will concerning creation has certain goals.

Now every rational being that is acting with his knowledge and his will towards goals possesses a plan for his actions. In an analogous way we have to say that God possesses a plan for his creation, not only that it comes to existence and not only as a whole but also for its development and also for the details. And insofar as his will has certain goals, his plan incorporates his will and knowledge concerning creation with which he directs his creation and creatures to certain goals. This plan according to which God guides and directs his creation and creatures to certain goals is called *providence*. Therefore it is necessary to attribute providence to God under the assumption that he has created the world (universe).

However that God acts according to his plan concerning the development and evolution of the universe does not mean that he executes everything himself. Likewise a king, although he possesses a plan for his government, delegates many things concerning the execution of the plan to his servants. Thus the plan (providence) of God concerning the universe is solely his own work. Concerning the execution of the plan however he delegates many things to his creatures by giving them the power of causality and higher abilities to contribute respectively to the development and evolution of the universe.[3]

---

2 Cf. Aquinas (1981), I, 14. Weingartner (2008a)

3 Cf. Aquinas (1981) I, 22, 3. and Aquinas (1954) qu.5.

2.3.1 Result of chapter 2

Thus we arrive at the following conclusion for this chapter:

T 2.1. *Under the assumption that God has created the world (universe) God has providence (providence is attributed to God).*

Theorem 2.1 can be proved along the justification given above:

1. $CR(g) \rightarrow [CKU(g) \wedge DWU(g)]$
2. $[CKU(g) \wedge DWU(g)] \rightarrow DGU(g)$

Premise 2. follows as an instance from the fact that every action of willing has an intention towards some goal.

3. $[CKU(g) \wedge DGU(g)] \rightarrow PLU(g)$

Premise 3. follows as an instance from the fact that everyone having knowledge and detailed goals about some domain must also have a plan about it.

4. $PLU(g) \rightarrow Prov(g)$

Premise 4. follows from the definition Df 1.1 (ch.1)

5. $CR(g) \rightarrow Prov(g)$

Conclusion 5. follows from premises 1.–4.

$CR(g)$ … God is the creator of the universe

$CKU(g)$ … God has complete knowledge of the universe (including its parts)

$DWU(g)$ … God has detailed will concerning the universe (and concerning its parts)

$DGU(g)$ … God has detailed goals concerning the universe (and concerning its parts)

$PLU(g)$ … God has a plan of the universe (including its parts)

$Prov(g)$ … God has providence (providence is attributed to God)

2.4 Answer to the Objections

2.4.1 (to 2.1.1)

Although it is correct to say that time is the time of this world (universe) and God is not time-dependent, providence can still be attributed to him. Because from possessing plan (providence) and knowledge about the timely development of things ordered towards an end it does not follow that the plan or the knowledge would be in time or change in time. Since from "God knows (plans) that thing x develops from being in state S_1 at t_1 to being in state S_2 in t_2 "(where t_1 and t_2 *refers* to a reference system of this universe) it does not follow that God would know and plan this also at a certain time (which one?). In other words it is a logical fallacy to conclude from "God knows that p happens at t" (symbolically: gKp_t) the sentence "God knows at t that p happens at t" (symbolically: gK_tp_t). If God is outside time then "God knows at t ..." does not make sense. What kind of t (time) we might ask, since we assumed that time is time of a reference system of this world (universe). Then it does not make sense to say God knows something at New York time or at Moscow time. It is clear from this consideration then that God's plan (providence) and knowledge can be outside time although it concerns things and events of creation (of the universe) which are in time and which are changing in time.

Therefore the conclusion of objection 2.11 is not proved and providence can be attributed to God.

2.4.2 (to 2.1.2)

From the fact that a rule orders changeable things it does not follow that the rule itself would change. For example the fundamental dynamical laws of physics like Newton's laws, Maxwell's laws or Einstein's laws of Special or General Relativity, rule and govern the change and the time development of physical systems. But the laws themselves don't change. Their space-time invariance is one of the most important properties of such fundamental laws of nature.[4] In the same way, God

4 For space-time invariance of laws of nature cf. Weinberg (1987) and Mittelstaedt and Weingartner (2005) ch. 6. If some fundamental constants of nature like G (gravitational constant) or h (Planck's constant) would change in time, then since they enter fundamental laws, also laws of

need not be changeable if changeable things are ruled and ordered by his plan, which is called providence.

nature would change in time. So far no such deviation in constants of nature has been discovered in despite of the most accurate measurements. But if it would turn out that the fundamental laws of nature are not anymore strictly time invariant they still would be stable enough – because of the extremely small change – to describe and explain nature.

3 Whether providence is concerned with creation?

3.1 Arguments Contra

3.1.1 First argument

Providence is concerned with the order of things. Now any order is ruled by laws of mathematics and logic. But laws of mathematics and logic do not seem to belong to creation since they are necessary in an absolute sense whereas things of creation are contingent.

Therefore providence seems to be concerned with laws of mathematics and logic but not with creation.

3.1.2 Second argument

All created things are changeable. But the rule, which orders the things, which are changeable, must not change itself. Now what is called providence is the rule, which orders the changeable things towards an end.

Therefore providence is concerned with something unchangeable, but not with (changeable) created things.

3.1.3 Third argument

God's knowledge extends to himself, to logic and mathematics and to his creation; since he knows everything about himself, about logic and mathematics and about his creation and creatures. But God's providence implies God's knowledge (as a necessary condition) because he has to know about everything that he orders towards its end by his providence. Thus it seems that also God's providence extends to himself, to logic and mathematics and to his creation.

Consequently providence is concerned not properly with creation but inclusively with creation.

3.2 Argument Pro

Providence is neither concerned with God nor with logic or mathematics. It is not concerned with logic or mathematics, because providence implies care and there cannot be care about logic and mathematics, viz. about the necessary principles of logic and mathematics.

Therefore providence is concerned with creation.

3.3 Proposed Answer

Providence – as it is usually understood – is the plan of God by which he orders things towards their ends. Now God cannot order himself towards an end, since he is the ultimate end. And further God cannot order logical or mathematical entities towards an end since these conceptual entities do not have an end and do not seem to have a relation to an end. On the other hand creatures and the creation as a whole can have an end.

Therefore providence must be concerned with creatures and creation as a whole.

That providence is concerned with creation is one feature of providence not immediately apparent from the above characterization of providence as a plan of God. There are others: Since a plan requires knowledge of what is planned, providence also requires knowledge about the things, which are ordered towards their ends. This is also manifest from the assumption that a creator has knowledge of what he has created. But in providence there is also a component of will: God's will that the things and events obey his plan and are directed towards a goal; and his permission w.r.t. those things or events for which there is freedom or chance and for those where he entrusts creatures to cause them.

Putting together these properties we may formulate the following definition for saying under what condition a thing or event comes under God's providence:

Df 3.1. A thing or event e belongs to God's providence iff

a) e belongs to creation

b) e happens at some time

c) God has complete knowledge about e

d) God wills that e happens or he permits that e happens

e) God causes that e happens or he entrusts creatures to cause that e happens

f) God directs e towards a goal or he subordinates e under a goal or he entrusts creatures to direct (or subordinate) e towards (under) a goal.

3.3.1 Result of chapter 3

From the considerations above it follows that providence must be concerned with creation (with the universe):

T 3.1. *Providence is concerned with creation.*

3.4 Answer to the Objections

3.4.1 (to 3.1.1)

It is correct to say that any order is ruled by laws of mathematics and logic in the sense that any order presupposes laws of mathematics and logic as underlying necessary conditions. Thus the shape of a solid body like a crystal satisfies laws of topology and geometry. On the other hand these laws explain only a part of the ordered structure of a crystal. Since the atomic structure of the crystal obeys laws of physics and its molecular structure obeys laws of chemistry for example those of chemical bindings. Therefore the ordered structure of a contingent thing (of creation) obeys – in addition to mathematical and logical laws – also laws of nature and the latter are concerned with creation.

3.4.2 (to 3.1.2)

Although providence as a rule, which orders changeable things towards an end is not changeable, this rule is nevertheless concerned with changeable things in the sense that they are ruled by it.

3.4.3 (to 3.1.3)

It is correct to say that God's providence implies God's knowledge in the sense that about everything, which he orders towards its end he has complete knowledge. But it is not correct to say that in everything of which God has knowledge he has also providence (as the objection suggests) since he has knowledge about himself but no providence. Thus there is no equivalence relation but only an implication in the direction from (God's) providence to God's knowledge but not the other way round.

If providence is the plan according to which the things are ordered towards their ends – as it was said in chs. 2. and 3. above – then it is necessary to show whether and how things are ordered towards their ends. Such an ordering is usually called *teleological*. Therefore it will be the task of the next sections 4, 5 and 7 to discuss and analyze different types of order and teleological order in things. Moreover it will be shown that there is also chance and randomness in things (see chs. 6 and 8) and that both order and chance are present in one physical, chemical or biological system. Under 'things' or 'systems', we understand things or systems of this universe. Although there might be creatures outside the universe we shall not deal with them here. We do not use the word 'design' since it has very different meanings in different contexts and especially biased connotations not free from prejudice.

4 Whether there is order in the change of things?

4.1 Arguments Contra

4.1.1 First argument

If change is not governed by dynamical-deterministic laws then change is not ordered. If change is governed by statistical laws then it is not governed by dynamical-deterministic laws. But many kinds of change like those in the domains of Thermodynamics and Quantum Mechanics are governed by statistical laws.

Therefore these kinds of change are not ordered and consequently not all kinds of change are ordered.

4.1.2 Second argument

Some kinds of change are chaotic. But chaotic change (chaotic motion) is not ordered.

Therefore not all kinds of change are ordered.

4.2 Argument Pro

All kinds of change are governed by laws. But everything, which is governed by laws is ordered.

Thus it seems that all kinds of change are ordered.

4.3 Proposed Answer

It is a fact that there is change in non-living things and that there is change and development in living things. This change is ordered by laws of nature. The change can be of different types. However in all the different types of change we find the order of laws of nature.

4.3.1 Change by movement

a) Change by movement can be such that the movement is approximately inertial movement (uniform velocity on a straight line or rest): translation in space (3 directions), orientation in space (3 directions), translation in time (1 direction), change of inertial systems (3 directions). This kind of change by movement of material or matter dependent bodies obeys Newton's Laws of Classical Mechanics; i.e. it is ordered by the laws of Classical Mechanics. The movement according to the 10 parameters above is called Galilean Movement. And the respective laws or ordering principles, which are invariant (i.e. do not change) with respect to the 10 possibilities of change by movement are called Galilei-invariant.

   Examples of such movements are the movements of stagecoaches, the movements of cars, trains and ships on earth if they move on a straight line without acceleration. The movements of the planets are physically not inertial because the planets rotate around the sun. Short pieces of an orbit are approximately inertial.

b) Change by inertial movement but up to the velocity of light. This kind of change by movement is no longer Galilean Movement. It is ordered and ruled by the laws of electromagnetism, which are Lorentz-invariant. The laws of Classical Mechanics when applied have to be adapted by the Lorentz-Transformation. The theory, which orders these kinds of changes by movement, is the Theory of Special Relativity. The properties of the non-living things (material or matter dependent bodies) are not all invariant with respect to such changes: although charge is invariant, mass, length, time and simultaneity are not.

   Examples are the movements of elementary particles in a linear (=straight) particle accelerator in those segments of the accelerator in which the particles (approximately) do not accelerate.

c) Change by arbitrary movement including acceleration and caused by gravitation. This kind of change by movement is ordered and ruled, described and explained by Einstein's field equations of General Relativity.

   Examples are movements of stars, galaxies and light rays through space.

In all the three cases of change by movement a), b), c) the laws of nature which order the things are dynamical laws. This kind of laws has special characteristics of which the following four are important:

D1 The state of the physical system S at any given time t_i is a definite function of its state at an earlier time t_{i-1}. A unique earlier state (corresponding to a unique solution of the differential equation) leads under the time evolution to a unique final state (again corresponding to a unique solution of the equation).

D2 Condition D1 is also satisfied for every part of the physical system, especially for every individual body (object) as part of the system, even if the individual objects may differ in the classical or in the quantum mechanical sense.

Dynamical laws have been applied successfully (i.e. such that the laws were confirmed by the application) to those physical systems which satisfy the following further conditions D3 and D4:

D3 The physical system S is periodic, that is, the state of S repeats itself after a finite period of time and continues to do so in the absence of external disturbing forces.

D4 The physical system S has a certain type of stability which obeys the following condition: Very small changes in the initial states, say within a neighborhood distance of ε, lead to proportionally small (no more than in accordance of a linearly increasing function of time) changes $h(\varepsilon)$ in the final state. This kind of stability, which survives small perturbations and leads to relaxation afterwards, is called *perturbative stability* and holds in many linear systems.[1]

If D4 is not satisfied the movement becomes chaotic although the underlying laws are dynamical laws. Chaotic motion lacks predictability and conservation of information. Nevertheless chaotic motion is not lawless; it is guided by dynamical laws (see 4.4.2 below).

1 For details on the properties of dynamical laws see Mittelstaedt and Weingartner (2005) ch. 7.2.3.2. For chaotic motion cf. H.G. Schuster (1989) and Weingartner and Schurz (1996).

A strong deterministic order of the universe which satisfies D1 and D2 was described by Laplace in his essay on probability:

> "We ought then to regard the present state of the universe as the effect of its anterior state and as the cause of the one which is to follow. Given for one instant an intelligence which could comprehend all the forces by which nature is animated and the respective situation of the beings who compose it – an intelligence sufficiently vast to submit these data to analysis – it would embrace in the same formula the movements of the greatest bodies of the universe and those of the lightest atom; for it, nothing would be uncertain and the future, as the past, would be present to its eyes."[2]

This idea can be illustrated by the following example: Assume a film is made of the world, i.e. of the events happening in the whole universe. After the film is developed we cut it into pieces corresponding to single film-pictures. Now we put the single pictures successively in time (in the order of time) into a long card index box like the cards of a library catalogue. Then one special state of the universe at a certain time t corresponds to one such card (film picture) of the catalogue. One can follow one trajectory across the (perpendicular to the) catalogue-cards. Interpreted with the help of this illustration Laplace's determinism means that it suffices to know the law(s) of nature and one single catalogue card (film picture) in order to construct all other cards of the catalogue, i.e. to predict and to retrodict all the other states of the universe. That means that Laplace's idea is a completeness claim with respect to the laws of nature: the correct laws of nature (known to a perfect intellect) plus one initial state of the whole universe are together complete in the sense that all true descriptions of states of the universe follow from them.

However, there are still some limitations to this kind of deterministic or mechanistic world view:

(i) D1 is not sufficient in a defining condition for determinism; because D1 does not guarantee further properties, like predictability or conservation of information etc. What is especially needed is that condition D4 is satisfied. Otherwise we have dynamical chaos which neither satisfies predictability nor conservation of information (cf. 15.3.1–15.3.2).

(ii) If the laws in Laplace's sense, the differential equations of motion were not defined everywhere, then these laws would also be incomplete.

(iii) If "physical system" in D1 and D2 is understood as macroscopic system (like the planetery system) then D2 holds for all macroscopic subsystems.

2 Laplace (1951) par.2.

This *presupposes* a concept of "individual object" that is unique and re-identifiable through time (as understood in Classical Mechanics). But if "physical system" in D1 and D2 is understood in such a broad way – as Newton said in his Principia – to comprehend all extended material bodies, then quantum mechanical objects should also be included. However, since they are not composable by Boolean operations and have only a restricted class of (commensurable) properties, the laws describing such objects are not complete.

(iv) Laplace's deterministic theory about the universe does not answer the questions whether there is a first state or a last state of the universe (according to the metaphor above: whether there is a first or last catalogue card): and consequently it does not answer the question whether the universe has a finite age.

The first philosopher who seems to have realized this was Thomas Aquinas. In his quarrel with Bonaventura at the University of Paris, he defended the view that the beginning of the world (universe) in time cannot be proved from universal principles of, or laws about the world.[3] Because universal principles like real universal definitions and universal laws together with the universal concepts or predicates contained in them abstract from *hic et nunc* (here and now):

> "We hold by faith alone, and it cannot be proved by demonstration, that the world did not always exist… The reason is this: the world considered in itself offers no grounds for demonstrating that it was once all new. For the principle of demonstrating an object … abstracts from the here and now (*hic et nunc*)."[4]

4.3.2 Thermodynamic change

The thermodynamic change is such that we have to distinguish two different levels: locally the change of the elementary particles or of the individuals appears

3 In contrast to Thomas Aquinas, Bonaventura argued that an infinite past of the universe is *logically* impossible. This argument goes back to Johannes Philoponos "*De aeternitate mundi: contra Proclum*" Philoponos (2004). For a short discussion of Philoponus' argument see Mittelstaedt (2008) p.125.

4 Aquinas (1981) I, 46, 2. Observe that by "demonstration" Thomas Aquinas means a rigorous proof from premises which essentially include necessary laws (of nature). What Thomas Aquinas has in mind here is – expressed in modern terms – the space time invariance of universal laws of nature and of the appropriate definitions.

to be lawless or random or by chance. But the greater the number of particles or individuals involved in the process of change the stricter is the emergence of a statistical law describing and explaining the respective global process and development. This situation was already characterized very well by Schrödinger in his inaugural lecture at Zürich (in 1922):

> "In a very large number of cases of totally different types, we have now succeeded in explaining the observed regularity as completely due to the tremendously large number of molecular processes that are cooperating. The individual process may, or may not, have its own strict regularity. In the observed regularity of the mass phenomenon the individual regularity (if any) need not be considered as a factor. On the contrary, it is completely effaced by averaging millions of single processes, the average values being the only things that are observable to us. The average values manifest their own purely *statistical regularity*."[5]

The large number of cases, Schrödinger is addressing, are all cases where statistical laws are successfully and adequately applied: Thermodynamic processes, processes of radiation, of friction, of electric transport, of diffusion, of measurement in quantum mechanics, of biology, of psychology, of cosmology.

In order to understand that more accurately it is necessary to compare the above given characteristics of dynamical laws D1 – D4 to the following characteristics of statistical laws:

S1 The state of the physical system at t_i is not a definite function of an earlier state at t_{i-1}. The same initial state may lead to different successor states (branching).

S2 Statistical laws describe and predict the states of the whole physical system, but they do not describe or predict the individual parts (objects) of this system.

S3 Statistical laws describe only physical or chemical or biological systems, which are non-periodic, i.e. systems with extremely improbable recurrence of the whole state of the system.

S4 The loss of information (and, consequently, the difficulty of prediction) about the state of an individual object (or a small part) of the whole system increases exponentially with the complexity of the system. On the other hand: The (accuracy of the) information about the average values of magnitudes (parame-

5 This lecture was later published under the title "Was ist ein Naturgesetz?" Cf. Schrödinger (1961) p.11.

ters) of the state of a huge number of individual objects (or particles) increases also with the complexity of the system.

It is easy to see that there is an essential difference between the conditions D1 and S1. Like D1 is necessary for dynamical laws, S1 is necessary for statistical laws. This presupposes, however, that we interpret S1 (and, by it, statistical laws) realistically (i.e. in an ontic sense). That is, we assume there is real branching in reality. An epistemic interpretation according to which branching is only a sign for our lack of knowledge, whereas in the underlying reality everything is determined (by hidden parameters and dynamical laws of which we are ignorant), we do not find justified.[6]

Similarly, D2 and S2 differ in an important point. Statistical laws are bound to huge ensembles; they describe physical systems consisting of a huge number of objects. The greater the number of objects, the more strict is the law about the whole ensemble. Though there is indeterminacy for every individual system, there is a strict law for the whole system if the ensemble is large enough. To some extent, such laws "emerge" from the "lawless" behavior of a large number of individual systems. In this sense, Wheeler spoke of "law without law".[7] This problem was clearly understood and emphasized already by Boltzmann and Poincaré: How can the law of entropy emerge from random behavior of individual systems?

A comparison of D3 and S3 shows that the difference between dynamical and statistical laws, which is usually viewed as the most striking one – time reversal invariance of the laws versus irreversibility of the laws – has to be taken with care. Strict time-reversal symmetry is no longer valid on the microlevel[8], and irreversibility on the macrolevel should be better replaced by very improbable recurrence.[9] However, the differences in this respect are sufficiently large to forbid reducibility in the one or the other way. But the more careful interpretation paves the way for the compatibility of both types of laws. That means that both, dynamical and statistical laws can be present in *one* physical, chemical or biological system and underlying dynamical laws are compatible with statistical behavior including degrees of freedom and chance on a higher level.

---

6 Cf. Weingartner (1998). For details concerning the differences between dynamical and statistical laws cf. Mittelstaedt and Weingartner (2005) ch.7.

7 Wheeler (1983). For details cf. Mittelstaedt and Weingartner (2005) section 12.2 and 12.3.

8 To establish this result several series of experiments have been made independently in CERN and FERMILAB within the last decade.

9 For more information on the comparison of D3 and S3 Mittelstaedt and Weingartner (2005) p.157–164.

The essential point in all such statistical processes is that within the same system there is chance and randomness in the sense of degrees of freedom on the one hand and order and lawfulness on the other. Some examples are: The molecules in a liter of gas; locally the microstates are changing randomly, globally they are ordered by the general gas-law $p \cdot V = RT$ and by the law of entropy. The process of forming stars is a random process in some local domains but an ordered process obeying laws of gravitation and General Relativity and obeying sophisticated principles of fine- tuning globally.[10] In the genetic processes, the mutation-rate and the distribution of male and female chromosomes in the recombination are random, but the production of the 20 amino acids or the screw-like folding of the double helix obey principles of chemical binding and principles of energy distribution. Behavior in animal populations appears random-like locally but follows general principles like evolutionary stabilized strategies globally.[11]

4.3.3 Quantum-mechanical change

Describing and explaining change in Quantum Mechanics (QM) cannot presuppose the usual conditions, which hold for objects of Classical Mechanics. One important reason is that for objects or systems of QM Kant's principle of "complete determination" is not satisfied for such objects.

> "Every thing as regards its possibility is likewise subject to the principle of complete determination according to which if all possible predicates are taken together with their contradictory opposites, then one of each pair of contradictory opposites must belong to it."[12]

A system (thing, object) of this kind possesses each possible "accidental"[13] property P, either as positive (P) or as negative ($not P$). In this case the dynamical law leads to a strict and complete determination of all properties. In particular it follows that such systems, things or objects possess always a well-defined position in space, i.e. they are permanently localized. A further presupposition is the im-

10 Many examples of cosmological fine-tuning are elaborated in Barrow and Tipler (1986) and Penrose (2005) chs.27 and 28.

11 Such strategies have been defined and investigated by Maynard-Smith (Maynard-Smith (1982)). Cf. Futuyma (1986) ch.9.

12 Kant (1929) B600.

13 Accidental properties are position, momentum, velocity, direction etc. Essential properties are mass, charge and geometrical shape.

penetrability of such objects. If both conditions are satisfied then each individual object can be characterized by its individual trajectory in space and time.

In QM the physical laws of measurements do not allow to determine jointly all possible properties of a given system or object. In any contingent situation, which is described by a state ψ only a subset P_ψ of properties where each two members of this subset are mutually commensurable can be measured jointly on the system. These properties can be called *objective* properties. However for any state ψ there are also *non-objective* properties (not included in P_ψ) whose measurement provides a material change of the state ψ of the system. For these properties Kant's principle is violated. This means that the change of objects (systems) in QM can only be described incompletely.

However despite of these difficulties change in QM is still ordered by laws. And this is so in a twofold way:

1. Laws in the sense of dynamical laws hold for the subset P_ψ of objective properties, which are given by the state $\psi(t)$. The temporal development of this state is determined by the Schrödinger equation according to D1 above. However in contrast to Classical Mechanics such a law, like the Schrödinger equation, does not hold for a particular object, but for kinds of objects, like an electron or a proton (i.e. D2 above does not hold). The indistinguishability of quantum objects of the same kind corresponds to *permutational invariance* of a many-body system.

2. Laws in the sense of statistical laws hold also for *non-objective* properties of objects or systems of QM. In a photon split beam experiment for an individual system it is undetermined whether the photon has the property A or the counter-property $non\text{-}A$. However, in spite of the objective indeterminacy of each individual system (object), for a sufficiently large ensemble of photons we observe a strict law.[14] This fact, that there are ordering laws for the whole (big ensemble) without there being laws for certain properties of the individual particles has been called "law without laws" by Archibald Wheeler.[15] Thus also in the domain of QM we have order by laws of nature.

14 Cf. the passage of Schrödinger's inaugural lecture at Zürich above.

15 Wheeler (1983). Cf. Mittelstaedt and Weingartner (2005) ch.12.

4.3.4 Result of chapter 4

There is law-guided order in the change of things. This has been shown concerning different kinds of change. First (4.3.1) concerning different kinds of movement which are governed by dynamical laws. Secondly (4.3.2) concerning thermodynamic change. This kind of change is ordered by statistical laws. Statistical laws order or govern huge ensembles of individual systems, like molecules, where the single particles have several degrees of freedom. This however does not mean that they are without order, although they move randomly, since they behave in such a way (within such borders) that a huge ensemble of them strictly and unambiguously satisfies a statistical law. Thirdly (4.3.3) concerning quantum-mechanical change. Although here the laws do not jointly determine all possible properties of quantum-mechanical objects, change in QM is still ordered by laws, either in the sense of dynamical laws (Schrödinger equation) for the subset of objective properties or in the sense of statistical laws for non-objective properties. Summarizing the result of chapter 4 we arrive at the following theorem:

T 4.1. *In all kinds of change (of things, systems) there is law-guided order.*

4.4 Answer to the Objections

4.4.1 (to 4.1.1)

As it should be clear from the difference between dynamical laws and statistical laws – which is manifest by comparing D1 with S1 and D2 with S2 – statistical laws govern the behavior of huge ensembles but allow freedom and chance for the individual (S2). And similarly: they govern the change of huge ensembles (of individuals or individual systems) but allow freedom and chance for the development of the individual system. On the other hand, dynamical laws, by governing huge ensembles, they at the same time govern every part of it and thus also the individual system (D2).

Therefore the conclusion of argument 4.1.1 is only partially correct. Although statistical laws allow some chance and freedom concerning the change of individual systems they govern and order every change of greater ensembles of individual systems.

4.4.2 (to 4.1.2)

There are mainly three different types of chaotic motion or chaotic change: Dynamical Chaos, Quantum Chaos and Cosmological Chaos.

(1) Dynamical Chaos
Dynamical Chaos is the one most widely investigated.[16] In dynamical chaos the underlying laws are dynamical laws and in this sense chaotic change is ordered change. Moreover chaotic motion (as Dynamical Chaos) is *bounded* motion. This means that the number of degrees of freedom is limited in different ways depending on the kind of chaotic motion. Also concerning such limitations the motion (change) is ordered.

But chaotic motion (change) violates predictability although it is governed by dynamical laws. The reasons for this are the following two properties (a) and (b):

(a) There is a separation of adjacent conjugate points (conjugate w.r.t. the starting point) which grows exponentially.

(b) There is a loss of information about the position of a point in an interval $[0, 1]$ after one iteration, which also grows exponentially. Both changing magnitudes (separation and loss of information) are measured by the Liapunov exponent (for the general more-dimensional case by the Kolmogorov entropy). Therefore there are degrees of freedom and in this sense there is chance and randomness concerning (a) and (b). But this chaotic motion is not without order since the exponential separation is measured by the Liapunov exponent or by the Kolmogorov entropy.

(c) Moreover there are weaker and stronger forms of Dynamical Chaos and these degrees can be measured by KAM-integrability. Strong Dynamical Chaos is not integrable, weak forms of it are partially integrable.[17] That means that also in this sense weaker and stronger forms of chaotic mo-

16 For properties of Dynamical Chaos see H.G. Schuster (1989), Chirikov (1996), Chirikov (1997), Weingartner (1996), Weingartner and Schurz (1996), Mittelstaedt and Weingartner (2005) ch.9.4, Ruelle (1990).

17 "KAM" is an abbreviation of Kolmogorov, Arnold and Moser who have solved several main problems of Dynamical Chaos especially the Price-Question of King Oscar II of Sweden of 1885. The price was given to Poincaré, although he did not solve the problem, but gave reasons and arguments. See: Mittelstaedt and Weingartner (2005) p.261ff.

tion correspond to stronger and weaker forms of order and to stronger or weaker forms of predictability.

(d) Three examples which show that order and chaos can be close to each other in one physical chemical or biological system. Bénard-experiment: A fluid layer heated from the bottom shows first heat conduction. After some time this state becomes unstable at a critical value (threshold) and so-called convection rolls are developed which represent a highly ordered structure. Observe that adjacent rolls turn like gear wheels and that the elements of the fluid go up (the warm ones) and go down (the cold ones) periodically. In this process different possible modes of movements are in competition. In the course of time successful ones (those modes which grow most rapidly) win over less successful ones and enslave them. The underlying principle – called the “Slaving-Principle” – says that the instable modes of slowly relaxing magnitudes enslave the relativity stable modes of quickly relaxing magnitudes. The result is a drastic reduction in the number of freedoms because the boundary conditions limit the number of rolls. An ordered hierarchy develops. If the temperature is increased further up to a certain threshold (measured by the Rayleigh number which is proportional to the increase of the temperature) then the motion begins to become chaotic.

Another example for order and structure in open dissipative systems is Karman’s water turbulence, which has an often observed characteristic picture emerging if a stick is put into a stream of water. Observe that the respective systems are *open* systems. The self-organization of order and structure does not violate the law of entropy because this law holds strictly for closed systems only.

Still another interesting example of a prototype of system, which satisfies the “Slaving Principle” is the laser.[18] Also these examples show that chaotic motion (change) is not without order.

(2) Quantum Chaos
Conditions (a) and (b) of Dynamical Chaos are not adequate for the description of Quantum Chaos. Whereas the Fourier spectrum of chaotic motion in the sense of Dynamical Chaos is continuous and its phase space is continuous, Quantum Chaos has a discrete spectrum of the motion and a discrete

18 Self-organizing structures of that sort have been studied intensively by Hermann Haken and his school. See Haken (1983), Haken (1987) and Haken et al. (1996).

phase space: In Connection with the uncertainty principle which allows only a finite size of the elementary cells of phase space, the frequency spectrum of quantum motion is discrete for the motion bounded in phase space. Moreover there are many forms of Quantum Chaos, which are representable by linear equations: linear wave chaos in quantum mechanics. This shows already that also Quantum Chaos is not without order, although we have order w.r.t. some parameters and degrees of freedom and chance w.r.t. some others.[19]

(3) Cosmological Chaos
Cosmological Chaos is the chaos of large Poincaré systems and has different properties from Dynamical Chaos and Quantum Chaos. Chaotic motion in large cosmic structures cannot be described by analysing trajectory routes but must concentrate on developing phase spaces of mutually interacting systems. The important point here is that such systems develop order and structure internally. Despite of a positive Liapunov exponent and growth of phase space and external increase of entropy they produce order, structure and information internally. Large galaxies having gigantic masses like that of 10^{15} sun-masses do not show repetitions or randomness in the structure and distribution of their building blocks. On the contrary they always show interesting new patterns and structures. Also the distribution of many of such galaxies does not satisfy any Poisson random statistics.

From this it follows that Cosmological Chaos in large cosmological systems is not without order but shows development of patterns, structures and information.[20]

It follows therefore from all the considerations concerning the three different types of chaos that chaotic change is not without order. Therefore the conclusion of the argument 4.1.2 is not proved.

4.5 Conclusion

It has been shown in ch. 4. that there is order in all the different kinds of change, even if the respective order is of different type. The different kinds of change,

19 Cf. Casati and Chirikov (1995a) and Casati and Chirikov (1995b).
20 For details see Prigogine (1977), Fahr (1997).

which contain order are change of movement, thermodynamic change, quantum-mechanical change and even chaotic change (cf. Theorem 4.1 of 4.3.4 above).

By showing that there is order in all these different kinds of changes the condition for the possibility of providence (recall the argument in 1.3.2) has been fulfilled w.r.t. order. It will be fulfilled w.r.t. both order and teleological order in chs. 5. and 7.

5 Whether there is teleological order in non-living things?

5.1 Arguments Contra

5.1.1 First argument

A teleological order is a development towards goals. But in non-living things there are no goals.

Therefore there is no teleological order in non-living things.

5.1.2 Second argument

A teleological order requires an irreversible process. But the laws governing non-living things are – to a great extent – dynamical laws; and dynamical laws do not prescribe irreversibility of the process (of the development between initial and final state), i.e. they permit reversibility.

Therefore there does not seem to be a teleological order in non-living things.

5.2 Argument Pro

Increasing order can be interpreted as teleological order. Now if there is growth, emergence of new properties and differentiation then there is increasing order. But among non-living things there is growth (for example growth of crystals), emergence (for example of new chemical compounds) and differentiation (for example new functions of the new chemical compounds).

Therefore there is teleological order in non-living things.

5.3 Proposed Answer

There is teleological order in non-living things. This is manifest, because there is not only *being* but also *becoming* in non-living things. But *becoming* (5.3.4) is a process leading away from equilibrium to non-equilibrium and new order. Thus *becoming* is a process of increasing order. Now every process of increasing order can be called teleological in a wider sense.

Therefore there is teleological order in non-living things. This will be substantiated more accurately in the following sections:

5.3.1 Things and systems

Under a thing we understand an individual with its properties.[1] A thing is not understood as a conceptual object (conceptual entity) like a number or a scientific theory. Objects may be divided into real objects (individuals with their properties) and conceptual objects (or constructs). Thus every thing is an object but not vice versa. A thing can have parts and the parts of a thing can also have properties. A thing consisting of linked parts is called a system. The following definitions Df 5.1–Df 5.10 hold for both non-living systems and living systems.

A system has at least the following three features: It has a composition, an environment and a structure.[2]

Df 5.1. $Comp(s) =_{df}$ the set of the parts of s.

Df 5.2. $Env(s) =_{df}$ those things y (which are not parts of s) such that

(a) s or some part z of s acts causally on y or

(b) y acts causally on s or on some part z of s

Examples: Water (y) acts on parts (z) of a salt mine (s); and parts (z) of the salt mine (s) act (hygroscopically) on water (y). Clean (or polluted) air (y) acts on the

1 For a detailed exposition cf. Bunge (1977) ch.3.
2 Cf. Prigogine and Stengers (1993) ch.3(4). Bunge (1979) ch.1.

lungs (z) of some animal (s). The vocal cord (z) of a bird (s) acts on the air (y) producing sound waves.

Input and *Output*: The set of activities of the environment on the system (or thing) may be called the *input* of the system (or thing); the set of activities of the system (thing) on the environment may be called the *output* of the system (thing).

The structure of a system consists in its internal structure and in its external structure. The internal structure consists in the relations of its parts, the external structure in the relations with the environment. These relations are twofold: relations of linkage (or bondage) and non-linkage relations. For example the electromagnetic force between electron and proton (in the system of an atom) is a linkage relation, the proportion of their masses ($m_p/m_e = 1836$) is a non-linkage relation. Thus we arrive at the following definition of *the structure of system* s:

Df 5.3. $Struct(s) =_{df}$ those relations R (R can be two-place, ... , n-place) such that

(i) R are linkage or non-linkage relations

(ii) R hold internally among the parts of s

(iii) R hold externally between the parts of s on the one hand and the things of the environment on the other.

Examples of systems having structure: A water molecule (H_2O) with internal forces (nuclear and electromagnetic) and external relations to other water molecules; other inorganic molecules; mountains, lakes, planetary systems etc.

A system may be called *closed* (at time t) if it has no environment (at time t). Otherwise the system is called *open*. The universe is a system, which is closed at all times. Most of the systems be they non-living or living systems are in fact open systems. But under certain conditions for isolation they may be interpreted as approximately closed. For example a crater-lake is closed w.r.t. the surrounding rocks but open w.r.t. air and sun. Or a cell is half open and closed because of its semipermeable membrane. This aspect is important for the question of the applicability of the Second Law of Thermodynamics (i.e. the law of entropy).

It has been presupposed so far that all these things and systems (5.3.1) have 3 spatial dimensions. This has an effect on all three points: their composition, their environment and their structure. And it is also fundamental for the higher types of order to be defined subsequently, first of all for Ord_2 (see Df 5.5 below). According to mathematical results there are no stable orbits for dimensions > 3:

> "There is one simple geometrical property unique to three dimensions that plays an important role in physics: universes with three spatial dimensions possess a unique correspondence between rotational and translational degrees of freedom. Both are defined by only three components."[3]

Moreover Hadamard has already shown that in general the transmission of wave impulses in a reverberation-free mode is impossible if the spatial dimensions have an even number.[4] The preferred odd-dimensional cases must obey Huygen's Principle.

5.3.2 Change and reversibility

A state S of a thing or system represents at least one property of it w.r.t. a reference system, i.e. at a certain time t and place $l(x, y, z)$. The thing or system s *changes* iff s transforms from state $S_1(t_1, l_1)$ to state $S_2(t_2, l_2)$. If the time difference is short, without considering intermediate states between S_1 and S_2, the change is called an *event*. If the time difference is extended with several or many intermediate states S_i between S_1 and S_2 the change is called a *process*. Thus every event and every process is a change but not vice versa.

Changes, events and processes can be reversible according to laws, which describe them, although they might in fact never be reversed. This is so because dynamical laws like that of Newton, Maxwell, Einstein and the Schrödinger Equation of Quantum Mechanics (QM) are time reversal invariant.[5] That means that in the differential equations of these laws we can replace the sign t (for time) by $-t$ without making the law invalid. Thus dynamical laws do not prescribe a direction of the process (event, change) described, i.e. they permit that the process may be reversed. For an example take the movements of the planets on their orbits, which are described by Newton's laws: given the state S_1 of the system of two planets and

3 Barrow and Tipler (1986) p.272 and p.260. Ehrenfest (1917) and Ehrenfest (1920) gives a lot of reasons for the 3 dimensions of space (stability of orbits of atoms, of atoms and of molecules, the unique properties of wave operators ... etc.) Similarly Weyl (1922) p.284 showed that only in $3+1$-dimensional space-times can Maxwell's theory be founded upon an invariant integral form of the action.

4 Hadamard (1923).

5 For details see Mittelstaedt and Weingartner (2005) ch.7, especially pp.147ff and 157ff.

the sun at time t_1 the laws describe the time development of the system such that one can predict the future state S_2 at t_2 of this system. These dynamical laws allow also the reversed movements back from S_2 to S_1 although the real movements of the planets depending on additional factors, like initial impetus, do not reverse; nevertheless there is recurrence of the state of the system after a finite period of time.

However most processes in nature are not reversible. Some examples are: throwing a stone into a lake, pouring a glass of wine into a barrel of water, radiation processes, processes of growth or of aging. Also on large scales in the universe time-reversal symmetry seems not to be satisfied: expansion and radiation suffice as examples. Such processes cannot be described by dynamical laws; they have to be described by statistical laws. In general: all processes which obey the second law of thermodynamics (the law of entropy) – i.e. those processes in which entropy increases – are not reversible. Or more accurately: the recurrence of the whole state of the system is extremely improbable. More critically we should speak about *very improbable recurrence* instead of *irreversibility*: Irreversibility and non-recurrence are not equivalent notions. This is manifest from processes of dynamical chaos where we have both, underlying dynamical laws which allow reversibility of the process and non-recurrence of the state of the system: the exact density of chaotic motion is always time-reversible but it is non-recurrent.[6] The following passage underlines the irreversibility of processes on the macrolevel:

> "Next we mention a very interesting symmetry which is obviously false, i.e. *reversibility in time*. The physical laws apparently cannot be reversible in time, because, as we know, all obvious phenomena are irreversible on a large scale: 'The moving finger writes, and having writ, moves on.' So far as we can tell, this irreversibility is due to the very large number of particles involved, and if we could see the individual molecules, we would not be able to discern whether the machinery was working forwards or backwards."[7]

But there are experiments, which seem to show that time-reversal symmetry seems to be violated also in processes on the microlevel. One is an indirect violation because *CP* (charge parity) invariance is violated but *CPT* (charge parity time) invariance is not. Thus *T* has to outbalance the difference. Some other recent experiments show direct violations.[8]

---

6 For more details see Chirikov (1996) ch.2.2 and Mittelstaedt and Weingartner (2005) p.160ff.

7 Feynman (1997) p.28.

8 Two different series of experiments have been made at CERN and FERMILAB. Cf. Mittelstaedt and Weingartner (2005) p.160.

5.3.3 Order

There are different types of order. The following three are applied to things or systems: (1) Ord_1 as structure (2) Ord_2 as Ord_1 where some of its relations obey special arithmetical or geometrical relations (3) Ord_3 as Ord_2 having a structure far from equilibrium. If any of these types of order are increasing we speak of *becoming*. There are other types of *order*, which are applicable only to events and processes. Thus we may say an event or process is ordered if it obeys dynamical or statistical laws; and respectively it is random if it is not law-like, i.e. if it neither obeys dynamical nor statistical laws. A further type of order is applicable to processes or sequences: a sequence or process is ordered if there is a code shorter than the process or sequence, which can produce the sequence (see below 6.3.5).[9]

Order_1 can be defined by structure (see above 5.3.1) for which we gave also some examples.

Df 5.4. A thing or system has Ord_1 (or is in order-state_1) iff it has structure (Df 5.3).

Df 5.5. A thing or system has Ord_2 (or is in order-state_2) iff it has a structure (Ord_1) and some of its internal or external relations obey special mathematical (arithmetical or geometrical) relations.

Examples: dunes and clouds with special patterns, cyclones, chiral systems, clouds and cells of a liquid having hexagonal structure, snowflakes, frostwork, fractal structures etc.[10]

Observe that Ord_2, presupposes, w.r.t. geometrical relations, which are obeyed by its internal or external relations, the 3-dimensional space. As has been said in 5.3.1 this fact is of enormous importance for the different types of orders of non-living and living systems, beginning from the lowest types in non-living systems to the highest types of order in living systems.

Another principle, which is of great importance for the atomic and molecular structure is the Pauli Exclusion Principle (two or more elementary particles of the

---

9 For different kinds of chance and randomness (in the objective sense) see Weingartner (2009a) and Weingartner (2010b).

10 For a systematic treatment of many examples of order_2 in nature see Haken and Wunderlin (1991).

same kind cannot agree in all 4 quantum numbers; i.e. no more than one particle of a particular kind and spin is permitted in a single quantum state). Among its enormous consequences are the Fermi-Dirac statistics, the stability of matter, the shell structure of atomic electrons and consequently the structure of the periodic system of the chemical elements.

To give a definition of Ord_3 we have to define *subsystem* first; since a system$_1$ can have Ord_3 only relative to another system$_2$, such that either system$_1$ is a subsystem of system$_2$ ($Subs(s_1, s_2)$) or system$_1$ has a different aggregate state from system$_2$, i.e. $Aggr(s_1) \neq Aggr(s_2)$[11]

Df 5.6. s_1 is a subsystem of s_2 ($Subs(s_1, s_2)$) iff

(i) $Comp(s_1) \subseteq Comp(s_2)$

(ii) $Env(s_2) \subseteq Env(s_1)$

(iii) $Struct(s_1) \subseteq Struct(s_2)$

Observe that if s_1 is a part of s_2 (i) then the environment of s_1 is s_2 plus the environment of s_2; thus the environment of s_2 is included in the environment of s_1 (ii). On the other hand the structure of s_1 is included in the structure of s_2 if s_1 is a subsystem of s_2 (iii). If two systems have the same chemical composition but are of different aggregate state ($Aggr$), as for example ice and steam, then (ii) may be satisfied and (i) is satisfied w.r.t. atomic composition ($AtComp$) but (iii) is not satisfied and therefore one cannot be the subsystem of the other.

Df 5.7. A thing or system s_1 has Ord_3 iff

(i) s_1 has Ord_2

(ii) There is an s_2 such that $Subs(s_1, s_2)$ or $Aggr(s_1) \neq Aggr(s_2)$ and $AtComp(s_1) = AtComp(s_2)$

(iii) s_1 is an open system

(iv) $Ent(s_1) \ll Ent(s_2)$

The third condition (iii) requires s_1 to be an open system. This means that s_1 can receive (input) (or give: output) energy or matter or both of them from (*to*) somewhere of its environment, where $Env(s_1) \subseteq s_2$ or $s_2 \subseteq Env(s_1)$.

11 The definition of *subsystem* is due to Bunge (1979) p.11.

The fourth condition (iv) says that the entropy of the system s_1 is much lower than that of system s_2. In this case the system s_1 is much farer from equilibrium than the system s_2. In order to push a system away from equilibrium it needs an input of energy.

However, the type of structure (Ord_3) established in s_1 by supplying energy is not necessarily dependent on the type of the supplied energy. The following examples will help to understand Df 5.7.

Examples: The part with dunes has Ord_3 relative to the desert (to which it belongs); clouds with special pattern embedded in huger systems of clouds; hexagonal liquid cells w.r.t. surrounding liquid (Bénard-Instability); target structures and spiral structures relative to surroundings in the Belousov-Zhabotinsky reaction; the earth relative to the system earth+moon.

These are examples where s_1 is a subsystem of s_2. The following ones are examples where s_1 and s_2 have different aggregate state but the same atomic composition: An ice crystal has Ord_3 relative to its respective steam; in the steam and in the fluid the molecules can move in all directions. The fluid or steam can therefore be described as a homogeneous material in which no space point is designated. But below the characteristic temperature (for water: $0°$ C) a crystal grating emerges (a case of Ord_3) and the translational symmetry is broken. A bar magnet (magnetic, because of the internal ordering of its elementary magnets) has Ord_3 relative to its heated state or relative to its melting state. The critical temperature of iron is $1044°$ Kelvin; above that there are no magnetic properties. The cooling down below the critical temperature means a phase transition (symmetry-breaking of rotational symmetry) with emerging internal ordering observable by magnetic properties; a metal in state of superconductivity has Ord_3 w.r.t. the same metal at higher temperature.[12]

The foregoing examples may suggest that Ord_3 decreases with increasing temperature. This is not true unrestrictedly: For example in the case of Bénard-Instability, the water in the pot has lower order before it is heated in such a way that the new structure of liquid rollers or of hexagonal liquid cells emerges (being of Ord_3).

If heating is continued and the water becomes noisy (before boiling) then this Ord_3 breaks down and we have some chaotic motion (which is again a different

12 For many examples of both types (with and without phase-transition) see Nicolis and Prigogine (1987).

lower state of order). Also the sun, although having 5600 degrees of Kelvin on the surface and some millions of it inside, has Ord_3 relative to the system: sun + planets. It is in a state far from equilibrium, since equilibrium would mean "heat death" of the planetary system. However w.r.t. the planetary system as a whole the law of entropy is applicable, since this system is approximately closed if we forget small external interactions like the cosmic background radiation or others from stars. That means that entropy increases in the planetary system as a whole. The message from the above considerations is that Ord_3 has to be defined as a relative term as in Df 5.7 in the sense that if a system s_1, has Ord_3 then there is another system s_2 to which it is related concerning its entropy.

Condition (iv) can also be interpreted in Boltzmann's sense: the number of microstates $Mk(s_1)$ which can realize the macrostate $MS1$ of system s_1 is much smaller than the number of microstates $Mk(s_2)$ which can realize the macrostate $MS2$ of system s_2: $Mk(s_1) \ll Mk(s_2)$. According to a genius idea, Boltzmann defined the entropy of a system s ($Ent(s)$) as the number of microstates $Mk(s)$ which can realize the (macrostate of) system s; This number is extremely large – in a liter of air at room temperature this number is about $10^{5 \cdot 10^{22}}$. He took the number of its numerals or the logarithm; and this has a deeper reason: whereas the microstates for realizing macrostates (or the respective probabilities) of two compared systems are multiplied, the logarithms have to be additive, i.e. the entropies are additive. Hence his famous principle: $Ent(s) = k \cdot log \cdot (number\ of\ microstates\ which\ can\ realize\ s)$, where k is the Boltzmann constant (a proportionality factor).

5.3.4 Becoming

Becoming is not a state but a certain transition from one state of a system at t_1 to another state of that system at t_2 ($t_2 > t_1$). Therefore *becoming* is an *event* or *process*. Moreover *becoming* is not just any transition, but a transition where order increases.

Df 5.8. B is a *process* of system s iff B is a transition from state $S_1(t_1)$ of s to $S_2(t_2)$ of s; where $t_2 > t_1$.

Df 5.9. B is a *process* of *becoming* of system s iff

a) B is a process of s

b) s in state $S_2(t_2)$ (denoted by s_2) has Ord_3 relative to s in state $S_1(t_1)$ (denoted by s_1).

Examples: The growing of an ice crystal or of frostwork on the window are processes of becoming; so are the formations of dunes or clouds with spacial pattern or of the liquid cells in the Bénard-Instability. There are a lot of processes of becoming in non-living and in living systems going on on the earth.

In each of these processes there is an increase of order and information and locally there may be a decrease of entropy. This is possible in accordance with the law of entropy because there is a permanent input of energy, which keeps the system in non-equilibrium. The balance of entropy of such systems far from equilibrium (dissipative systems) can be described (according to Prigogine) by $\Delta(Ent) = \Delta_I(Ent) + \Delta_e(Ent)$ where $\Delta_I(Ent)$ is the change of entropy according to irreversible processes and is measured by the entropy production per time unit; it is always positive. On the other hand $\Delta_e(Ent)$ may be negative, if the system is an open system and receives energy or matter from its environment. Thus $\Delta(Ent)$ may also be 0 or negative in such an open system, where there is permanent entropy production and entropy transport. A case in point for an important principle of order is what Prigogine called Boltzmann's ordering principle:

> "It is of outstanding significance, because it describes an enormous multiplicity of structures, among them those which are rather complex and of such a fragile structure as snowflakes."[13]

The principle states the probability that a system (for example a molecule) – which is at Kelvin temperature T in equilibrium state with its environment – be in one particular (of the possible) levels (states) of energy.

To come back to the example of the earth receiving energy from the sun: The earth receives high-grade energy as electromagnetic radiation (with Planck temperature of 5600 Kelvin) from the sun and passes on low-grade energy as heat radiation (with Planck temperature of only about 300 Kelvin) into its environment. The received energy has low entropy and a respectably lower number of degrees of freedom (i.e. of possible microstates which can realize a macrostate), whereas the delivered energy has high entropy and a much greater number of degrees of freedom. It is also understandable that the earth *with* living organisms (including men) produces more entropy than it would produce without. It should be mentioned, however, that, although the flow of entropy is not balanced, the flow of energy (received per time unit and delivered per time unit) is balanced. That means that the earth, and also all living systems, convert high grade energy, by passing it through their systems, into low grade energy, and by that process they are able to

13 Prigogine (1977) p.95. For details about Boltzmann's ordering principle cf. ibid ch. IV, 1.

create order, quality and differentiation. The Earth (and living systems) are open systems of non-equilibrium, which permit a loss of entropy which does not violate the law of entropy, since in the whole system sun-earth-cosmic environment, entropy still increases. But it shows that, locally, the law-like direction of the thermodynamic processes (towards higher entropy) can be reversed such that order and information can be produced.[14]

It should be mentioned in addition that such a production of order and information is strongly dependent on the selection of the electromagnetic spectrum first by the solar radiation and then by the atmosphere of the earth. There are many coincidences necessary in order to permit and promote the different levels of order in non-living things and eventually carbon-based life.[15]

Observe that a process of becoming is usually not a transition (from state $s_1(t_1)$ to $s_2(t_2)$ solely guided by dynamical laws. The final state is only rarely but usually not uniquely determined from the initial state (cf. conditions D1 and S1 of ch.4). As we shall see later, this fact is important for defining teleology (teleological order, teleological process and teleological system).

5.3.5 Teleological order

In every process of becoming (of a system s) there is an initial state $S_1(t_1)$ of lower order and a final state $S_2(t_2)$ of higher order. If the system s is a non-living system there cannot be consciousness and consequently there cannot be a conscious intention to reach the state of higher order. In this sense, therefore, we cannot speak of an intended *telos* or *goal*. On the other hand there is a wider sense of *telos* or *goal*, defended already by Aristotle, according to which a state of higher order can be called a relative *telos* or *goal* w.r.t. (relative to) the respective state of lower order from which it developed. The property of such a process of becoming which develops from a state of lower order towards a state of higher order as its *telos* or *goal*, can be called *teleological order*. And in this wider sense then there is teleological order in non-living things.

Df 5.10. TO is a *teleological order* of a process B of system s iff

a) B is a process of becoming of a non-living system nls

b) the final state $S_g(t_g)$ of higher order of nls is a relative goal w.r.t. other states of lower order of nls from which it developed or to which it is compared.

---

14 Cf. Fahr (1997) and Penrose (2005) p.705f.

15 See especially ch. 3 “The Fitness of the Light“ of Denton (1998).

Example: According to the *Anthropic Principle* the process from the beginning of the universe to the emergence of carbon-based life is a process that has teleological order, since the present state (carbon-based life) is interpreted as a goal w.r.t. the earlier states.

According to Aristotle there is an internal teleological order in every process of growth of both non-living and living systems. Thus a crystal grows towards its crystalline form, a plant towards its mature state in which it can have flowers and fruit (where the state of flower and the state of fruit are also goals relative to an initial state in spring). An animal also grows towards its mature state in which it is able to produce descendants.

5.3.6 Values and goals in non-living systems

In order to be more accurate concerning definition Df 5.10 of teleological order, we have to define values and goals of non-living systems (nls).

Df 5.11. A property or process C of a nls or a thing X of the environment of nls is a *primary value* for nls iff meeting C or X is necessary to increase order of nls relative to its environment.

Df 5.12. A property or process C of nls or a thing X of the environment of nls is a *secondary value* for nls iff meeting C or X is necessary to keep or regain a certain level of order relative to its environment.

Df 5.13. A primary or secondary value of nls is called a *basic value* of nls.

Df 5.14. B is a *higher value* of nls iff

(a) B is a process of becoming of nls

(b) B is a basic value of nls (Df 5.13)

(c) B contributes to the continuation of the history of nls or B contributes to the conservation of nls and its basic values

Df 5.15. X is a *relative goal* of a nls iff

(a) X is a state of $S(t)$ of a process B of becoming of nls

(b) B is a basic value or a higher value of nls (Df 5.14)

(c) X has a level of order such that

(i) it is the highest level of order L_m relative to other states of B

(ii) L_m is compatible with laws of nature, fundamental constants, and contingent initial conditions.

Observe that Df 5.15 defines goal as a *relative goal*. This means that neither goals nor values are understood in an absolute sense. Basic values are defined relative to a certain level of order (not to the highest level of order) and relative to a certain environment. Goals are defined as states of highest value relative to other states in a process of becoming. This need not be the final state of this process since order may decrease later. Therefore teleological order does not imply a straightforward progress to a predetermined goal, even if such a situation is not ruled out either. Moreover teleological order does not exclude chance, since there may be chance-like events during the process of becoming. Teleological order does not imply harmony since there might be competition w.r.t. goals during the process of becoming. And finally there is no need for teleological order to be realized always and everywhere.

5.3.7 Result of chapter 5

We may formulate the results of chapter 5 in the following theorems:

T 5.1. *Every non-living thing (system) has Ord_1 (i.e. structure).*

T 5.2. *Many non-living things (systems) possess Ord_2 or Ord_3.*

T 5.3. *Some non-living things (systems) possess teleological order (TO).*

In order to avoid misunderstandings, we want to emphasize the following points:

(1) Values are not understood (defined) as absolute values

(2) Goals are not understood (defined) as absolute values or goals

(3) TO does not imply a straightforward progress to a predetermined goal

(4) TO does not exclude chance

(5) TO does not imply harmony (there is also fight and competition in w.r.t. goals)

(6) TO is not (need not be) always realized

5.4 Answer to the Objections

5.4.1 (to 5.1.1)

Although it is correct that in non-living systems there cannot be goals as the target of intentions of individuals – as it is the case with the living systems – there can nevertheless be goals in a wider sense like that of Df 5.10: goals in the sense of final states of higher order relative to the respective initial states of lower order.

5.4.2 (to 5.1.2)

To this objection we may reply several things: (1) Although dynamical laws permit time-reversibility the real processes cannot be reversed; i.e. we cannot reverse the direction of the rotation of the planets or stars. (2) Moreover on the microlevel time reversibility does not seem to be satisfied (cf. section 5.3.2). (3) We know phenomena of systems (for example: dynamical chaos) which obey dynamical laws permitting reversibility, but which have no recurrence of the state of the (whole) system. This shows that reversibility and recurrence are not equivalent notions. (4) Disordered or even chaotic behavior (dynamical chaos) of the molecules of a fluid can develop (when heated from below as an *open system*) into emergence of macroscopic ordering ("self organization") as the hexagonal cells of the Bénard Instability show. In such a process there is increasing order, which can be interpreted as teleological order according to Df 5.10. A Bénard-cell has a length of about 1 millimeter and there are about 10^{21} molecules in such a cell. The emergence of order means that this immense number of 10^{21} molecules (per cell) shows completely coherent behavior. In this case we have underlying dynamical laws, though non-recurrence of the state of the system. (5) As is evident from section 4.3.2, many physical, chemical or biological phenomena obey statistical laws, not dynamical laws. In this case we have irreversible, or better: non-recurrent, processes for which *teleological order* can be defined if there is an increase of order.

5.5 Conclusion

It has been established in this chapter that there are different types of order in the non-living things of this world. There are weaker types of order in the sense of structure; and there are stronger types of order, which require in addition specific external or internal relations (Ord_2) and lower entropy relative to another system (Ord_3). Beyond these types of order there is teleological order (TO), which presupposes a process of becoming and a relative goal.

The establishment of these types of order together with teleological order satisfies the antecedent-condition of the proof in ch. 1 that providence is possible. The respective statement 7 of section 1.3.4 says: If there is order and teleological order then providence is possible.

In the terminology of chapter 1. this reads:
If p belongs to the states of affairs which describe the order (Ord_1 or Ord_2 or Ord_3) in change and in the development of (non-living) things and (moreover) if p belongs to the states of affairs which describe the directedness of these things towards their ends, i.e. its teleological order (TO) then it is possible that p belongs to God's providence. Since the antecedens of this implication has been established in this chapter, the conclusion – i.e. the possibility of God's providence (for those states of affairs p) – follows.

6 Whether there is chance and randomness in non-living things?

6.1 Arguments Contra

6.1.1 First argument

In non-living things there is order of different degrees, even teleological order as has been substantiated in chapter 5. above. But order is the opposite of chance and randomness.

Therefore there does not seem to be chance and randomness in non-living things.

6.1.2 Second argument

The behavior of large domains of non-living things (for example: movement) is governed by dynamical laws. In this case the trajectories of the non-living things are strictly predictable and there is no chance or randomness.

Therefore there is no chance and randomness in large domains of non-living things.

6.1.3 Third argument

The behavior of great ensembles of non-living things (like the molecules of a gas or of a fluid) obeys statistical laws. In this case the macrostates of such ensembles are predictable with probability close to 1 such that there is no chance and randomness.

Therefore there is no chance and randomness in great ensembles of non-living things.

6.2 Argument Pro

There are several areas in physics and chemistry where the processes obey statistical laws and the respective macrostates can be predicted by such laws. Examples are thermodynamic and decay phenomena. On the other hand, there are many degrees of freedom for the respective microstates of these processes, such that it is justified to say that they occur by chance or randomly.

Therefore there are several areas in physics and chemistry, which show that there is chance and randomness in non-living things.

6.3 Proposed Answer

There is chance and randomness in non-living things. This is so for the following reason: Many processes (of non-living systems) in physics and chemistry obey only statistical laws but not dynamical laws. That means that there are (several or many) degrees of freedom for the respective microstates of these systems, which are not ruled by the statistical laws for the whole ensemble. But to interpret these degrees of freedom only epistemically, i.e. as lack of knowledge or as degrees of ignorance, is untenable, since in this case there would be (unknown) hidden parameters, which ultimately render possible the system to be deterministic, that is obeying dynamical laws. But many attempts of this sort have been shown to be clashing with experimental results.[1] Therefore the degrees of freedom of the microstates have to be interpreted realistically, that means, as belonging to reality. Now insofar as these microstates are not ruled by statistical laws for the whole ensemble (i.e. those laws which rule the macrostates); they (the microstates) can be said to occur by chance or to occur randomly (cf. 6.3.3–6.3.6 below).

There is also a second reason for the existence of chance and randomness in non-living things. The first reason considered above is dependent on the interpretation of chance and randomness as contrary to dynamical-deterministic laws. The second reason depends however on the interpretation of chance and randomness as opposite to teleological order: since there are processes of non-living things

---

1 The respective attempts concerning Quantum Mechanics and their refutations by the experiments of Clauser (Clauser et al. (1969)), Freedman (Freedman et al. (1972)), Aspect (Aspect et al. (1982)), Kwiat (Kwiat et al. (1995)) and Weihs (Weihs et al. (1998)) became well-known.

of which the final state cannot be interpreted as a goal w.r.t. its earlier or initial state from which it developed one can speak of chance or randomness in the sense that such processes cannot be referred to some appropriate goals (cf. 6.3.7 below).

Therefore there is chance and randomness in non-living things or systems. This is a preliminary answer. It will be substantiated more fully in what follows.

6.3.1 Extreme positions

(1) According to the mechanistic worldview all real things or systems are – if analyzed in their inmost structure – ultimately mechanical systems. That is to say that all things or systems of the world, however complex they ever are, like gases, swarms of mosquitoes or clouds, are ultimately – if analyzed according to the detailed interaction of their particles – like clocks (which were viewed as paradigm examples for mechanical systems). For this worldview we may use Popper's words in his A. H. Compton Memorial Lecture: "All clouds are clocks".[2] The theoretical background of this worldview is expressed by Laplace's famous passage in his essay on probability:

> "We ought to regard the present state of the universe as the effect of its anterior state and as the cause of the one which is to follow. Given for one instant an intelligence which could comprehend all the forces by which nature is animated and the respective situation of the beings who compose it – an intelligence sufficiently vast to submit these data to analysis – it would embrace in the same formula the movements of the greatest bodies of the universe and those of the lightest atom: for it, nothing would be uncertain and the future, as the past, would be present to its eyes."[3]

The view expressed in this passage is that everything is ruled by dynamical laws. Forgetting about dynamical chaos[4] not known at the time of Laplace, this means that a strict determinism governs all events in this world. And in this case there is no room for chance, randomness or freedom.

(2) Although this extreme position was defended also by some physicists up to 1900, the discovery of thermodynamics (already within the 19-century) and

---

2 Popper (1965) p.210. For more details see Mittelstaedt and Weingartner (2005) ch.7.2.3.1, p.147ff.

3 Laplace (1951) ch.2. Cf. the explanation in section 4.3.1 above.

4 In this case there are underlying dynamical laws but no recurrence of important variables of the system (like amplitude, conductivity etc.) and no predictability. For details see H.G. Schuster (1989), Weingartner and Schurz (1996) and Weingartner (1996).

that of Quantum Mechanics led to some general doubts concerning a mechanistic worldview and a completely deterministic interpretation of the world. As a reaction this doubt led to another extreme position. Could it not be the case that all laws are statistical and the deterministic outlook is only on the surface of macroscopic phenomena? That is, all complex systems (things) of the world are in fact – in their inmost structure, i.e. on the atomic level – like gases or swarms of mosquitoes or clouds. Such considerations led to another extreme picture labeled by Popper as: "All clocks are clouds." The theoretical background of this view is that nothing is ruled by strict dynamical-deterministic laws but everything ultimately obeys statistical laws, which allow degrees of freedom, chance and randomness on the microlevel and in individual cases.

If one of these extreme positions were true, either all laws of nature should be ultimately reducible to dynamical laws or all laws of nature should be ultimately reducible to statistical laws. But such a reduction is not possible in either way. Nor is it possible just for the fundamental laws of nature.[5]

(3) For each of the above extreme positions there is even one more extreme subsidiary position. Concerning the first view according to which everything is ruled by dynamical laws the word "everything" is also extended to initial conditions, boundary conditions, constants of nature etc. This goes beyond Laplace's view; since initial conditions, although known by Laplace's intelligence, are not determined by the dynamical laws. But although we cannot decide this question in application to a beginning of this universe (Big Bang) we can certainly show that it must be wrong when applied to the present state of the universe. This can be shown as follows:

All possible microstates in a liter of air (see section 6.3.4 below) are compatible with the laws (both statistical and dynamical laws). Let us imagine now all possible microstates and all possible initial conditions of the whole universe at present. All of them are compatible with all the laws of nature, because this is just the understanding of what a law is: something invariant w.r.t. a change of initial conditions or microstates. The number of all possible microstates and initial conditions of the whole universe is so big that it is clearly impossible that each of them could be realized in the universe at some time, under the assumption that the universe has a finite age and has a finite future; otherwise, if the universe is infinite in time, even the huge number of microstates

5 This has been shown in detail in Mittelstaedt and Weingartner (2005) ch.7.2.

and initial conditions could possibly be played through. But since we assume in agreement with the General Theory of Relativity that the world is finite in space (closed space coordinates) and in time (no closed time like curves, but finite) it is impossible that all these microstates or initial conditions could be realized (played through) during the finite lifetime of the universe. This means that both the microstates and initial conditions that have been realized and those which are not realized (not yet or never) are not ruled by laws of nature and are in this sense random or chance-like. A further consequence of this consideration is that the laws of nature are valid also in other universes, which differ from our universe only with respect to microstates or initial conditions[6].

(4) There is also a more extreme version concerning the second view (2). According to (2), ultimately, everything is ruled by statistical laws. The still more extreme version says that since statistical laws do rule only the macrostates of a great number of things or systems and emerge only when the behavior of huge ensembles is described the individual things or systems and the single particles on the microlevel are not ruled by any law; they are just behaving randomly and by chance such that chance and randomness is the basis of everything: Chance alone is the source of every innovation, of all creation in the biosphere. Pure chance, absolutely free, but blind...[7] Even if there is some restriction mentioned w.r.t. the biosphere this does not hinder that the underlying laws on the atomic and molecular level are physical and chemical laws. Although it is not wrong to say that the respective atoms and molecules have certain degrees of freedom and insofar behave randomly it has to be stressed that they behave randomly *relative* to the physical and chemical laws the obey. Therefore Monod's slogan "Chance alone..." is more than a tolerable exaggeration. This point, that different kinds of chance and randomness can only be defined relative to order and law, will become clear from the following sections.

6.3.2 Randomness in arithmetic and geometry

There is already a kind of randomness or contingency in both arithmetic and geometry. There are questions of arithmetic, which cannot be answered by any law

6 For a detailed argument of that sort see Weingartner (1996) section 7.
7 Monod (1972) p.110.

of arithmetic. For example it has been proved by Juri Matijasevic in 1970 that Hilbert's 10th problem, i.e. the question whether a diophantine equation (that is an equation which contains only integers) has a solution in integers, is equivalent to the question whether a computer program comes to a stop: i.e. both questions are undecidable. Similarly the question whether a diophantine equation has finitely or infinitely many solutions cannot be decided by any mathematical laws. Thus arithmetically random and algorithmically random can be defined relative to laws of arithmetic or to an algorithm or computer program respectively:

Df 6.1. The state of affairs p is arithmetically random (algorithmically random) iff p is not ruled (decided) by any law of arithmetic (by any algorithm or computer program).

In contradistinction to Riemann: "Über die *Hypothesen*, welche der Geometrie zugrunde liegen" Helmholtz named his work: "Über die *Tatsachen*, welche der Geometrie zugrunde liegen"; he was pointing to the *contingency* of certain facts which determine the choice of the geometrical framework. Thus Helmholtz proved a theorem, which says that if we assume rigid bodies of finite extension that are freely movable in space (as measurement rods) then the geometry is of constant curvature i.e. it is eucledean, elliptic or hyperbolic. On the other hand if the rigid bodies freely movable in space are sufficiently small then the geometry is Riemannean.[8] According to the above consideration we may formulate Df 6.2:

Df 6.2. The state of affairs p is geometrically contingent iff p is dependent on the existence of rigid bodies, which are freely movable in space.

The conditions for measuring rods expressed in the definiens of Df 6.2 – to be freely movable in space and to remain rigid in the sense of not changing its properties – are contingent empirical and also falsifiable facts: they are not universally valid or satisfiable as we know from the Theory of Special Relativity.

8 For more on that see Mittelstaedt and Weingartner (2005) ch.4.

6.3.3 Kinds of chance and randomness concerning *dynamical* laws of nature

The laws of nature can be divided into two groups: into dynamical laws and into statistical laws. According to our knowledge today all physical chemical and biological laws are either dynamical laws or statistical laws[9]. Examples for dynamical laws are Newton's laws of motion, Maxwell's equations of electromagnetism, the Schrödinger equation; examples for statistical laws are the laws of thermodynamics[10], the law of radioactive decay, the Hardy-Weinberg law of population genetics.

In order to explain chance and movement we need to distinguish something, which changes relative to something, which does not change. That what changes (moves) is thought to be contingent (random, not necessary) relative to the not changing (or even not changeable) necessary principle or law. From this it follows that chance and randomness (w.r.t. non-living systems) can only be defined relative to a law, which is not random, stable and necessary. This is done by the subsequent definitions:

Df 6.3. A law is naturally necessary iff it is invariant under a change of initial conditions.

This definition expresses an essential property of laws of nature, i.e. their invariance under certain inessential conditions. Under these the space-time invariance is the most important and also the oldest invariance. The content of Df 6.3 can also be expressed in this way: A law is naturally necessary iff it holds in all possible worlds (universes) that differ from our world (universe) – if at all – only w.r.t. initial conditions[11].

On the other hand states of affairs which represent descriptions of initial conditions (for example individual space-time points) are random or accidental relative to those (dynamical) laws of nature:

---

9 For a justification cf. Mittelstaedt and Weingartner (2005) ch.7.1. For properties of dynamical laws see ch. 4.3.1 above.

10 With some proviso. Since if the laws of thermodynamics are viewed just as phenomenological descriptions of macrostates they seem to be not statistical but only stating the coexistence of phenomena. But as soon as one incorporates their deeper foundation on the microlevel they are statistical laws obeying criteria S1–S4.

11 This formulation goes back to a definition of natural necessity given by Popper in his Logic of Scientific Discovery (Popper (1959) p.433)

Df 6.4. p is not naturally necessary (or: empirically random or accidental) w.r.t. dynamical laws iff p can change without changing any (fundamental) dynamical law.

According to this definition we might ask the general question: What is the set of all changes, which do not change (dynamical or just any) laws of nature? Steven Weinberg called this set “the symmetry group of nature” and said about it:

> “It is increasingly clear that the symmetry group of nature is the deepest thing that we understand about nature today … Specifying the symmetry group of nature may be all we need to say about the physical world beyond the principles of quantum mechanics.”[12]

But how can we determine the set of all changes, which leave the laws invariant? This would mean to know the line of demarcation between contingent initial conditions and necessary and invariant laws. It would mean to know which constants when changed do not affect laws and which do[13] and which initial conditions and boundary conditions would affect the laws when changed and which would not. Are the laws of nature invariant with respect to a change of the amount of energy (mass) of the whole universe (which is constant by the law of conservation of energy)? Or could we change the ratio of electron and proton mass slightly without changing laws? From these questions it is clear that invariance (or symmetry) in this wide sense incorporates all the groups of symmetries which are known today in physics: and it may even concern further ones of which we are ignorant so far.

Examples:

1. Whether the orbits of the planets are circles or ellipses is not determined by Newton’s laws, thus it is empirically accidental according to Df 6.4. Galileo defended circles, may be partially because of esthetic reasons, but partially perhaps he has understood that the circles are the simplest solutions of rotationally symmetric laws.

2. That the orbit of a planet lies in one plane which contains the sun is determined by the laws, i.e. is naturally necessary according to Df 6.3. But which plane it is or better which angle this plane has with respect to say another

---

12 Weinberg (1987) p.73.

13 We know of course that constants like G (gravitational constant), h (Planck’s constant), e (elementary charge), m_e (mass of electron) and c (light velocity in vacuum) must not be changed since these enter fundamental laws and so a change of them would change the laws. Other constants are dependent on them like $\alpha = e^2/\hbar \cdot c$.

star is not determined by the laws, i.e. is empirically accidental according to Df 6.4.

3. The distances of the planets from the sun and their proportions are also not determined by Newton's (or Kepler's) laws. Kepler thought that they have this proportion for the purpose of harmony. But today one knows that Kepler was right in the sense that these proportions play a role for the stability of the whole planetary system in such a way that chaotic motion (to a greater extend)[14] can be avoided.

Here we could continue with other kinds of randomness relative to dynamical laws: for example the randomness present in chaotic processes, which is twofold. One type is concerned with the process of motion or the respective trajectory; the other with the loss of information about the position of a point in an interval after one iteration.[15] However since this chapter is not one on chance and randomness in general, but serves only to guarantee the fact of chance and randomness in non-living things we need not to go into more details concerning dynamical laws. On the other hand, it is necessary to deal with at least some kinds of chance and randomness relative to statistical laws of nature.

6.3.4 Kinds of chance and randomness concerning *statistical* laws of nature

Chance and randomness are usually connected with statistical laws. The main reason is that statistical laws have some properties in which they differ essentially from dynamical laws. Two very important ones, responsible for chance and randomness, are the following:

(1) In contradistinction to dynamical laws the state S_2 at t_2 of the physical system is *not* a definite function of an earlier state S_1 at t_1. The same initial state S_1 at t_1 may lead to different successor states (branching).

(2) Whereas dynamical laws if they hold of the whole system they hold also for their parts, statistical laws describe and predict the states of the whole system, but they do not describe or predict the states of the individual parts (objects)

14 The orbits of the first four planets are (large-scale) chaotic to a small degree (Mercury most, then Mars, Venus and the Earth is the most quiet, especially because it is a balanced system with the moon). Cf. Laskar (1994).

15 For details cf. Weingartner (2009a) section 4 and Weingartner (1996) p.57 and p.59.

of this system, i.e. statistical laws permit *degrees of freedom* for the parts (individual objects, particles) of the system.[16]

Property (2) was expressed already very clearly in Schrödinger's inaugural lecture at the ETH (Zürich) in 1922:

> "In the observed regularity of the mass phenomenon the individual regularity (if any) need not be considered as a factor. On the contrary, it is completely effaced by averaging millions of single processes...The average values manifest their own purely statistical regularity."[17]

Though there is indeterminacy for every individual system, there is a strict law for the whole system if the ensemble is large enough. To some extent, such laws "emerge" from the "lawless" behavior of a large number of individual systems. In this sense, Wheeler spoke of "law without law".[18]

According to the above considerations we may define *statistically random* as follows:

Df 6.5. Assume p to be an individual state, event or process. Then p is statistically random (statistically accidental) iff p can change without changing any (fundamental) statistical law. Similarly, one may define *thermodynamically random* and *quantumstatistically random*.

Examples: In a liter of gas (air) at temperature $T = 0°$C and sea-level pressure there are $2,7 \cdot 10^{22}$ molecules. This system can be in a huge number of different microstates ($10^{5 \cdot 10^{22}}$) so as to realize the macrostate "liter of air under the mentioned conditions". Thus a change from one microstate to another does not change any law of thermodynamics with the help of which one can predict for example a certain velocity distribution (as a macrostate) of the system. Therefore any such individual microstate is statistically random. In big ski resorts in Austria the lifts and cable cars can take up about 60.000 people per hour. The state or skiing process of a particular skier is statistically random relative to the statistical behavior of the whole system of 60.000 skiers which obeys certain statistical laws describing for example the average velocity, the average difference in altitude, the average direction etc. An individual mutation event is statistically random w.r.t. the average mutation-rate r (within the limits of $1 : 10^5 \geq r \geq 1 : 10^8$. It should be mentioned however that the mutation is not random w.r.t. the place where it oc-

16 For more on differences between dynamical and statistical laws see Mittelstaedt and Weingartner (2005) ch.7.2.

17 Published later as "Was ist ein Naturgesetz". Schrödinger (1961) p.11.

18 Wheeler (1983).

curs in the DNA; nor is it random w.r.t. the exchange of a letter or base pair (which obeys physico-chemical laws) nor w.r.t. influence of the environment. There is on the other hand randomness of the mutation event w.r.t. the usefulness for the living system (see below 8.3.3).

6.3.5 Complexity and randomness of sequences

A further domain of chance and randomness is the structure of sequences. DNA, RNA are examples of sequences of living systems, chains of inorganic elements or compounds are examples of sequences of non-living systems. One important property of such sequences is its complexity. According to an idea of Kolmogorov[19] the degree of complexity of a sequence can be defined as the minimal length of a code that can produce the sequence:

Df 6.6. The Kolmogorov Complexity KC of the sequence $sq =_{df}$ the minimal length of a code cd such that cd can reproduce sq.

In all cases where the minimal length of cd is shorter than sq, the sequence sq can be "compressed", i.e. it can be represented by a shorter code. The following examples show such cases: Examples: The sequence of Euclid's Elements can be represented by Hilbert's axioms + derivation rules of his *Grundlagen der Geometrie*, which are a code of minimal length for that sequence. The Kolmogorov Complexity KC of the sequence of states of the planetary orbits of the last 2000 years can be understood as the "code" of Newton's laws + one initial condition, which are both (approximately[20]) sufficient to reproduce all the other states of the system. The KC of the sequence of proteins of a higher animal is the minimal length of that part of DNA, which can reproduce the sequence of proteins. Concerning the whole human DNA however one does not know exactly whether all of it is necessary for all the tasks it has (i.e. whether it is G-random or better G-complex). Earlier one thought that the part of DNA for reproducing the proteins is the most important and the largest one such that the rest might be at least partially redundant. But according to our knowledge today "the rest" is about 98% and thus cannot be redundant. First one knows there are a lot of important regulative functions fulfilled

---

19 Cf. Kolmogorov (1963), Kolmogorov (1965).

20 'Approximately' means here that the calculation would have to incorporate some perturbations, especially of the first four planets, the orbits of which are not completely smooth but slightly chaotic. Cf. Laskar (1994).

by those 98% and secondly one knows that repetitions of sequential parts of the DNA accomplish important tasks. Moreover that part of the DNA which is specifically human (ca. 30 million letters out of 3 billions) is not protein producing. Of these things research has been done only very partially so far, even if it is done recently all over the world.[21] Suppose now that the KC of some sequence sq is not shorter than sq; i.e. the minimal length of the code which can reproduce sq is not shorter than sq. Then one may look for another code, which is shorter. But if there is not any shorter code for sq than sq itself, then such an sq is called "random" by Gregory Chaitin[22] (called G-random below):

Df 6.7. A sequence sq is G-random iff the minimal length of any code or algorithm cd, such that cd can reproduce sq, is not shorter than sq itself.

Observe however that a sequence which is G-random need not to be without order or structure. This can be seen from the following application of Df 6.7: Let us take a famous piece of literary art like Shakespeare's Hamlet, Goethe's Faust or Dostojewski's Brothers Karamazov. Can these texts be completely represented by a shorter text? If not, they are G-random. But it would be ridiculous to say that they have no order or structure. What these considerations show is only that one has to focus on that very aspect which the respective definition describes. And as it is clear from Df 6.6 this kind of randomness is a measure of the complexity of the sequence, but it is not a measure of its order or structure. Or in different words: this kind of randomness is a measure for the incompressibility of the sequence, not of its structure. Therefore the DNA- and RNA-sequences have a very high Kolmogorov-complexity. In contradistinction to that two valued propositional logic, or better to say the infinite sequence of valid sentences of two valued propositional logic have low Kolmogorov-complexity: the code may be truth tables or the three axioms of Lukasiewicz plus the rule Modus Ponens. A similar consideration is true of Euclid's Elements and its axioms or of Peano Arithmetic with its axioms.

However, the sequence of the planetary orbits has a much higher degree of Kolmogorov-complexity. Although shorter, the code itself is considerably more complex (Newton's laws: differential equations): and so is the sequence of proteins since its code is already quite complex.

---

21 Cf. Pollard (2009) and Geraci (1996).
22 Chaitin (1966).

There is an important general result concerning Kolmogorov complexity KC due to Chaitin (1974): A formal system S possessing degree k of Kolmogorov-complexity cannot prove whether a binary sequence has a Kolmogorov-complexity of degree higher than some constant m (where m is determined by k). This means also that KC is not a computable function.[23] From this it follows that the randomness of a sufficiently long sequence (for example of length m) cannot be proved with the help of S. Moreover it holds that for every system S there is such an m.

6.3.6 Kinds of chance and randomness w.r.t. structure and order

It will have become evident from the preceding sections that all different kinds of chance and randomness cannot be defined "absolutely" or "independently" but only relative to some law (dynamical or statistical) or to some rule or order. This will become manifest also from the following definitions which relate chance or randomness to different types of order defined in sections 5.3.3–5.3.5 above.

At first sight it might seem that we could define a kind of chance and randomness of some system s by saying that s lacks structure (defined by Df 5.3) or that s only partially fulfills the conditions (ii) or (iii) of 5.3. But at a closer look this does not seem reasonable because any thing or system will have some internal relations among their parts and will have some external relations between its parts and things of its environment. For this reason it seems more suitable to define those kinds of chance and randomness, which are related to different types of order in such a way that some structure is always satisfied, but some additional properties or relations are lacking.

Therefore one type of chance or randomness can be related to Ord_2 (5.3.3, Df 5.5):

Df 6.8. A thing or system s is random w.r.t. Ord_2 iff s does not have Ord_2 in the sense that its internal or external relations do not include special arithmetical or geometrical relations.

---

23 Cf. Chaitin (1987) and Suppes (2002) ch.5.4.

Examples: A crystal has Ord_2, but the respective smashed crystal is random w.r.t. Ord_2. A magnet has Ord_2, when the magnet is demagnetised it is random w.r.t. Ord_2.

Df 6.9. A thing or system s_1 is random w.r.t. both Ord_3 and system s_2 iff conditions (i)–(iii) of Df 5.7 are satisfied, condition (iv) of Df 5.7 is not satisfied. This means that s_1 does not have much lower entropy than s_2 (s_1 may have even higher entropy than s_2).

Examples: A crystal or a fullerene C60 has Ord_3 but the melted crystal or fullerene is random w.r.t. Ord_3. A magnet at low temperature has Ord_3, but at very high temperature when the elementary magnets all fluctuate it is random w.r.t. Ord_3.

Df 6.10. A process B from $S_1(t_1)$ to $S_2(t_2)$ of system s is random iff there is no entropy decrease but only an entropy increase from $S_1(t_1)$ to $S_2(t_2)$ w.r.t. the whole system s. In such a case there is no becoming from $S_1(t_1)$ to $S_2(t_2)$ w.r.t. the whole system s according to Df 5.9 (section 5.3.4).

Examples: There are lots of examples for such random processes: radiation processes, the burning processes of stars, all processes tending towards equilibrium or balance etc. Observe however that some subsystems of system s may be still involved in the opposite process of decreasing entropy and building up order (recall Df 5.7 of Ord_3).

6.3.7 Kinds of chance and randomness w.r.t. teleological order

As the considerations so far have shown it holds that every kind of chance is related or can be defined only w.r.t. some kind of order. But the kind of order may be also a network of goals or a hierarchy of values. And thus a thing or event or process can be called *random* in the sense that it cannot be subordinated under or directed towards some goal; or if it cannot be integrated into some hierarchy of values.[24] In this case the final state is not a relative goal w.r.t. the initial state of the respective system (cf. Df 5.10).

---

24 Cf. Soontiens (1991).

Df 6.11. A process B of system s is random w.r.t. teleological order iff either

(1) B is not a process of becoming of s or

(2) it is not the case that the final state $S_2(t_2)$ of higher order of s is a relative goal w.r.t. the initial state $S_1(t_1)$ of lower order of s from which it developed

(3) both (1) and (2) are the case.

Examples: All processes of increasing entropy (decreasing order) of a system, which has no subsystems of increasing order. All chaotic processes, which lead to increasing disorder.

6.3.8 Results of chapter 6

T 6.1. *There is chance and randomness in things (systems) (or states of affairs concerning such things) in the sense that they can change without changing either dynamical or statistical laws (cf. 6.3.3 and 6.3.4).*

T 6.2. *There is chance and randomness in things (systems) in the sense that sequences of them have a certain degree of complexity (cf. 6.3.5).*

T 6.3. *There is chance and randomness in things (systems) in the sense that they do not possess Ord_2 or that they do not possess Ord_3 or that they have no processes of* becoming *(cf. 6.3.6).*

T 6.4. *There is chance and randomness in things (systems) in the sense that some of their processes do not possess teleological order (cf. 6.3.7).*

6.4 Answer to the Objections

6.4.1 (to 6.1.1)

As has been shown in section 6.3.6 (Df 6.8,Df 6.9) there is a certain type of chance and randomness related to the type of Ord_2 and of Ord_3 (cf. section 5.3.3). This proves already that there is chance and randomness in non-living things. But there are still other types of chance and randomness related to dynamical and to statistical laws as is clear from sections 6.3.3 and 6.3.4.

6.4.2 (to 6.1.2)

All changes which do not change any fundamental dynamical law are random w.r.t. this law (recall Df 6.4). Therefore those things, which are not governed by dynamical laws, like initial conditions, are random w.r.t. them. Moreover several parameters of chaotic behavior (belonging to dynamical chaos) are random, although the underlying laws are dynamical laws.

6.4.3 (to 6.1.3)

As it is already pointed out in the *Argument Pro* (6.2) nothing hinders that the microstates of a big ensemble behave randomly whereas the macrostates are strictly predictable. Moreover this is an important point in understanding statistical laws: random behavior and law-like behavior is together compatible in the same physical, chemical or biological system. And in addition to that: different properties of one such system may be governed by dynamical and by statistical laws in such a way that both types of laws are compatible with each other in one system.[25]

---

25 Cf. Mittelstaedt and Weingartner (2005) ch.7.2.3.5.

7 Whether there is teleological order in living things?

7.1 Arguments Contra

7.1.1 First argument

Teleological Order requires the existence of goals. But goals seem to exist only in those living things that have consciousness.

Therefore it generally does not seem to hold that there is teleological order in living things.

7.1.2 Second argument

Teleological order in living things requires that carbon-based life can evolve. A necessary condition that carbon-based life can evolve is that the observed values of all physical and cosmological quantities take on very special values. Therefore: If there is teleological order in living things then the observed values of all physical and cosmological quantities take on very special values. But this whole argument is based on the Anthropic Principle. And "It is hard to see … how the Anthropic Principle can ever be used to make a testable prediction, because any physical theory that is inconsistent with our existence is manifestly incorrect anyway."[1]

Therefore the conclusion or some premises might not be correct and consequently there might not be teleological order in living things.

1 Davis (1982) p. 129.

7.2 Arguments Pro

7.2.1 First argument

The DNA is a subsystem (Df 5.6, 5.3.3) of every living system. It has also Ord_3 w.r.t. its respective living system + environment. Moreover the process DNA $\rightarrow$ RNA $\rightarrow$ Protein occurring in living systems possesses teleological order according to Df 5.10 (5.3.5).

Therefore there is teleological order in living things. That processes in living systems possess also higher level of teleological order will be shown subsequently (Df 7.7, 7.3.5).

7.2.2 Second argument

If it can be defended that there is teleological order already in non- living systems the more it is defendable to be present in living systems. In this sense Hull says:

> "If anything is to count as a teleological system, living organisms must."[2]

But it has been shown in ch. 5 (Df 5.10) that there is teleological order in non-living systems.

Therefore it must be defendable that there is teleological order in living systems.

7.3 Proposed Answer

It has been shown in section 5.3 that there is teleological order in non-living things. This has been substantiated by the fact that there is *becoming* in non-living things, i.e. a process leading away from equilibrium to non-equilibrium and new order. But in living things there is *becoming* even in an intensified sense: living things (living systems or biosystems) possess *metabolism*, *self-regulation*,

2 Hull (1974) p.104.

propagation and *adaption* concerning changes of environment. Within a certain period of lifetime they also possess growth. Therefore: There is teleological order in living things (living systems, biosystems). This conclusion will be substantiated more accurately in the following sections.

7.3.1 Living system (Biosystem)

Df 7.1. ls is a living system (biosystem) iff the following conditions are satisfied:

(i) ls consists of chemical and biochemical subsystems (cf. Df 5.6, section 5.3.3) containing water, proteins, nucleic acids, carbon hydrates and fats where the parts of ls are in interaction and the border of ls is a flexible and semipermeable biomembrane

(ii) ls possesses metabolism

(iii) ls possesses self-regulation

(iv) ls possesses a genetic subsystem (DNA-structure) which controls propagation if available

(v) ls possesses adaption concerning some changes of the environment (of ls).

An important example of a living system[3] (biosystem, ls) is the cell. It is probably the smallest unit of a living system. The cell may be a eukaryotic cell having a cell nucleus or a prokaryotic cell having no cell nucleus (as in bacteria). But also systems of cells like tissues or organs are ls. An *elementary biosystem* is a biosystem such that its components (parts) are no biosystems themselves. An organism is an elementary or compound biosystem (ls), which is not a species-like subsystem of another ls. All elementary ls (biosystems) seem to be cells; but not the other way round, because some cells may have as their parts alga-cells in symbiosis. Molecules are not ls, although molecular biology investigates those molecules, which are parts of ls.

Condition (i) says that living systems (biosystems) are partially open systems because of their biomembrane (recall Df 5.7, condition (iii), section 5.3.3). Physically speaking, cells are thermodynamic systems that are open and far from equilib-

3 The above definition of living system is – concerning its main parts – due to Mahner and Bunge (2000) p.137.

rium. They maintain chemical concentrations that are far from equilibrium. To do this they take in matter and energy from the environment, hence are *open* thermodynamic systems.[4] Condition (ii) requires metabolism as a necessary condition for ls. Consequently viruses, since they have no metabolism, are not ls; an isolated virus may have a crystalline structure. However, the compound virus-cell system may be called a ls. It should be remarked though that metabolism can be reduced for some time in living systems as it is, for example, in spores and seeds.

Condition (iii) says that self-regulation is a necessary condition for ls; but from this it does not follow that self-reproduction is a necessary condition for ls. For example tissues or organs are ls but have no self-reproduction. Therefore it says in condition (iv) "if available". This is the case for living individuals or organisms. Aristotle, when he spoke of living things, had in mind living substances, i.e. usually higher living individuals or organisms. And then his three essential characteristics: growth, nutrition and propagation would be correct.

Finally, condition (v) says that adaption concerning changes of the environment are necessary although adaption may not be possible if these changes are too big and too sudden.

7.3.2 Order and teleological order in living systems

From definitions Df 5.3 and Df 5.4 (sections 5.3.1 and 5.3.3) it is evident that living systems have order of type 1, i.e. structure. From conditions (i) and (iv) of Df 7.1 it is also clear that ls possess order of type 2 (Ord_2). According to condition (i) ls contains subsystems (Df 5.6, section 5.3.3) and is itself a subsystem w.r.t. its environment. From condition (i) it follows that ls is a partially open system. Furthermore any ls has lower entropy w.r.t. its environment. From these points it follows that ls satisfies Df 5.7 (section 5.3.3) that is ls has Ord_3 relative to the environment of ls. Thus, living systems (biosystems) possess Ord_1, Ord_2 and Ord_3.

According to Df 7.1 every ls possesses metabolism and self- regulation. Both metabolism and self-regulation are ordering processes in the sense of *becoming*; i.e. they satisfy Df 5.9. This holds also for adaption and for propagation if the latter is available. Moreover all four, metabolism, self-regulation, adaption and propagation possess *teleological order*, since they are ordering processes of becoming and since any relative final state $S_2(t_2)$ of higher order is a relative goal

4 Kauffman (2008), p.47.

w.r.t. the initial state $S_1(t_1)$ of lower order from which it developed (Df 5.10 of section 5.3.5).

Since all these four processes possess teleological order and since all living systems possess at least metabolism and self- regulation it follows that all living systems possess teleological order.

7.3.3 Values in living systems

In addition we may consider the question in what sense or under what conditions such processes or the relative goals of such processes are valuable for the respective ls.

7.3.3.1 Primary, secondary and basic good of a living system

Either a property or a process of ls and a thing of the environment of ls can be primary, secondary or a basic good for ls.

Df 7.2. A property or process C of ls or a thing X of the environment of ls is a *primary good* (primary value) (or primary need) for ls iff meeting C or X is necessary for ls to stay alive in its environment.

Df 7.3. A property or process C of ls or a thing X of the environment of ls is a *secondary good* (or secondary need or value) for ls iff meeting C or X is necessary to keep or regain health in the environment (including society) of ls.

Df 7.4. A property or process C of ls or a thing X of the environment of ls is a *basic good* (basic value) for ls iff C or X is either a primary or a secondary good (value) for ls.

Examples[5]: All four processes of ls, metabolism, self-regulation, adaption and propagation are primary, secondary and basic goods of ls according to definitions

5 The definitions Df 7.2 – Df 7.4 are similar to that of Bunge (1989) p.35. Cf. Weingartner (2003) pp.26ff and Haring and Weingartner (2014b).

Df 7.2 – 4. Moreover the properties of ls described in (i) of Df 7.1 are also basic goods for ls. Concerning environment basic goods of ls are: sufficient and sufficiently clean air and water, adequate food ... etc.

Df 7.5. A *basic evil* of ls is a lack of a basic good for ls (i.e. is a lack of a primary or of a secondary good for ls).

Or in the terminology of the above definitions: A basic evil of ls is a property (state, process) C of ls or a thing X of its environment iff avoiding C or X is necessary for ls to stay alive or keep (regain) health in the environment of ls.

7.3.3.2 Goods and values

In order to define 'good' (primary, secondary, basic) we may presuppose other goods or values. In other words: 'good' or 'value' can be defined relative to other goods and values. Thus Df 7.2 presupposes that to stay alive is an essential good or goal for any living system; and also to keep or regain health is an essential good for any living system. There are people who deny this. But this seems to deny and refuse the most accessible, the obvious and the matter of course. They are presupposing implicitly – at least concerning our knowledge about values – that man is constructed in such a bad way that he has always to deny and refuse that which is to him most obvious and most easily accessible by experience.

However there is also a possibility to connect essential goods for ls with activities of ls. In this case the essential goods are not connected to other goods or values (at least not directly). Thus we may connect staying alive or preserving survival with striving after or aiming at in the following way: All living systems are striving after (are aiming at) staying alive or preserving survival. Moreover: All ls are striving after (are aiming at) keeping or regaining health. The idea of such connecting principles – or *bridge principles* as they are called in modern theories of the foundations of values or of ethics – goes back to Aristotle. He tried to define "essential good (value) for ls" by those goods, which are strived after by all individual living systems or organisms.[6]

The activities "striving after" or "aiming at" have to be understood in their widest sense; even if Aristotle had in mind higher animals in the sense of individual sub-

6 Aristotle. (1985) 1094a. On this idea the Natural Law-theory is based. Cf. Weingartner (1983b).

stances. Examples are a tree, a worm, a fish, a bird, a horse or an individual man. Aristotle did not know of bacteria (in general: prokaryotes) and all his examples of living things belong to higher-level eukaryotes. But even then the activities "striving after" or "aiming at" have to be taken without presupposing consciousness and in an analogous sense.

For the present purpose it suffices though, that *staying alive* or *survival* and *to keep* or *regain health* are essential goods or goals for any ls. From this it does not follow, however, that these goods or goals of the respective ls are also the highest goods or goals under all circumstances or conditions. This need not always be the case, since the survival or health of parts of ls which are ls themselves, like the cells or organs, may be sacrificed for the survival or for regaining health of the whole individual ls.[7]

7.3.4 Values concerning the history of ls

Considering staying alive or survival and keeping or regaining health we may even ask whether there are more comprehensive goals for the whole living system. This only makes sense however if we select only those eukaryotic[8] living systems, which are compound ls (biosystems) not being species-like subsystems of another ls (biosystem) (cf. 7.3.1 above); tissues or organs are ruled out. Then one reasonable "comprehensive goal" is (the ability of) continuing the respective species-history of the ls in question. The continuation of the species-history and consequently the conservation of the species was *the* goal of the species (as a whole) already for Aristotle.[9]

7 Basic values can be sacrificed for some higher values also consciously by humans in exceptional situations (cf. 15.3.5.2 2, below).

8 For prokaryotic ls the concept of "species" is more difficult to define. Scientists therefore use practical demarcations.

9 Observe also the rehabilitation of the concept of "species" in biology by the *Synthetic Theory* and its founders and defenders like Dobzhansky, E. Mayr, Stebbins and others. Especially E. Mayr has focussed on the concept of species. A closer look or a more accurate definition of species (for example in his Mayr (1998) p.178) shows however several shortcomings. Cf. the critical remarks in Mahner and Bunge (2000) pp.249ff. We agree with Aristotle and Mahner and Bunge that the common (for Aristotle: essential) properties which define a species ultimately belong to the individuals who are members of the species, but cannot belong to populations (of individuals) as Mayr claims in his definition. Other definitions of species as lineages of ancestral descendent populations or of species as individuals suffer from similar weaknesses, cf. Mahner and Bunge (2000) pp.251ff.

Df 7.6. Assume C to be a property or a process of an eukaryotic compound ls (i.e. of an individual organism). Then C is *species-valuable* to ls iff possessing or having access to C contributes to the continuation of the species-history of ls or contributes to the conservation of the species of ls. Otherwise C is either neutral of harmful to ls.

In[10] the sense of Df 7.6 all four processes of ls, metabolism, self- regulation, adaption and propagation are valuable to ls. Since they are necessary conditions contributing to the continuation of the species-history viz. contributing to the conservation of the species of ls.

7.3.5 Higher-level teleological order

It has been shown in section 7.3.2 that every ls has Ord_1, Ord_2 and Ord_3. Moreover that the important processes of every ls, metabolism, self-regulation, adaption and propagation are processes of becoming and possess teleological order. In sections 7.3.3 and 7.3.4 it was shown that there are values in ls in the sense that properties or states or processes of ls are basic goods and goals of ls. Depending on these values we can say that there is also higher-level teleological order in living things in the sense given by the following definition:

Df 7.7. Process C of ls possesses higher-level teleological order (HTO) iff

(a) C is a becoming of ls (Df 5.9, section 5.3.4)

(b) the final state $S_2(t_2)$ of higher order of ls is a relative goal w.r.t. the initial state $S_1(t_1)$ of lower order of ls, in the sense that

  (i) $S_2(t_2)$ is closer to the basic good (value) of ls (Df 7.4) than $S_1(t_1)$ or

  (ii) $S_2(t_2)$ is closer to the continuation of species-history of ls (Df 7.6) than $S_1(t_1)$.

Df 7.8. X is relative goal of a ls iff

(a) X is a state $s(t)$ of a process C of becoming of ls

(b) C is a basic goal (value) of ls or C is a HTO of ls

10 A similar definition is due to Mahner and Bunge (2000) p.151.

(c) X has a level of order such that

   (i) it is the highest level of order L_m relative to other states of C

   (ii) L_m is compatible with laws of nature, fundamental constants and contingent initial conditions

7.3.6 Higher human values

Df 7.9. A property (event, process) C is a *higher human value* iff C is the intentional object of a higher human desire which follows a series of judgements of the human intellect about that object.

Df 7.10. X is a *legitimate higher human desire* of person b, living in society d iff X can be met in d

(a) without hindering the satisfaction of any basic good (value) of any member of d and without doing basic evil to any members of d

(b) without endangering the integrity of any valuable subsystem of d much less of d as a whole.

Df 7.11. A property (event, process) C is a *legitimate* higher human value iff

(a) C is a higher human value and

(b) C is the intentional object of a legitimate higher human desire

7.3.6.1 Different kinds of higher values

Higher values can be of three sorts: first, values which are connected to human nature; second, personal or individual values; third, values which go beyond human nature.

(1) Higher values of the first kind are legitimate desires (or contribute to them) of mankind as a species, i.e. of all men. Examples: Increasing knowledge in

11 Definition Df 7.10 is, in its main parts, due to Bunge (1989) p.35, Def 1.13.

accordance with abilities and interests, improving control of natural forces, human life in peace and average welfare.

(2) Higher values of the second kind are legitimate wants (or contribute to them) of the individual person. Examples: Choosing a particular profession, a particular study, a particular wife or husband, ... etc.

(3) Higher values of the third kind are legitimate desires (or contribute to them) of religious people.[12] Examples: Happiness in another life after this life; to do justice to everybody; practising their religion; ... etc.

These groups of higher values are (at least partially) legitimate by the Human Rights or by similar constitutions of different countries. But in some countries they cannot be realized or their realization is hindered even if they are legitimated in the constitution.

7.3.6.2 Values and norms

There is no direct connection between these values and the respective norms, which would require that these values be realized. Nor is there such a connection to the validity of the norm that these values and the human rights connected to them should not be violated or "are" inviolable rights. To state such a connection is not a fact, but an additional *assumption*. We cannot derive a norm from a statement about facts or from evaluations (value judgments) which are factual. This is only possible with the help of *bridge principles* which connect facts with norms like: if survival is a value of mankind then it should be realized.[13] Thomas Aquinas proposed the most general bridge principle, which he understands as the first self-evident normative principle of ethics: the good should be done, the bad should be avoided.[14] However, if these principles are not accepted as self-evident, they have to be assumed explicitly. Here we take the Human Rights as norms which require the realization of certain values of mankind.

12 "Religious people" can be characterized by the following description, which is due to Cicero: A man is said to be religious from "religio" because he often ponders over, and, as it were, reads again (religit) the things which pertain to the worship of God.

13 A detailed study of bridge principles can be found in chs. 11 and 12 of Schurz (1997).

14 Aquinas (1981) I-II, 94, 2.

7.3.7 Projected teleological order

If we apply definition Df 5.2 (of environment) to human actions, we receive a part of the human environment which we may call *action space*[15]. This action space consists of non-living systems (like houses, chairs, computers) and living systems (like other human persons, animals and plants). The respective definition is this: Let x be a human person; then the *action space* of x is defined as follows:

Df 7.12. $Actionspace(x) =_{df}$ those things y (which are not parts of x) such that x or some part z of x acts on y.

According to chs.5 and 7 these systems (living or non-living) possess different types of order and teleological order in the sense of the definitions given there. From these definitions it is clear that these types of order and teleological order and also the kinds of values involved are *objective* in the sense that they represent certain structures in the things (systems).

There are, however, also *subjective* types of order which are, so to speak, "projected" by the person who produces them by actively interpreting his or her environment and by hypothesizing about it. These projected types of order and teleological order correspond only partially to some type of order (teleological order) in the real thing or system. We may call this kind of "produced" environment the *projected action space*. Let x be a human person. Then the projected action space of x is defined as follows:

Df 7.13. *Projected Action Space(x)* $=_{df}$ those things y (which are not part of x) such that x believes that x or a part z of x acts on y.

Examples: The politician believes that he convinced his audience with his talk. The parent believes that the child accepts his advice. The chancellor believes that the net tax system leads to a more just distribution of goods in the country. Such beliefs may be partially or totally wrong.

Moreover, there is an additional important feature. It is the aspect of projected evaluation and projected teleological interrelations: the person projects values, goals and teleological order onto things and systems which may not or only partially possess them in an objective sense. A relevant example is described in de-

15 For more details see: Haring and Weingartner (2012) and Haring and Weingartner (2014b).

tail in the book "Vehicles" by Braitenberg[16], where a triangle, a rectangle and a circle move around. Certain movements are immediately interpreted as goal directed and teleological: If for example the triangle approaches the circle with one of its edges and the rectangular moves in between the two, this is interpreted as intended attack and protection. Instead of *objective* and *subjective* types of order, Boesch speaks in a similar way of *denotative* and *connotative* meaning:

> "However, all these denotations are associated with personal experiences, personal or cultural beliefs or evaluations; these *connotations* are not expressed by the denotative label. They may even, to a considerable degree, remain unconscious and therefore difficult to communicate."[17]

Boesch illustrates his statement on connotations within an action range concerning one's home:

> "Thus the home forms a base for planning and initiating action, as well as a target for terminating it. These home-valences, obviously, are related to external valences of places, objects and people… In other words, the things surrounding us will be increasingly structured into patterns; the home not only forms a structure of intimate familiarity, but by its power to exclude non-desired or threatening impacts of the external world takes on the quality of shelter."[18]

Let x be a human person. Then the projected teleological order of x can be defined as follows:

Df 7.14. *Projected Teleological Order (x)*$=_{df}$ those things y (which are not part of x) such that x, when acting on y, believes that the things y are ordered in a relation of means and goals.

7.3.8 Result of chapter 7

The result of this chapter (7.) is that living systems possess first of all that teleological order, on a lower level, which is possessed already by non-living systems (recall Df 5.10 of section 5.3.5). In addition to that living systems (ls) possess teleological order on a higher level in the sense defined by Df 7.7. That means especially that w.r.t. ls we can find out some of their most important basic values and its re-

---

16 Braitenberg (1984). There are several other purely mechanical vehicles and their movements described in this book which also immediately receive a goal directed interpretation.

17 Boesch (1991) p.23. Cf. Haring and Weingartner (2014b)

18 Boesch (1991) p.33

spective goals (staying alive and keeping or regaining health). And this holds generally for all *ls*. The result of ch. 7. can therefore be summarised in the following theorems (cf. also 7.5 below):

T 7.1. *All living systems possess teleological order (cf. 7.3.2).*

T 7.2. *All living systems possess basic goods or values (cf. 7.3.3).*

T 7.3. *All living systems possess higher-level teleological order and relative goals (cf. 7.3.5).*

Observe however that from these theorems it does not follow that all living systems possess the mentioned three features for all their properties or processes. Living ssystems can have some processes, which are neither teleological nor meet goals or values (cf. 8.3.6 below).

7.4 Answer to the Objections

7.4.1 (to 7.1.1)

Those living things that have consciousness, know their goals in a special way and possess some degrees of freedom when choosing the means for reaching the goal. But also when there is consciousness only very partially concerning the goal and less partially concerning the means, like in animals guided by instinct, the existence of goals and their achievement is manifest. Birds flying several thousand kilometres to the south before winter in order to find food and to survive is an example. An example on a much lower prokaryotic level is a bacterium, (E. Coli), the activities of which in order to survive are described by the following passage:

> "Its talents are legion, but its size is minuscule. E. Coli is a cylindrical organism less than 1 nm in diameter and 2 nm long … . Yet it is adept at counting molecules of specific sugars, amino acids, or dipeptides; at integration of similar or dissimilar sensory inputs over space

and time; at comparing counts taken over the recent past; at triggering an all or nothing response; at swimming in a viscous medium ..."[19]

From these examples (which could be continued) it follows that one can talk of basic values and goals (in living systems) in a reasonable and scientific way also in cases where there is only partial consciousness or no consciousness at all.

7.4.2 (to 7.1.2)

Independently of the validity of the Anthropic Principle the argument in 7.1.2 has the following structure: Teleological order in living things (T) implies that carbon-based life can evolve (C). C implies that the observed values of all physical and cosmological quantities take on very special values (O).

Therefore: T implies O. This is logically valid, because it is just the logical principle of Hypothetical Syllogism or in other words the principle of the transitivity of implication which is this: $T \to C$ and $C \to O$ together imply $T \to O$. But this argument cannot prove T to be a fact, although O is a fact; i.e. the observed values of all physical and cosmological quantities take on very special values indeed. But from this one cannot conclude T, since O is only a necessary condition of T (but not a sufficient one). However the fact that O is the case, supports T in the sense that at least a very important necessary condition for T is fulfilled. Therefore the first part of the argument in 7.1.2 (without the remark about the Anthropic Principle) is not contra teleological order but indirectly supports teleological order by stating an important necessary condition (O).

The Anthropic Principle. One possible form of the Anthropic Principle (AP) is this: $C \to O$; i.e. if carbon-based life evolves then the observed values of all physical and cosmological quantities take on very special values. This form is close to what Barrow and Tipler call the *strong* AP:

> "The universe must have those properties which allow life to develop"[20]

From the formulation of SAP above one can see that "those properties of the universe" are necessary conditions for life to develop, just as it is asserted in: $C \to O$. Concerning testability of SAP or of $C \to O$ one has first to realize that both C and

---

19 H. C. Berg, Cold Spring Harbor Symposium on Quantitative Biology 1990. Cited in Denton (1998) p.211.

20 Barrow and Tipler (1986) p.21. This principle is abbreviated there as SAP.

O are true and have been confirmed by severe tests. C is true, since it is just a fact that carbon-based life exists in many different forms and on different levels up to the existence of man. And O is true in the sense of extraordinary specialness. Numerous observations and calculations have shown the fine-tuning of all physical and cosmological quantities. To give only two of a great number of examples:

(1) If the numerical proportion of the strong nuclear force to the electromagnetic force (about $1 : 10^{-2}$) were slightly different then there would not be any carbon-based life.

(2) If the proportion of the number of protons to the number of photons ($\approx 1 : 10^8$) in the universe were slightly different then there would not be any carbon-based life.[21] According to a calculation of Penrose the creator of the universe had to meet an accuracy of 1 part in $10^{10^{123}}$ in order to create a universe with as special a Big Bang as that we actually find.[22]

From these considerations one can see that also O (i.e. the observed values of all physical and cosmological quantities take on very special values) is very well confirmed. Since both C and O are very well confirmed it follows that also the material implication $C \rightarrow O$ (if C then O) is very well confirmed. From this however it does not follow that $C \rightarrow O$ can be interpreted as a law-statement expressing a law of nature; although it can be interpreted as a well- confirmed hypothesis.

Concerning the question of Davis whether AP can be used to make testable predictions about carbon-based life and especially man we agree that this is hardly possible for two reasons: First the fact of the existence of man and many scientific results about man have been offered by a lot of other sciences like anthropology, anatomy, physiology, medicine etc. (without much use of physics). Secondly AP can hardly be interpreted as claiming that the special values of physical and cosmological quantities are sufficient conditions for predicting something about mankind or carbon-based life in general; i.e. AP can hardly be interpreted as $O \rightarrow C$ (which would be the opposite implication of $C \rightarrow O$). In this sense we agree with Davis and this was one of the reasons that we have interpreted the fact that the observed values of all physical and cosmological quantities take on very special values (O) as a necessary condition for carbon-based life, but not as a sufficient one. This holds also for the two examples (1) and (2) above: the numer-

---

21 Cf. Barrow and Tipler (1986) p.5. This book contains numerous examples of that sort.

22 Penrose (2005) p.5. An explanation of such fine-tuning facts with the help of "pure chance" is therefore completely impossible. See ch. 8 below.

ical proportion of the strong nuclear force to the electromagnetic force in (1) and the numerical proportion of protons and photons in (2) are *necessary conditions* for carbon-based life. And therefore AP can help to make further predictions concerning these special values of physical and cosmological quantities; but not the other way round.

Concerning teleological order, SAP is usually interpreted in the sense that carbon-based life or the emergence of man is a final state in the development of the universe, which can be considered a goal. Then the process which reaches that goal possesses teleological order according to Df 5.10 (section 5.3.5) and it possesses higher-level teleological order according to Df 7.7 (section 7.3.5). Moreover the many different necessary means for reaching this goal (under those come also the special values of physical and cosmological quantities) are states or processes of systems, which obey different levels of order in the sense of Ord_1, Ord_2 and Ord_3 (cf. section 5.3.3). In addition to that the different necessary means can also be understood as basic goods or basic values according to Df 7.4. Since the goal is not just the existence of carbon-based life and the existence of man but also its survival and its health.

7.5 Conclusion

What has been established in ch. 5 (see section 5.5) for non-living things has been shown in ch. 7 for living things: It has been shown that there are different types of order and teleological order in living things. Moreover one can speak of goods and values and goals w.r.t. living systems and w.r.t. their histories. With the help of these concepts one can also define *higher-level teleological order* of a process belonging to a living system. In other words: Concerning living systems scientific research can find out their most important basic values (like staying alive and keeping or regaining health) and their respective activities to reach them as their goals. As it has been said already in section 5.5 the establishment of these types of order and teleological order (also in the sense of values and goals) in living systems satisfy the antecedent-condition of the proof in ch. 1 that providence is possible. And for living systems this condition is satisfied on a higher level since the presence of teleological order is substantiated by special values and goals.

8 Whether there is chance and randomness in living things?

8.1 Arguments Contra

8.1.1 First argument

It has been shown in ch.7 above that there are different kinds of order and also teleological order in living things. But this seems to exclude the existence of chance and randomness in living things.

Therefore there does not seem to be chance and randomness in living things.

8.1.2 Second argument

If different kinds of chance and randomness are only describing our different degrees of ignorance then there are no objective degrees of freedom as the basis of chance and randomness in reality. Thus every event must ultimately occur according to deterministic-dynamical laws while only its phenomenal appearance looks undetermined due to hidden variables not known to us. And as a consequence, there is no chance and randomness in living things but only in our mind as ignorance. As Ruse says chance and randomness are only describing our degrees of ignorance:

> " 'Chance' is not a thing or an objective entity. It is a confession of ignorance".[1]

Therefore there does not seem to be chance and randomness in living things but it exists only as ignorance in our mind.

1 Ruse (2001) p. 121.

8.2 Argument Pro

All living things, which possess the ability (and activity) of learning, possess the ability (and activity) of using trial and error. To possess the ability to use trial and error presupposes degrees of freedom for the actions of these ls. Such real degrees of freedom are degrees of chance and randomness in the actions of ls.

Therefore there is chance and randomness in living things.

8.3 Proposed Answer

There is chance and randomness in living things. The reason for this is similar to that given in section 6.3 above. Many processes of living systems obey statistical laws. Statistical laws do not satisfy condition D1 (cf. section 4.3.1) of dynamical laws but allow branching according to condition S1 (4.3.2). Moreover statistical laws obey condition S2 and not D2, i.e. they do not describe, explain or predict the individual parts (objects) or the microstates of the huge ensemble of living things to which they apply; but they describe, explain or predict its macrostate. Therefore there are (several or many) degrees of freedom for the respective microstates or for the behavior of the individual system. Moreover we cannot interpret these degrees of freedom subjectively or as degrees of ignorance as has been justified in section 6.3 above. In other words, the degrees of freedom of the microstates have to be interpreted realistically, i.e. as genuine degrees of freedom in biological reality. Therefore – insofar as these microstates are not ruled by statistical laws – they are said to occur by chance or to occur randomly. Therefore there is chance and randomness in living things.

This preliminary answer will be complemented more fully by the subsequent sections.

It has been shown in section 6.3.2 that there are different kinds of chance and randomness already in arithmetic and geometry and also in the domain of dynamical laws of nature. In sections 6.3.3 and 6.3.4 chance and randomness have been treated w.r.t. dynamical and statistical laws. In 6.3.5 chance and randomness have been discussed w.r.t. complexity of sequences and in 6.3.6 w.r.t. types of order and structure. In 6.3.7 it was eventually treated w.r.t. teleological order. Although the focus of interest of ch. 6 was non-living systems, many important features, which also concern living systems, have been discussed there. These will be presupposed now and the respective definitions will be used too. The following section will focus on the question of randomness of the DNA; first concerning the sequence itself then concerning its emergence and third concerning mutation. Further sections will deal with randomness and chance in higher-level systems and w.r.t. the Hardy-Weinberg equilibrium.

8.3.1 The question of randomness of the DNA-sequence

As a first question we might ask: Is the DNA G-random or G-complex (recall Df 6.7, section 6.3.5)? It has already been stated there that this question is hardly decidable w.r.t. the human DNA.

According to an earlier view, the main task of the DNA (RNA) was thought to be the production of all the proteins. A motive was the so-called *central dogma of molecular biology*: DNA $\rightarrow$ RNA $\rightarrow$ Protein. Based on this understanding some parts of the human DNA were interpreted as *redundant* since they could be dropped without affecting the protein-production. This view was refuted recently by discovering that only about 2% of the DNA-sequence is responsible for the production of all the proteins.[2] Therefore it became impossible to claim that 98% of the DNA was redundant. The exact function of these 98% is still unknown to a large extent, although extensive research has been done on that part and also on the specific human part; the latter concerns about 30 million of DNA-letters out of 3 billion ($3 \cdot 10^9$).

From these remarks it is understandable that the question whether human DNA can be compressed or represented by a shorter code is not yet known. And as a consequence of the result of Chaitin (1974), mentioned in section 6.3.5, the randomness of the DNA may hardly be provable.

In claims like "the DNA is a product of chance" at least two things are confusing: whether the DNA-sequence is a random sequence (see the remarks above and this section) or whether the sequence emerged exclusively from random processes. In this section (8.3.1) we shall deal with the first question. The second question, the chance hypothesis, will be dealt with in 8.3.2.

Df 8.1. A biological sequence (specifically the DNA) is random iff it has no structure.

2 Cf. Pollard (2009) and Geraci (1996).

A consideration of the definition Df 5.3 of structure and of the following facts shows that the DNA is not random in the sense of Df 8.1. The facts are as follows:

a) It is a double strand helix.

b) It has 4 subunits with linkage-relations; special nucleotides (phosphate, ribose, GCTA).

c) It has geometric perfection: guarantees the right degree of stability: 5 hydrogen bonds with bond lengths at the energy maximum.

d) The rolled up ball or cluster is not arbitrary: it obeys laws of energy distribution.

e) It possesses metastability: it stabilizes its own structure.

This shows that the DNA has a very sophisticated structure. It further shows that the DNA is also *not random* in the sense of Df 6.8 and Df 6.9 (section 6.3.6). That means it possesses higher types of order. It is not random in the sense of Df 6.8 because its internal relations obey special geometrical principles according to a), c) and d) above.

It is not random in the sense of Df 6.9 since (iv) of Df 5.7 is satisfied, i.e. the DNA has lower entropy than its environment; this is also confirmed by e) above since the stabilization of its own structure means increasing of order (decreasing of entropy) w.r.t. its environment.

These considerations show that the DNA-sequence is not random in the sense of Df 8.1, Df 6.8 or Df 6.9; it is a highly complex and ordered sequence.

8.3.2 The question of randomness and chance in the emergence of the DNA-sequence

The claim that the emergence of the DNA resulted from a random process by pure and blind chance alone was later called the "chance hypothesis". One of the most vigorous proponents of it was Jacques Monod:

> "Chance alone is the source of every innovation, of all creation in the biosphere. Pure chance, absolutely free, but blind ... All forms of life are the product of chance."[3]

3 Monod (1972) p. 110. Cf. also Monod (1975).

This passage contains at least two claims: One is that there is chance in some absolute sense. The other is the *chance hypothesis*, i.e. that life (and consequently also the DNA) is a product of processes of chance.

A reflection on the different types of chance defined so far (cf. Df 6.7–Df 6.10 and Df 8.1) reveals that the first claim is rather nonsense or at least scientifically useless. Understood as scientific concepts, chance and randomness are – like most scientific concepts – relative and not absolute. That means that "chance" and "randomness" are only definable relative to order or law or law governed structure; and consequently: a special type of chance or randomness is only definable relative to a special type of order or law or law-like structure. In other words, "pure chance", "absolutely free but blind" do not exist and the respective concepts are not scientific concepts.

The second claim, the *chance hypothesis*, can be formulated more specifically w.r.t. the DNA as follows: The specific sequence of the nucleotides in the DNA-molecule of the first organism came about by a purely random process in the early history of the earth.[4] Let us see what this means w.r.t. different living systems. For the following examples we assume that all sequence alternatives (or permutations) are physically equivalent.

(1) The smallest catalytically active protein (enzyme) has $\approx 10^{130}$ sequence alternatives (sqa).

(2) The RNA-sequence of the virus specific unit of the $Q_{\beta -}$ replicase consists of ≈ 1000 nucleotides, i.e. has $\approx 10^{600}$ sqa.

(3) The genome of a simple bacterium (E. Coli): $4 \cdot 10^6$ nucleotides, i.e. $10^{2,4mill}$ sqa.

(4) The human genome: $3 \cdot 10^9$ nucleotides, i.e. $10^{600mill}$ sqa.

A suitable numerical example is this: A Coli bacterium has about the same chance (according to the "chance hypothesis") of arising purely randomly (by pure chance) as a 4-volume textbook of biochemistry (420 pages per volume) has of arising by random-mixing of its letters.

If the "chance hypothesis" i.e. claims for the origin of life in terms of "blind chance", "pure chance" or "chance alone" were correct, an emergence of life would be excluded:

4 Küppers (1990) p. 59.

> "No matter how large the environment one considers, life cannot have had a random beginning … there are about two thousand enzymes, and the chance of obtaining them all in a random trial is only one part in $10^{40.000}$, an outrageously small probability that could not be faced even if the whole universe consisted of organic soup."[5]

> "Our statistical discussion has shown that we will for fundamental reasons never be able to determine the frequency of appearance of living systems in the universe. This is because a well-founded answer to this question could only be given if we possessed sufficient knowledge of the functional properties of all the alternative sequences of a biological information carrier. However, this extremely large number of sequence alternatives makes it impossible to obtain such knowledge, by theoretical or empirical means, for even the lowest levels of macromolecular complexity."[6]

The above considerations show that the *chance hypothesis* is no reasonable answer. To split the improbabilities into handy pieces[7] does not help for the explanation of the emergence of living systems. This can be seen as follows. The age of the universe is about 10^{17} seconds.[8] If we grant 10^9 evolutionary steps per second then we get 10^{26} evolutionary steps since the Big Bang. This number is ridiculous small in comparison to the number of sequence alternatives of the smallest catalytically active protein ($\approx 10^{130}$).

In Dawkins' book (Dawkins (1996)) there are other great mistakes concerning probability, which show ignorance or great misunderstandings of thermodynamic principles. On the first pages of ch. 3 of his book Dawkins claims that the scrap yard is as improbable as the Boeing 747 (when considered as past events) since its parts could also be arranged differently. According to thermodynamic probability – which is essential w.r.t. a comparison of order and disorder in non-living and in biological systems – the macrostate "Boeing 747 at a time t" (B) is much more improbable for many orders of magnitude than the macrostate "scrap yard of Boeing 747 at time t" (Sc). Because the number of microstates which can realize Sc is much greater (greater in the sense of many orders of magnitude) than the number of microstates which can realize B. And this is independent

5 Hoyle and Wickramasinghe (1981) p. 148f.

6 Küppers (1990) p. 65f.

7 Cf. Dawkins (1996). Dawkins' view seems to be at least ambiguous if not inconsistent. On the one hand he says that Darwinism cannot be a theory based on chance because of the huge improbabilities, on the other, he thinks he only needs to split them into small pieces.

8 Even if this number would be incorrect for several orders of magnitude (recent research assumes that it is greater) – because a universal cosmological time is hardly definable (cf. Mittelstaedt (2008)) – the proportion to the numbers of sequence alternatives mentioned above would be roughly the same.

of whether the permutations of greater or smaller parts of B or Sc, or even the permutations of atoms of B or Sc are meant.

Further reasons against the *chance hypothesis* are:

(1) The physical and chemical laws at the bottom permit degrees of freedom (w.r.t. statistical laws) but forbid "absolute", "pure" and "blind" chance.

(2) A modern interpretation of selection does not use absolute or pure or blind chance, although it uses possible degrees of freedom, i.e. restricted chance when explaining

(i) the stabilization of certain structures

(ii) feedback properties

(iii) self-reproduction

(iv) messenger mechanism (transformation of information)
… etc.

One of the first rigorous interpretations of selection and the above properties with the help of a mathematical model was the *hypercycle* of Eigen and Schuster.[9]

8.3.3 The question of the randomness of mutation

Two further domains where randomness occurs are mutation and recombination, the most important causes for genetic variation. We shall deal here with mutation of genes (not of chromosomes and not of genomes) caused by recombination mistakes. Mutation of genes can also be caused by the environment, for example by radiation. In fact the process of genetic copying is very precise. It can be as precise as illustrated by a "picture" from Peter Schuster:[10] Just one mistake (this is a point mutation of one letter) within a sequence which is written down in 100 books, each having 300 pages (i.e. within 30.000 pages). Concerning such a small number of deviations (mistakes) or exceptions one would think immediately of a dynamical law. But dynamical laws are usually interpreted in such a way that the

9 Cf. Eigen and Schuster (1979).

10 P. Schuster (2007). This rate corresponds to the DNA of bacteria per base pair. The rates are different for different genes. On the average between $1:10^5$ and $1:10^8$.

law not only holds for huge ensembles of systems or bodies but also for each individual system or body (recall condition D2 of section 4.3.1). This however would not be a correct understanding of the situation here. On the other hand a statistical law is a law, which allows degrees of freedom for the individual case (instance) and is thus not disconfirmed by such exceptions.

This type of randomness, the so-called mutation-rate is usually presupposed and taken for granted. Because it is that kind of randomness which is well known as a characteristic of statistical laws; be they in the domain of physics, chemistry or biology (recall conditions S1, S2 and S4 of section 4.3.2).

Before giving a definition of what is usually understood (by biologists) when they talk of the randomness of mutations, we shall first list the cases w.r.t. which a mutation is not random:

(i) The probability of mutations is (on the average) not the same for all places in the DNA;

(ii) Mutations are dependent of the environment; for example they may be caused by radiation. This dependence is calculable to some extent.

(iii) The process of exchanging letters in the DNA is governed by physical and chemical laws.

The important point is, however, that the probability of the event (occurrence) of a mutation is independent of the question whether the mutation could be *useful* (for example for adaption or fitness).[11] This however does not mean that mutations cannot be useful or harmful. It is a fact that they sometimes have a negative effect for propagation (for example white eyes or cut wings for Drosophila) and sometimes a positive effect for the phenotype. The negative or positive effect also depends on the environment and can be changed by it from the negative to the positive. This kind of randomness of mutations can be characterized by the following definition:

Df 8.2. Let p be the state or event of a mutation of the DNA of a living system ls. Then p is mutationally random iff the probability of p does not depend on the usefulness of p for ls.

---

11 Cf. Futuyma (1990) p. 86.

This definition could also be expressed in the following way: p is mutually random iff a change of p does not necessarily (regularly) change the usefulness of p for ls.

8.3.4 Randomness and chance in the emergence of higher-level biological systems

Living systems of higher level are never random or chance-like in the sense of not possessing higher types of order in the sense of Df 5.5, Df 5.7, Df 5.10 or Df 7.7. But some living systems may be more random than others w.r.t. a special type of order.

Df 8.3. Living system ls_2 is less random than living system $ls_1 =_{df}$

(i) ls_1 and ls_2 have structure (Df 5.3, section 5.3)

(ii) ls_2 can build new structures and stabilize them (if this offers any selection advantage) – more efficiently than ls_1

(iii) ls_2 can change its shape (if this offers any selection advantage) – more efficiently than ls_1

(iv) ls_2 can store and transmit (by self-reproduction) more information than ls_1
$\ldots$

(v) $Ent(ls_2) < Ent(ls_1)$.
The number of microstates, which can realize ls_2 is much smaller than the number of microstates which can realize ls_1.

8.3.5 Randomness concerning the Hardy-Weinberg equilibrium

The Hardy-Weinberg law is a kind of further development of Mendel's laws. It says that under five important conditions the genetic proportions remain constant. The five conditions – in fact unrealistic assumptions or idealizations – are the following:

(1) No genetic drift (realizable by very large populations)

(2) Random-mating populations of diploids (also realizable by large populations)

(3) No unbalanced mutation

(4) No unbalanced migration (no immigration)

(5) No selection

Suppose in a homozygote population the frequency of AA-individuals is P and that of aa-individuals is Q such that $P + Q = 1$ (meaning that together they constitute 100% of the population) where A are dominants produced by AA and a are recessives produced by aa. Then the Hardy-Weinberg law says: If conditions (1)–(5) are satisfied then the genotypic proportions of the next generation is $P^2 AA + 2PQAa + Q^2 aa = 1$. This law is relatively robust w.r.t. many departures from equilibrium conditions, which usually take place in populations. Therefore we could ask what is the set of changes within degrees of freedom which would not change the equilibrium determined by the Hardy-Weinberg law. This gives us a further kind of randomness:

Df 8.4. Let p be a state of affairs describing some condition like (1)–(5) above or some other condition concerning genetic frequencies. Then p is HW-random iff a change of p does not change the Hardy-Weinberg equilibrium (where 'HW' stands for 'Hardy-Weinberg').

8.3.6 Chance and randomness concerning goals and teleological order

In section 6.3.7 it has been shown that there is chance and randomness w.r.t. teleological order in non-living things (cf. Df 6.11). To claim that all living things (ls) are teleological or directed to some goal in the sense that every property or process of ls possesses teleological order or is satisfying a basic good of ls or is valuable to ls (cf. definitions Df 7.4, Df 7.6, Df 7.7) seems to be not only an exaggeration, but cannot be true. This is evident from the fact that there exists also basic evil of ls according to definition Df 7.5. In general there are properties and processes of ls, which do not possess any internal teleological order or purposiveness or directedness to some goal. That means that w.r.t. such properties or processes none of the definitions Df 7.2–Df 7.4, Df 7.6, Df 7.7 are satisfied. In such cases we might speak of chance or randomness as contrary to teleological order, to purposiveness or to directedness to some goal:

Df 8.5. A process B of a living system ls is random iff

(1) it does not satisfy definition Df 7.4 or

(2) it does not satisfy definition Df 7.6, i.e. it neither contributes to the continuation of the species-history of ls nor to the conservation of the species of ls or

(3) it does not satisfy condition (b) of definition Df 7.7 for higher-level teleological order.

Examples: Any process of illness that neither contributes to staying alive or to surviving or to keeping or regaining health nor contributes to the species-history. All processes which cannot be subordinated to some hierarchy of goals or to some higher-level teleological order. Observe however that although ls cannot be teleological in the sense that all its properties or processes possess teleological order etc., they are teleological in the sense that their essential properties (Df 7.1) i.e. metabolism, self-regulation, propagation, adaption and many properties or processes possess teleological order or are satisfying some basic good etc. (cf. ch. 7).

8.3.7 Conclusion concerning chance and randomness

One could go on to define other types of chance and randomness. And some additional types may also contribute some new aspects. But the diversity shown so far by Df 6.1, Df 6.2, Df 6.4, Df 6.5, Df 6.7–Df 6.10 and Df 8.1 is sufficient to draw a number of more general conclusions.

(1) Every kind of chance and randomness is called so relative to some order or law. In other words: every state or event or process or sequence is called random relative to a law-like or law-guided state or event or process or sequence. That means there is no state or event or process or sequence, which is random in an absolute sense. Claims like the ones of Monod (section 8.3.2) are useless exaggerations because they lack this relation to order and law. That "chance alone" (whatever that may be) is not sufficient, should be evident from the different types of chance and randomness investigated so far[12]; and it will also become clear fom the following points.

(2) No state, event, process, sequence is random in every aspect. It is random w.r.t. a particular order, rule, law L but it is not random or even ordered,

12 i.e. in ch. 6 and ch. 8. For still more types of chance and randomness see Weingartner (2009a) and Weingartner (2010b).

ruled, planned w.r.t. another order, rule, law L'. For example, the trajectory of chaotic motion is random w.r.t. the dependence on the initial conditions and w.r.t. the loss of information about its position and consequently random concerning predictability; but it is not random w.r.t. its boundaries or its stable points (fixed points) and it is also not random w.r.t. a "strange attractor". The movement of the particular molecules of a gas are statistically random, but their collective behavior, i.e. their collective properties like velocity or temperature are not random, they are ruled by the laws of thermodynamics (recall the quotation from Schrödinger in section 4.3.2). Some parts of the changes in the process of recombination are random since they concern degrees of freedom w.r.t. Mendel's laws or Hardy-Weinberg's law. But the same changes in the recombination are not random w.r.t. another statistical law, which makes the recombination of neighborhood genes less probable than that of more distant genes.

(3) Although randomness and chance is typical w.r.t. statistical laws, there is also randomness and chance if the underlying laws are dynamical (i.e. dynamical chaos, recall section 4.4.2) and even if the laws are those of arithmetic and geometry (recall section 6.3.2).

(4) There is no incompatibility that randomness and chance on the one hand and order and law on the other are present in the same physical, chemical or biological system. In fact this is the normal situation. In order to avoid confusion one must only observe that some state, event, process, sequence cannot be random and not random w.r.t. the same aspect, property or law. But – as is clear from (2) above – it is random w.r.t. the law L and not random w.r.t. L'.

(5) Finally, every definition of chance or randomness presupposes the existence of some state, event, process, sequence. If there is nothing there, there cannot be chance or randomness; and without an existing state, event, process, or at least some sequence of entities, chance or randomness cannot be defined. Therefore contentions like "the world developed from nothing (to something) by chance" are sheer nonsense.

8.3.8 Results of chapter 8

The results of ch. 8 can be summarized as follows:

T 8.1. *The DNA-sequence is not random in the sense that it has no structure. On the contrary it has many very sophisticated structural features (cf. 8.3.1).*

T 8.2. *The so-called "chance hypothesis" (cf. 8.3.2) is not a possible scientific explanation for the emergence of life or of the DNA.*

T 8.3. *Mutation is random concerning the* mutation-rate *and concerning its usefulness for the ls, but it is not random in many other aspects (cf. 8.3.3).*

T 8.4. *There may be relative randomness of high-level ls in the sense that ls_1 is more random than ls_2, but never in an absolute sense (cf. 8.3.4).*

T 8.5. *Every ls has also several properties or processes, which are random in the sense that they are neither basic goods, nor valuable for the conservation and continuation of the species, nor possessing higher-level teleological order.*

8.4 Answer to the Objections

8.4.1 (to 8.1.1)

Already from sections 8.2 and 8.3.6 it should be clear that chance and randomness on the one hand and law and order on the other are not only mathematically compatible but are factually present in one and the same physical, chemical or biological system. More specifically it became evident that, for example, mutation is random w.r.t. the mutation-rate and w.r.t. the usefulness for the living system but not random w.r.t. the place in the DNA, to the environment and to the process of exchanging letters, which is governed by physical and chemical laws.

Therefore it is no hindrance that both chance and randomness on the one hand, and law and order on the other, are present in living things.

8.4.2 (to 8.1.2)

The claim of Ruse is that there is no chance or randomness in the objective sense; but only in the sense of degrees of our ignorance. But this claim cannot be true. This can be shown (i) by considering its consequences and (ii) by an analysis of statistical laws:

(i) As it has been said correctly in the argument 8.1.2 if there are no objective degrees of freedom in reality then every event or process must ultimately occur according to deterministic-dynamical laws. However there are many events and processes which – at least according to our knowledge at present – cannot be explained with the help of deterministic-dynamical laws but only with the help of statistical laws. Such events or processes are: quantum-mechanical processes, cosmological processes of expansion, radiation, friction, heat, diffusion, electric transport, conscious mental processes ... etc. Therefore there are two possibilities:

(a) The respective statistical laws are genuine laws and their degrees of freedom for the single event or process are objective. In this case there is chance and randomness for branching in the objective sense.

(b) The respective statistical laws yield only a preliminary explanation on the surface; but an ultimate explanation would find the hidden variables, which determine all apparent degrees of freedom such that those events and processes can be described by deterministic-dynamical laws. Controversy concerning the interpretation of quantum mechanical processes arose between two groups of physicists: one group defending deterministic-dynamical laws or hidden variables or both (among them Albert Einstein defending dynamical laws and David Bohm defending both), the other rejecting hidden variables and defending a probabilistic description (among them Niels Bohr and Heisenberg).[13]

Several *Gedankenexperimente* and theories have been constructed to save the deterministic and dynamical interpretation with the help of hidden variables. The most famous *Gedankenexperiment* was that of

13 For a detailed elaboration of hidden variable theories cf. Jammer (1974) p. 253ff.

Einstein-Podolski-Rosen (abbreviated as EPR-experiment)[14]. The most famous theoretical attempt was that of David Bohm.[15]

Einstein himself, although hoping for an ultimate solution with the help of dynamical laws, was not convinced by Bohm's proposal:

> "Ich glaube aber nicht, dass diese These sich halten lässt".[16]

The first decisive arguments against hidden variable theories were the discoveries of John Bell. In 1964 he proved what is now called Bell's theorem: A local hidden variable theory cannot reproduce all statistical predictions of quantum mechanics. He showed that if the spin of the electrons in the EPR-experiment were indeed controlled by local hidden variables, then the determination of the spin of electron 2 by a measurement on electron 1 could not take place instantaneously as it does according to quantum mechanics.[17] By including the basic assumptions we may put it this way: Accepting the two basic assumptions of EPR (a) *locality* (two sufficiently separated particles do not influence each other) and (b) *reality* (if without in any way disturbing a system, we can predict with certainty the value of a physical quantity, then there exists an element of the physical reality corresponding to this physical quantity, EPR p. 777) and applying it to the spin measurement of the two par-

---

14 Einstein et al. (1935). A somewhat similar *Gedankenexperiment* was published by Popper 1934 of which he sent a copy with a letter to Einstein in December 1934. Einstein replied that this experiment could not be carried out since to predict position and momentum of particle B, both time and energy of particle A have to be measured simultaneously which is impossible. Jammer considers the possibility that Popper's *Gedankenexperiment*, which Popper assumed to be refuted by Einstein's reply, might have influenced Einstein for the EPR-*Gedankenxperiment* (Jammer (1974) p. 178f.). This letter of Einstein is reprinted in Popper's Logic of Scientific Discovery (Popper (1959) p.461f). However Popper didn't use his *Gedankenexperiment* to defend determinism or hidden variables, since he argued that most parts of physics are indeterministic:

> "Most systems of physics, including classical physics and quantum physics ... are indeterministic in perhaps an even more fundamental sense that the one usually ascribed to the indeterminism of quantum physics (insofar as the unpredictability of the events ... is not mitigated by the predictability of their frequencies)." Popper (1950) p.117.

15 Bohm (1952) part I and II. The first paper proposes an interpretation of Quantum Mechanics with the help of a hidden variable theory, the second adds a new theory of measurement in conformity with it.

16 In a letter to Renninger of May 3, 1953; cited in Jammer (1974) p. 254.

17 Bell (1964) and Bell (1966). For more on Bell's theorem and EPR see Bell (1981), Mittaelstaedt (1998) 4.4(c) and Mittelstaedt and Weingartner (2005) p. 290ff.

ticles leads to the four Bell-inequalities. Since these Bell-inequalities were shown to be violated experimentally (by Aspect and others)[18] in accordance with quantum mechanics this leads – via modus tollens – to a violation of one of the basic assumptions. Independently of this, the probabilistic forms, the set theoretical forms and the propositional-logical forms of Bell's inequalities can be shown to presuppose principles of classical logic, which are too strong such that their application to several empirical domains leads to difficulties.[19] Observe that these results confirm the necessity of a statistical and (where possible) probabilistic description but not automatically Bohr's "Copenhagen Interpretation".[20]

The negative results concerning hidden variables in the domain of quantum mechanics show already that a general interpretation of statistical laws with the help of degrees of ignorance and a reduction to dynamical laws with the help of hidden variables is not even possible on the lowest level, i.e. on that of microphysics.

(ii) An analysis of statistical laws and a comparison between dynamical laws and statistical laws shows that neither the first can be reduced to the second nor vice versa. This should be clear from the conditions of dynamical (D1–D4) and statistical laws (S1–S4) and its comparison in sections 4.3.1 and 4.3.2.[21] On the other hand it is shown in these sections above that both types of laws are compatible and may be both present in the same physical, chemical or biological system.

18 Aspect et al. (1982).

19 See Weingartner (2009b) section 4.3.2 and Weingartner (2010a) section 2.

20 See Bell (1987) p. 155f. and Mittaelstaedt (1998), 1.2(a).

21 For a detailed justification see ch. 7.2 of Mittelstaedt and Weingartner (2005).

9 Whether providence is compatible with both order and chance?

9.1 Arguments Contra

9.1.1 First argument

In ch. 5 it was shown that non-living things possess Ord_1 since they have structure and they possess Ord_2 since they have in addition some special arithmetical or geometrical relations. What already has order need not to be given order w.r.t. it's end. But by providence one understands a God given order to the things w.r.t. their ends.

Therefore providence does not seem to be compatible with the existing order of non-living things.

9.1.2 Second argument

Many processes of becoming, i.e. of increasing order emerge through self-organisation as for example the Bénard instability. As Haken says:

> "The phenomenon of self-organization is familiar from many biological processes. Here we can see the emergence of structures without any special influence from outside... By self-organization we understand that certain structures emerge in systems on their own."[1]

But the order emerging through self-organization is not a given order from outside. The order provided by providence however is a given order from outside.

Therefore providence must be incompatible with order emerging through self-organization.

1 Haken and Wunderlin (1991) p. 150. (Author's translation).

9.1.3 Third argument

What possesses order obeys laws of nature. What obeys laws of nature occurs by necessity. What occurs by necessity need not be ordered towards its end. But what occurs through providence needs to be ordered towards its end.

Therefore: What occurs through providence does not possess order. And thus providence seems not to be compatible with order.

9.1.4 Fourth argument

Providence implies order. But according to Df 6.8 (ch. 6) a thing or system is random iff it does not have order.

Therefore, if a thing or systems is random it does not come under providence. And thus providence does not seem to be compatible with randomness or chance.

9.1.5 Fifth argument

If an event happens under providence it happens according to a plan which orders it towards its end. But, as Inwagen says, if an event happens by chance it does not happen according to a plan which orders it towards it's end:

> "What I shall mean by saying that an event is a "chance" occurrence, or a state of affairs, a "matter of chance" or "due to chance" is this: The event or state of affairs is without purpose or significance; it is not part of anyone's plan; it serves no one's end; and it might very well not have been."[2]

Therefore providence and chance are incompatible notions.

2 Inwagen (1995) p. 50.

9.2 Argument Pro

If God is the creator of the universe then it must hold: Everything which occurs in the universe comes under God's providence. According to chapters 5, 6, 7, 8, both order and chance occur in the universe.

Therefore: If God is the creator of the universe then it must hold: Order and chance come under God's providence. And since what comes under God's providence cannot be incompatible with his providence, order and chance are compatible with God's providence.

9.3 Proposed Answer

Providence is compatible with both order and chance. This can be substantiated as follows.

9.3.1 Providence is compatible with any kind of order which is realized in the universe

Since, according to chapter 3, providence is concerned with creation and since the universe is part of creation providence is concerned with the universe. Therefore it has to be shown that providence is compatible with any order realized in the universe. On the other hand it is not required that providence is also compatible with the order of other possible universes that are not factual (real): Although providence extends also to future events of this real (factual) universe which are not yet factual.

In order to proceed more accurately we shall first give some definitions of compatibility. They can be applied to things, systems, properties, events, processes, but also to predicates or concepts. Furthermore they can be applied to states of affairs and to propositions.

Df 9.1. Two things or systems which are not human thoughts are compatible iff they coexist, i.e. iff both exist in reality.

This definition presupposes that we do not adhere to a doctrine which claims that there are contradictions inbuilt into reality. Contradictions are solely in our imperfect thinking about reality but not in reality itself. It follows from Df 9.1, that all things (systems) which exist in the universe are compatible with each other. Observe that the question of coexistence of things or systems depends severely on the distance in space and time. Thus water and fire can coexist at a certain distance of space or time, but not at the same place at the same time (relative to some reference system). This is true with many other things, for example, boiling water and ice, bodies at rest and moving bodies, systems in equilibrium and dissipative systems, system with low entropy and system with high entropy etc. Concerning time we have to add that simultaneity of existence can only be defined locally, not for the whole universe; i.e. there is no designated reference system relative to which we could say that all things of the universe coexist simultaneously. This is so if we adopt realistic situations, i.e. if rotating parts and gravitation are not excluded.[3]

Df 9.2. Two properties (or events or processes) P_1 and P_2 are incompatible w.r.t. the thing or system x iff x possesses P_1 implies not: x possesses P_2; In other words: iff possessing P_1 precludes possessing P_2.That is iff: $\forall x(P_1 x \rightarrow \neg P_2 x)$

Df 9.3. Two properties (or events or processes) P_1 and P_2 are compatible w.r.t. the thing or system x iff they are not incompatible. That is iff $\exists x(P_1 x \wedge P_2 x)$.

For example a system of Classical Mechanics like a planet of the solar system possesses both a sharp position (spatial localisation) and a sharp velocity value; i.e. these properties are compatible w.r.t. the planet. On the other hand a quantum-mechanical microsystem does not have, both sharp position and sharp momentum (or velocity) value; i.e. these properties are not compatible w.r.t. the QM-microsystem.

Observe that there are several relationships between two properties which are sufficient (but not necessary) for their compatibility. For example if there is homomorphic or isomorphic mapping between them, then they are compatible but not vice versa. Thus a map of a piece of land (understood as a certain structure of a material piece of paper) is homomorphic to the (structure of the) real piece of

3 For details on this see Mittelstaedt (2008). Moreover a certain value for the age of the universe is reasonable only under several presuppositions and restrictions like the Friedmann solutions of Einstein's field equations.

land; therefore both structures are compatible. If analogy is defined as a homomorphic or isomorphic relation between relations of things or systems[4] then also the analogy between two things or systems may be sufficient at least for partial compatibility of the respective properties (relations).

Df 9.4. Two predicates (or two concepts) C_1 and C_2 are incompatible iff their extensions exclude each other.

Df 9.5. Two predicates (or two concepts) C_1 and C_2 are compatible iff their extensions do not exclude each other; i.e. iff their extensions have at least one common element: $\exists x(x \in Ext(C_1) \wedge x \in Ext(C_2))$. This condition may be written in PL1 also in this form: $\exists x(C_1 x \wedge C_2 x)$.

Df 9.6. Two propositions p and q are compatible iff p does not contradict q and there is no consequence of p which contradicts any consequence of q and vice versa.

Df 9.7. Two states of affairs are compatible iff the propositions which represent them are compatible.

Df 9.8. Two human thoughts are compatible iff the propositions which represent them are compatible.

Providence is usually understood as the plan of God by which he orders things towards their ends. (For more details concerning providence see ch. 10 below) That this plan is compatible with any kind of order of this world can be shown as follows:

1) God's plan by which he orders things or by which he creates order is compatible with any kind of order in the universe according to Df 9.1 because both God's plan exists and the respective type of order in the universe exists.
2) Providence – God's plan by which he orders things or by which he creates order – is also compatible with any kind of order in the universe according to Df 9.3. Both are not incompatible if interpreted as properties. A similar consideration holds if we interpret them as predicates (Df 9.5) belonging to a lan-

4 For precise definitions of analogy see Weingartner (1979) and Weingartner (1976) II, 1 ch. 3.64.

guage (of philosophy or theology) in which we describe both, features of the world and supernatural things like God as creator of the world.

3) Assume that $\{p \in T(Prov)\}$ is the set of the theorems (true propositions) concerning providence and $\{q \in T(Ord)\}$ is the set of theorems concerning the different structures of order in the world. Then, since both $\{p \in T(Prov)\}$ and $\{q \in T(Ord)\}$ are two sets consisting of only true propositions they must be compatible in the sense of Df 9.6. And if these propositions are interpreted as representing states of affairs then both sets of states of affairs are compatible according to Df 9.7.

In all three cases 1)–3) order may be understood as Ord_1 (structure) or Ord_2 (structure + arithmetical or geometrical relations) or Ord_3 (Ord_2 + conditions (ii)–(iv) of Df 5.7, chapter 5). The aspect of goal or end will be incorporated in point 4) below.

4) If we speak more specifically of providence in the sense of God's plan by which he orders things towards their ends, that is if we speak of processes directed to goals and ends, then we have to refer to the *process of becoming* (Df 5.9) and to *teleological order* (Df 5.10) of chapter 5.

Moreover we have to recall that according to ch. 7 all living systems (ls) possess teleological order (cf. 7.3.2); moreover that all living things (ls) possess several properties or processes which are basic goods for them (for ls) and which contribute to the conservation and continuation of the species of them (of ls) (cf. Df 7.4, 6). In this sense some processes of living systems possess higher level teleological order (cf. Df 7.7). Concerning *becoming*, *teleological order* and *basic goods* we can show the compatibility again in the senses 1)–3) as above:

1) Both God's plan for becoming, for teleological order and for basic goods is compatible with becoming, teleological order and basic goods in the world because they coexist (Df 9.1).

2) They are compatible again in the sense of Df 9.3.

3) Also the sets of true propositions concerning God's teleological plan (by which he orders things towards their ends) and the sets of true propositions concerning *becoming*, *teleological order* and *basic goods* in the world are compatible according to Df 9.6 (and Df 9.7, if interpreted as states of affairs).

9.3.2 Providence is compatible with any kind of chance which is realized in the universe

This can be justified as follows:

(1) Order and chance are compatible by Df 9.1 since they coexist in one physical, chemical or biological system.

(2) Compatibility is transitive according to all definitions of *compatible* given in section 9.3.1 (Df 9.1,Df 9.3,Df 9.5,Df 9.7,Df 9.8). That means that if A is compatible with B and B is compatible with C then also A is compatible with C.

(3) It has been shown in section 9.31 that providence is compatible with order.

Therefore it follows that providence is compatible with chance.

That premise (1) above is true, i.e. that order and chance coexist in one system, can be grasped already from chapters 5, 6, 7 and 8.[5] In addition it can be justified as follows:

a) Already from definitions (Df 6.1) and (Df 6.2) it is clear that randomness (or chance) in mathematics can only be defined relative to arithmetical or geometrical laws and order; i.e. something is random, because it is not ruled or not directly dependent on some laws. But both order and laws and some specific kind of chance or randomness coexist in arithmetic and in geometry.

b) A second kind of randomness or chance was defined relative to dynamical laws (Df 6.4). There are degrees of freedom of initial conditions within the borders of dynamical laws. And both order, in the sense of dynamical laws, and chance or randomness in the sense of initial conditions coexist in one physical system. Since laws and initial conditions are best formulated as propositions (representing states of affairs) they both are compatible according to Df 9.6–Df 9.7. The following example shows this coexistence and this kind of relativity in case of dynamical chaos, where the underlying laws are dynamical laws: The trajectory of chaotic motion is random w.r.t. the dependence on the initial conditions and w.r.t. the loss of information about its position and consequently random concern-

5 That teleology or teleological order and chance are compatible and moreover that teleology is necessary for evolutions is also shown in Soontiens (1991).

ing predictability; but it is not random w.r.t. its boundaries or its stable points (fixed points) and it is also not random w.r.t. a "strange attractor".

c) A third kind of chance or randomness was defined relative to statistical laws (Df 6.5). There are degrees of freedom of individual microstates within the borders of statistical laws. Again, both order in the sense of statistical laws, and chance or randomness in the sense of individual microstates coexist in one physical (non-living) system. They also coexist in living systems but chapters 4, 5 and 6 are concerned with establishing order, chance, and their compatibility with providence w.r.t. non-living systems. Similar to (b) above, the respective compatibility of statistical laws and microstates are expressed by definitions Df 9.6–Df 9.7.

d) As it was shown in section 6.3.5 a sequence which is G-random is not therefore without order or structure. On the contrary the examples discussed there (DNA, the letters or musical notes of a work of art ... etc.) show the coexistence of chance in the sense of Df 6.7 and order.

e) A further type of chance or randomness was defined relative to the types of Ord_2 and Ord_3 (cf. 6.3.6). But it is already apparent from the definitions of order and from the discussion there that no state, event, process, or sequence is random in every aspect. It is random w.r.t. a particular order O. But not random or even ordered w.r.t. another order O'.

f) Different further kinds of chance have been discussed in ch. 8 (8.3.1–8.3.5). They all concern living systems and especially the DNA sequence. Like in ch. 6 the results of ch. 8 showed that chance and randomness on the one hand and structure and order on the other are compatible with each other and coexist in one biological system. Since God's plan is compatible with any kind of order in the universe which either he has created or which has been caused by his creatures (ch. 13) it is also compatible with any kind of chance since this is in turn compatible with the kinds of order in the universe. Another reason for this is that any creator who does not determine everything and who wills the cooperation of creatures concerning the development of the universe permits chance and degrees of freedom as action space for the creatures. And there are many reasons for assuming that God wills the cooperation of creatures to which he has given the power of causality:

> "In another way one is said to be helped by a person through whom he carries out his work, as a master through a servant. In this way God is helped by us; inasmuch as we execute his orders, according to 1 Cor. 3, 9: We are God's coadjutors. Nor is this on account of any defect in the power of God, but because he employs inter-

mediary causes, in order that the beauty of order may be preserved in the universe; and also that he may communicate to creatures the dignity of causality."[6]

g) In sections 6.3.7 and 8.3.6 a kind of chance was defined which is contrary to teleological order and contrary to the satisfaction of basic values (of ls) and to conservation and continuation of the species of ls. In this sense this kind of chance does not seem to be planned. However one has to observe that what is not planned locally or what cannot be directed to some goal locally can still be planned globally or can be subordinated globally to some goal. Examples: The *slaving principle* described by Haken[7] governs microscopic parts which are locally not ordered and subordinates them globally under order parameters to produce macroscopic ordered patterns. Recall the quotation of Schrödinger (1922) in section 4.3.2 and the examples given there. They show that it is the frequent (or normal) case in the huge area of thermodynamics that randomness locally is governed by laws globally.

   Moreover observe that there is also the opposite possibility: Globally something may not look as planned or ordered, but locally it is.

   Example: According to the *Cosmological Principle* the universe is isotropic and homomogeneous *globally* and therefore it looks globally symmetric and disordered such that no point and no direction in space is designated. However from a *local* point of view there are galaxies, stars, planetary systems and planets with carbon-based life on it and even with consciousness and rationality. This shows different types of order and structure such that *locally* the universe is structured and ordered to a high degree. According to the *Anthropic Principle* this structure and order is highly teleological and planned.[8]

9.3.3 Result of chapter 9

The result of ch. 9 can be summarized as follows:

T 9.1. *God's providence is compatible with any kind of order which is realized in the universe. This is true for different types of compatibility defined as coexistence, non-*

---

6 Aquinas (1981) I, 23, 8 ad 2.
7 Haken (1988)
8 Cf. Barrow and Tipler (1986) chs. 4 to 8.

exclusion of properties or predicates, non-contradiction of propositions or states of affairs.

T 9.2. *God's providence is compatible with any kind of chance which is realized in the universe. This holds for different types of compatibility defined as coexistence, non-exclusion of properties or predicates, non-contradicting propositions or states of affairs.*

9.4 Answer to the Objections

9.4.1 (to 9.1.1)

Since we assume that God is the creator of the universe, every order which exists in the universe originates in God, either as in his plan or as in both his plan and his execution (of the plan). Concerning the plan every order is given (by God); concerning the execution of the plan God entrusts his creatures with the power of causality to produce order themselves. Like the master builder lays out the plan of the house but he entrusts the different engineers and workers with the execution of the plan. A particular order which is already there among non-living things may have been established by creatures. But the general plan - and this is called providence in the first place – is not incompatible with any such particular order.

9.4.2 (to 9.1.2)

As has been said above (9.3.2 (3).e); 9.4.1) the execution of God's plan (providence) is done to a great extent by the creatures. Thus it does not hinder that many processes of becoming, i.e. of increasing order, emerge through self-organization by creatures. But from this it does not follow that they would be incompatible with providence, i.e. with God's plan.

9.4.3 (to 9.1.3)

Things can be ordered towards their (or some) goals in different ways. One is by laying down laws, either for meeting the goal in all cases (dynamical laws) or for meeting the goal in most cases (statistical laws); another is by entrusting the creature with rationality to find his (her) goal him- or herself. In both cases the plan for ordering towards an end (i.e. providence) is not incompatible with order. On the contrary, since what is ordered by necessity (by law), may very well have (and reach) a goal.

9.4.4 (to 9.1.4)

To this objection we may answer two points: (1) As has been said in section 9.3.2, 9.3.2 (3).e) no thing or event is random in every aspect. It is random w.r.t. a particular order O but not random or even ordered w.r.t. another order O'. In this sense it then comes under providence. (2) Since order and chance coexist, i.e. are present in the same system (cf. 9.3.2 above) to provide order implies to allow chance. In this sense chance comes under God's providence because (according to the definition of providence) everything that God permits comes under his providence.

9.4.5 (to 9.1.5)

As it is clear from section 4.3.2 if things or events are ordered by statistical laws i.e. if they obey statistical laws, the singular thing or event or the singular microstate has degrees of freedom and in this sense is chance-like or random. Nevertheless the huge ensemble of things, events or microstates obeys strict statistical laws. Thus for example a huge ensemble of things, events or microstates obey the law of entropy which directs them towards a macrostate of equilibrium. But the singular things, events or microstates behave in a chance-like way. Therefore things, events or microstates can happen under a plan or law globally but still be chance-like locally. And consequently providence in the sense of the global plan is not violated by local chance which is also permitted by providence, because it is compatible with it.

Inwagen, when telling us how he understands "chance" is claiming at least two different things: (1) The respective event is without purpose and not part of anyone's plan. (2) The event might very well not have been. Beginning with (2) we may point out that this claim is important and correct. Recalling different definitions of chance, like Df 6.1, Df 6.2, Df 6.4, Df 6.5, Df 6.8–Df 6.10, Df 8.2, Df 8.4 shows that what occurs by chance need not have been at all or (as in the definitions) need not have been that way, but could have been different. Observe that this is not against the respective laws but left open or permitted by those laws. The claim (1) however might be understood in two ways. First, as a kind of communication about Inwagen's understanding of "chance" in the sense of an non-committal information. In this case we cannot speak of a true or false opinion but only of a more or less adequate usage of the word. Secondly, claim (1) might be understood as stating some important property of chance, where chance is understood in an objective sense according to one of the definitions just mentioned above. In this case claim (1) is wrong. As has been said in section 9.3.2 and above (9.4.5) a plan or order or law can coexist globally with a local chance in one and the same physical, chemical or biological system (recall definitions Df 5.4,Df 5.5,Df 5.7,Df 5.9,Df 5.10 of ch. 5 and Df 7.7 of ch. 7 and the respective examples there). Moreover any kind of chance and randomness can only be defined relative to some structure, order or law (recall definitions Df 6.4, Df 6.5, Df 6.8–Df 6.10 of ch. 6 and Df 8.1–Df 8.4 of ch.8 and the respective examples there).

10 Whether everything that happens comes under God's providence

10.1 Arguments Contra

10.1.1 First argument

What comes under God's providence is ruled or ordered towards its end. Thus providence means an intervention of God in the sense of ordering things towards their end. But as Susskind says, scientists deny any divine intervention:

> "But scientists – real scientists – resist the temptation to explain natural phenomena, including creation itself, by divine intervention. ... So we resist, to the death, all explanations of the world based on anything but the laws of physics, mathematics, and probability."[1]

Therefore it seems that no natural phenomena comes under God's providence; and consequently: not everything that happens, comes under God's providence.

10.1.2 Second argument

As has been shown in chapters 6 and 8 there are several types of events that happen by chance. These are roughly those which are not ruled by dynamical laws but by statistical laws (i.e. indeterministic laws) which allow degrees of freedom for the individual case. But according to Inwagen events happening by chance do not come under God's providence:

> "Since the natural physical world seems in fact to be indeterministic, it is plausible to suppose that there are a great number of states of affairs which are not part of God's plan ...".[2]

Since God's providence is God's plan, what does not come under God's plan, does not come under his providence.

Therefore: Not everything that happens comes under God's providence.

1 Susskind (2006) p. 355
2 Inwagen (1995) p.55

10.1.3 Third argument

It is impossible that everything what happens comes under God's providence. This can be seen as follows: Under providence we understand God's plan together with it's execution by which the developments of things and events of this world (universe) are ordered. As a special case God's plan contains also his Ten Commandments by which human actions are ruled. But there are events which violate the Ten Commandments, as for example immoral human actions (sins). Thus they also violate God's plan. God cannot have planned the sins of men, otherwise he would contradict himself having decreed his Ten Commandments.

Therefore occurring immoral actions (sins) cannot come under God's providence. And consequently not everything that happens comes under God's providence.

10.1.4 Fourth argument

Instead of saying "everything that happens" we could also say "everything which is the case or which is a fact". Now there are also facts of mathematics or of logic like "the diagonal in the square is not rational" or "the consequences of true premises are true". Such facts cannot come under God's providence since they cannot be directed towards an end.

Therefore: not everything that happens or what is a fact comes under God's providence.

10.1.5 Fifth argument

God himself is not directed to an end; on the contrary he is the ultimate end. And also facts about God, like that he exists or that he is omniscient and omnipotent, are not directed to an end nor do they come under God's plan.

Therefore: Not everything that happens comes under God's providence.

10.2 Argument Pro

As has been said already in ch. 3 God's providence presupposes God's knowledge about his creation. But since God is omniscient he knows everything that happens (is the case) concerning his creation. Thus he might take care w.r.t. everything that happens concerning creation. And if he is good, he will take care of it such that it comes under his providence. Therefore everything what happens concerning creation comes under God's providence.

10.3 Proposed Answer

In Chapter 3 it has been shown that providence is concerned with creation and since the universe is part of creation, providence is concerned with the universe. In chapter 9 it was shown that providence is compatible with all processes and events of the universe, be they processes and events ordered by dynamical or statistical laws or random-processes and chance-like events.

This chapter will defend that all processes and events which occur in the universe come under (or belong to) God's providence. This is done in the following way: First, a definition with several necessary conditions is given for what it means that a process or event, or more generally a state of affairs, belongs to God's providence. Secondly, it will be defended that these necessary conditions are satisfied. This will be done in this chapter for conditions (a) and (b), but in subsequent chapters for conditions (c)–(f). The definition is basically similar to Df 3.1 of ch. 3 but is here formulated more generally for states of affairs, viz. for the propositions which represent them. Moreover some additional supplementations are added. Thus we may speak of the set of true propositions (called: theorems) concerning providence, in symbols: $\{p \in T(Prov)\}$ or the set of theorems concerning the universe: $\{p \in T(U)\}$.

10.3.1 Definition of 'providence'

Df 10.1. The proposition p (representing a state of affairs) belongs to the theorems of God's providence iff the following conditions (a)–(f) are satisfied:

(a) p belongs to the theorems concerning creation and to the theorems concerning the universe.

(b) p is the case at all times t (omnitemporal) or at some time(s); where t is a time relative to a reference system of the universe and where some specific t may be past, present or future relative to that reference system.

(c) God knows that p is the case

(d) God wills that p is the case or God permits that p is the case.

(e) God causes that p is the case or God entrusts creatures to cause that p is the case

(f) God directs p towards some goal or integrates p into a network of goals.

The constant 'g' for 'God', which is used in Df 10.2 below, has been introduced in section 1.3.3 with a definition.

A more symbolic version of Df 10.1 is this:

Df 10.2. $p \in Tg's(Prov)$ iff

(a) $p \in T(CR)$ and $p \in T(U)$, where $T(U) \subset T(CR)$

(b) $(\forall t)p_t$ or $(\exists t)p_t$, where t is as above

(c) gKp

(d) $gWp \vee gPp$

(e) $gCp \vee gEtr(crCp)$

(f) $(\exists x)(Goal(x) \wedge gDir(p/x)) \vee (\exists y)(NGoal(y) \wedge gInt(p/y))$

The expressions 'K' 'W' 'P' 'C' 'Etr' 'Dir' 'Int' are understood here as truth-functional operators applied to propositional variables; for these propositional variables the usual rules of substitution hold. As is known such operators and other epistemic, volitive or deontic operators can be defined implicitly by an axiom system. The operator K together with the other operators G (for strong belief), B (for weak belief) and A (for assumption) have been shown to be also definable by a decidable many valued logic.[3]

Definitions Df 10.1 and Df 10.2 are more general than definition Df 3.1 (ch. 3). This is so because they are formulated with propositions representing states of affairs

3 Cf. Weingartner (1981) and Weingartner (1982)

rather than with things or events. Things or events are too restricted, since we want also to say that, for example, laws of nature or states or the respective facts about the numerical values of constants of nature (fine tuning) or about genetic sequences or mutation rates... etc. can come under God's providence.

Since the theorems concerning the universe U are included in the theorems concerning creation $T(U) \subset T(CR)$, it might seem we need to mention only the latter. But since we do not deal here with those creatures which do not belong to the universe (angels for example) it is necessary to mention the additional restriction to the universe as condition (a).

10.3.2 Omnitemporal and temporal states of affairs (Df 10.1 (b))

Some states of affairs which come under God's providence exist (or: are the case) for all times. Thus fundamental laws of nature are – according to our knowledge today – time-translation invariant; i.e. they do not change through time. In a similar way the fundamental constants of nature, for example, G (gravitational constant), h (Planck's constant) c (light velocity in vacuum) do not change through time. This is also the case with purely numerical dimensionless values, for example that of the fine structure constant $\alpha(= 1/137)$ or that of the ratio of proton mass to electron mass (1836).[4]

There are other states of affairs of the universe which hold only for some time. To these belong the initial conditions or states of the universe at its beginning but also later states and events at a certain place and time (relative to a reference system of spacetime). In particular also states and events and processes (more general: states of affairs) of non-living and of living systems including those of men and his free-will decisions.

The first type of those states of affairs which hold for all times, the laws of nature, can also be called *necessary* in the sense of physically or empirically necessary.

---

4 These constants of nature are really constant according to the most exact measurements known today. But whether they nevertheless are changing very slowly beyond the threshold of today's most accurate measuring instruments and – methods is in fact not known. If these constants would change very slowly indeed, then also the respective fundamental laws of nature in which they enter, would change very slowly too. Still both constants and laws couldn't have developed by natural selection since they must have been fixed at the beginning of the universe in order to make its evolution possible. Cf. Denton (1998) p. 13f.

According to a proposal of Popper this means that they are valid in all possible universes (including ours) which differ from ours only w.r.t. initial conditions.[5] Concerning the constants of nature it is not known in what sense they could be called necessary in dependence of the laws of nature. But it is known quite well that their present values are necessary for the development of carbon-based life on earth. (This is some weak form of the *Anthropic Principle*.)

> "However, it is well to bear in mind that many of the (experimental) limits on varying constants have a rather questionable status. No precise theory is yet available which allows any particular parameter one wishes to possess arbitrary space-time variations and still be consistent with other constraints and laws."[6]

Similarly it is not known why the other dimensionless constants like α and m_p/m_e have the value they have, but again it is known that with different values the known cosmological evolution would have been different let alone the development of carbon-based life. It has to be stressed that these types of states of affairs of the universe which hold for all times seem not to be subject of evolution or selection:

> "We have found nature to be constructed upon certain immutable foundation stones, which we call fundamental constants of nature. We have no explanation for the precise numerical values taken by these unchangeable dimensionless numbers. They are not subject to evolution or selection by any known natural or unnatural mechanism."[7]

Those states of affairs of the universe, however, which hold for some time only, may all be subject to evolution or selection. But even if the fundamental constants of nature would turn out to be not absolutely constant and consequently if the laws of nature would not be completely time-translation invariant, they both would be stable enough to speak of invariant laws of nature and fundamental constants of nature compared to the innumerable kinds of changes concerning states, events, processes, developments of non-living and living systems of the universe. And even a slightly different value of the fundamental constants must have been fixed at the very beginning and could not have been subject to evolution or selection.

---

5 Cf. Popper (1959) p. 433.

6 Barrow and Tipler (1986) p. 238. The complicated network of the fundamental constants of nature has been investigated in detail by Barrow and Tipler (1986). Cf. also Denton (1998) for consequences in the domain of biology.

7 Barrow and Tipler (1986) p. 31.

10.3.3 Both states of affairs, those which hold for all times and those which hold for some time, come under God's providence

(1) The states of affairs which hold for all times are necessary conditions for the universe. If God is the creator of the universe he has to create also these necessary conditions of the universe; and since what he creates he incorporates into his plan and his plan belongs to his providence it holds that the states of affairs which hold for all times belong to his providence. This is also manifest from the following facts:

Those fundamental constants of nature which are dimensionless like $m_p/m_e = 1836$ and $\alpha = 1/137$ and others of this type must have been fixed at the beginning of the universe. And thus they can be hardly a result of evolution and selection. This holds in a similar way of the other constants like G, c, h and e and also of the fundamental laws of nature; without them the evolution of the universe couldn't have started. Therefore if God is the creator of the universe he must have determined these fundamental laws and constants too. And thus they come under God's providence in the sense of both his plan and his execution of the plan.

(2) Those states of affairs of the universe which hold for *some* time, are subject of the time development according to dynamical and statistical laws; in so far they may be also subject to evolution and selection, since especially statistical laws allow degrees of freedom and chance for the individual cases (be they objects, systems, states, events or processes). However to these kinds of states of affairs belong also the first initial states or events at the beginning of the universe. That they do not follow from any fundamental law of nature was already clearly recognized by Thomas Aquinas: Since the universal laws abstract from here (hic) and now (nunc) they do not allow to demonstrate a certain point of time or of space.[8] In modern terms: from a law no singularity can be deduced. This is also connected with a deep question concerning the scientific description and explanation of nature: with the distinction between what changes relative to what does not change which goes back to the Greek ideal of science elaborated in detail by Plato and Aristotle: To describe and explain the visible, observable, concrete, particular, changing, material world by non-visible, non-observable, abstract, universal, non-changing and immaterial principles.

8 Cf. Aquinas (1981) I, 46,2

> "The world is very complicated and it is clearly impossible for the human mind to understand it completely. Man has therefore devised an artifice which permits the complicated nature of the world to be blamed on something which is called accidental and thus permits him to abstract a domain in which simple laws can be found. The complications are called initial conditions; the domains of regularities, laws of nature".[9]

The distinction between initial conditions and laws of nature can be very well justified in classical mechanics but is more complicated in other domains of physics.[10] However the first initial conditions at the beginning of the universe must certainly be different from the laws of nature. And also w.r.t. these it holds that without them the universe could not start. Thus if we accept God as the creator of the universe he must have determined these first initial conditions too.

Since spacetime must be assumed together with the first change and the first initial condition cannot have developed by change or chance, it cannot be included in spacetime. This is pointed out by Barrow and Tipler w.r.t. the Friedman and Einstein universe:

> "The key point to note is that neither in the expanding Friedman universe, nor in the Einstein universe, is the 'beginning' (in t or τ time) included in space-time".[11]

Or similar w.r.t. a quantum theoretical approach concerning the beginning of the universe:

> "This approach is consistent with the view that there is no time at the most fundamental level".[12]

The same point was also underlined concerning creation by Thomas Aquinas:

> "The phrase about things being created in the beginning of time means that the heavens and earth were created together with time; it does not suggest that the beginning of time was the measure of creation."[13]

Also from this consideration it follows that God as creator of the universe must have determined the first initial condition too. And in this sense the first initial condition comes under God's providence concerning its plan and its execution of the plan.

---

9 Wigner (1967) p.3

10 For such a justification see Mittelstaedt and Weingartner (2005) ch. 8.1.

11 Barrow and Tipler (1986) p. 442. Cf. Jammer (2006).

12 Halliwell (1994) p. 375.

13 Aquinas (1981) I, 46, 3 ad 1.

However, concerning other states of affairs which hold for *some* time, God need not and does not determine all of them. Under these there are states of affairs which are determined by dynamical laws; others which obey statistical laws w.r.t. huge ensembles and are chance-like, having degrees of freedom w.r.t. the individual case; human free will decisions are falling under the latter category. All these states of affairs come under God's plan, but concerning the execution of the plan, God entrusts his creatures to which he gave the power of causation. Observe however that falling under God's plan does not mean that the state of affairs is determined by him, since foreknowledge of an event does not imply willing or causing that event (see below chs. 11, 12. and 13.) But everything which comes under God's plan comes under his providence and therefore also states of affairs which hold only for some time come under his providence.

10.3.4 Result of chapter 10

The result of ch. 10 can be summarized as follows:

T 10.1. *Everything that happens comes under God's providence.*

What this means is more accurately described in definition Df 10.1 by conditions (a)–(f). Of these the first two have been established as theorems in this chapter (Theorem 10.2 and Theorem 10.3 below). The remaining conditions (c)–(f) will be the results of chs. 11–14.

T 10.2. *Everything that happens in creation (in the universe) belongs to God's providence.*

T 10.3. *Everything that happens omnitemporally and everything that happens at some time (where time is the time of a reference system of our universe) belongs to God's providence.*

10.4 Answer to the Objections

10.4.1 (to 10.1.1)

(1) The first thing to say to this objection is this: It has been shown in chapter 9 that both order and teleological order in this world and chance and randomness in this world are compatible with God's providence. This has been shown to hold with different notions of compatibility. From this the following rather trivial facts follow:

(i) The set of true propositions about scientific results and of true scientific laws on the one hand and the set of true propositions about God's providence including his divine intervention in the world on the other, cannot be incompatible. Since any two sets of true propositions are always compatible on logical grounds. And this fact of logic cannot be hindered or prevented by any kind of "resistance" of some scientist.

(ii) An incompatibility can only arise if one (or both) of the domains contains a false proposition due to misinterpretation or by going beyond their competence. For example if scientists add to their domain some ideological superstructure or world-view or if philosophers or theologians misinterpret and misuse some scientific results as a support for some of their statements.

(2) The methodological rule that natural phenomena should be explained by science and its methods as completely as possible, without introducing God as a deus ex machina or as a stopgap, is fully acceptable. This applies also to "creation itself" if the respective scientists are critical enough to admit that beyond a special level (say the Planck scale) there are mainly conjectures and no hard results. Even if it can be admitted that there are different cosmological models which are mathematically consistent. But from this it does not follow that they are physically (cosmologically) correct.

(3) Concerning the quotation in 10.1.1 it has to be observed that from accepting the methodological rule above (2) nothing follows concerning facts about God's plan, God's providence or God's intervention. To claim that there cannot be an intervention of God as a consequence of such a rule would just be a simple logical fallacy. Therefore the conclusion in 10.1.1 that natural phenomena do not come under God's providence is not proved.

10.4.2 (to 10.1.2)

In order to answer the objection of Inwagen we have to distinguish two different senses of the expression God's plan:

(i) A state of affairs p (or an event e) pertains to God's plan iff p (e) is known (and foreseen) + willed + directed to an end by God. In this sense indeterministic states of affairs (events) – to which belong also human free will decisions – do not come under God's plan because they are not directly willed by God. And if "God's plan" is interpreted in this narrower way Inwagen's claim concerning free will decisions is correct.

(ii) On the other hand, if we define God's providence and God's plan in a wider sense as in section 10.3.1 then also indeterministic states of affairs (events) come under God's providence and plan. Since certain indeterministic states of affairs (events), like human free will decisions, God permits and integrates into a network of goals. Therefore, if "God's plan" is interpreted in this wider sense, Inwagens claim is not correct (see also below 11.3.2).

10.4.3 (to 10.1.3)

The answer to this objection is similar to that of 10.1.2 (in 10.4.2). God has not planned the sins of men in the sense that he had willed them or caused them. But he knows them without willing or causing them. And he permits them since he created man with free will. And further he is able to integrate them into a network of goals in the sense that a global goal (good) need not to be hindered by local events (sins) violating local goals (goods). Just as a master builder will eventually reach his goal of building a house with a group of workers, some of whom work in an excellent way, others in a good way and still others who work ineffectively, partially hindering the team. Or in the words of Geach:

> "God is the supreme Grand Master who has everything under his control. Some of the players are consciously helping his plan, others are trying to hinder it; whatever the finite players do, God's plan will be executed."[14]

---

14 Geach (1977) p. 58

10.4.4 (to 10.1.4 and 10.1.5)

It is correct as it is said in the objections that facts of logic and mathematics do not come under God's providence.

And furthermore, facts about God himself, such as his existence, or that he knows and loves himself ... etc. do not come under God's providence. The reason is that God's providence is concerned with his creation as has been established already in ch. 3. Therefore the question of ch. 10 "Whether everything that happens comes under God's providence" has to be interpreted according to what has been said in ch. 3, i.e. as "everything that happens in creation" or "everything which is a fact in the universe".

11 Whether everything that comes under God's providence is known by God

11.1 Arguments Contra

11.1.1 First argument

What belongs to God's providence is concerned with creation. Among the states of affairs of creation there are also contingent future states of affairs. Let p be such a contingent future event; then if it is known at t_o (t_o = present) that p will occur at $t_1 > t_0$ then p must obtain at t_1 and cannot not obtain. This must hold particularly of God's knowledge since it is infallible such that whatever is known by him is true. From this it follows that every contingent future event (also a human free will decision) is determined by God's knowledge connected with his providence, and consequently there are no indeterministic states of affairs contrary to what has been established in chs. 4, 6 and 8 and what is known by modern physics:

> "Once instability is included, the meaning of laws of nature changes radically as they have to be formulated on the statistical level. They no longer express 'certitudes' but 'possibilities'."[1]

Moreover, it has been mentioned already several times that a great part of physics and also of chemistry and biology does not obey exclusively dynamical – deterministic laws and so uses statistical laws for many indeterministic phenomena.

Therefore: Since this – that there are no indeterministic states of affairs – is absurd it does not seem to be true that everything that comes under God's providence is known by God.

11.1.2 Second argument

Contigent future states of affairs, like actions of free will, must belong to God's providence since they belong to creation (to this universe). And according to ch. 3 God's providence is concerned with creation. But as the following argument seems

1 Prigogine (1996) p. 3

to show certain contingent future states of affairs cannot be known by God, because it seems impossible that both: he knows that they will occur at the future time t_3 and they are actions of free will at t_3.

(1) Assume to the contrary that: God knows the future state of affairs that a person A acts (in such a way) that p (is the case) at time $t_3 > t_0$ (where t_3 is in the future relative to t_o at present) and person A acts freely that p (is the case) at time t_3.

(2) We assume that it holds that whatever God knows, he necessarily knows.[2]

(3) Moreover, it holds that whatever God knows is (or will be) the case (is true) since his knowledge is infallible.

(4) Therefore if God knows that person A acts (in such a way) that p_{t_3} (where $t_3 > t_0$) then it is necessary that person A acts that p_{t_3}.

(5) If it is necessary that person A acts that p_{t_3} then person A does not act freely that p_{t_3}.

(6) Hence: If God knows that A acts that p_{t_3} then A does not act freely that p_{t_3}.

(7) Therefore: If person A does act freely that p_{t_3}, then God does not know (the future state of affairs) that person A acts freely (in such a way) that p_{t_3}.[3]

(8) And consequently: Not both: God knows that A acts that p_{t_3} and A acts freely that p_{t_3}.

---

2 This thesis has been defended at length in my book on omniscience Weingartner (2008a), ch. 2.

3 Linda Zagzebski discussses an argument with a similar structure (Zagzebski (1997), p. 291f). The difference is that there, time indexes (of the past) are attributed to God's knowing and so necessity is introduced as *necessity per accidens* as William of Ockham called the necessity of the past. Here the view is defended that time indexes cannot be applied to God's actions and they cannot be applied to truth (or a truth operator), either, because both God and truth are timeless. Time can only be applied to events or states which are in space time of this world (creation). However, necessity can be introduced here via premise (2) according to ch.2 of Weingartner (2008a). This leads to the same difficulty of God's knowledge (of future state of affairs) and human freedom as in the case of the argument discussed by Linda Zagzebski.

11.2 Argument Pro

If God has created the universe he must know everything concerning the universe. In addition we may assume that he knows everything about his other creation (for example angels). Since providence is concerned with creation and inclusively with the universe, everything which comes under God's providence is known by God.

11.3 Proposed Answer

It has been shown elsewhere[4] in detail that God is omniscient in the sense that

(i) his knowledge is infallible, i.e. that whatever he knows is true and

(ii) he knows everything about himself, about logic and mathematics and about creation.

Moreover, it has been defended there: that God does not know at some time, although he knows that something happens at some time of the world (relative to some reference system of the world); that whatever he knows he necessarily knows; that his knowing does not imply causing; that he knows also singular events, past events and future events. In this sense the proposed answer here is much more incomplete, than the analysis there, since here God's knowledge is that connected with providence (cf. Df 10.1, condition (c)), whereas there it concerns God's knowledge in general. Since God's providence is concerned with creation, the knowledge implied by providence is knowledge about creation. Since we shall not be concerned with other creatures outside the universe (for example angels) we shall restrict creation to the universe. Under the assumption that God has created the universe, God knows everything concerning the universe. In other words: If God has created the universe, God knows every theorem (true proposition) which belongs to the theorems of the universe. We might define the fact that proposition p (representing a state of affairs) belongs to the theorems concerning the universe (U) as follows:

4 Weingartner (2008a).

Df 11.1.

$p \in T(U) \leftrightarrow p \in T\text{-}Law(U) \vee p \in T\text{-}Const(U) \vee p \in T\text{-}State(U) \vee p \in T\text{-}Init(U) \vee p \in T\text{-}Event(U)$

$p \in T\text{-}Law(U) \ldots$ p belongs to the law-theorems of U

$p \in T\text{-}Const(U) \ldots$ p belongs to the theorems about the value of fundamental constants of U

$p \in T\text{-}State(U) \ldots$ p belongs to the theorems describing states of U

$p \in T\text{-}Init(U) \ldots$ p belongs to the theorems describing initial conditions of U

$p \in T\text{-}Event(U) \ldots$ p belongs to the theorems describing events or processes of U.

Condition (c) of definition Df 10.1 of God's providence says then that God knows all theorems concerning laws, fundamental constants, states, initial conditions and events and processes of the universe.[5]

11.3.1 Does God know all laws and constants of the universe?

Assume that God has created this universe, but would not know some laws or constants. Since we know from today's science that any slight difference in laws or constants would result in a rather different universe an ignorance of some laws or constants would mean that he could not have had control over them and consequently could not have created this universe. Since this is contrary to the assumption we have to say that God knows all theorems concerning laws and constants of U.

5 For a comprehensive elaboration of God's knowledge of the universe see Weingartner (2008a) chs 4., 7., 11 and 13.23.

11.3.2 Does God know all states, events, processes and initial conditions in the universe?

(1) First we consider those states, events, processes and initial conditions which are determined by dynamical laws provided that other initial conditions are given (presupposed). In this case God must know them. Since they follow – given some other initial conditions – from the laws. To think that God could be ignorant of this type of states, events (processes) and initial conditions would be completely absurd, since already scientists know many of them.

(2) Secondly we consider indeterministic states, events and processes. In the case of statistical laws there are degrees of freedom for the individual event. Such degrees of freedom for "chance-like" events exist already at the atomic level but also on higher levels, for example in learning behavior via trial and error (recall sections of 4.3.2–4.3.3, 6.3.4–6.3.6 and ch. 8). On a still higher level this is also the case if the event is a human free will decision. Some have said that God's knowledge about his creatures is law-like knowledge such that God cannot know singular events. Firstly this cannot be true of those singular events which are predictable even for humans (cf. above) since we cannot assume that God's knowledge is weaker than that of his creatures. Secondly, this cannot be true of past and present singular events. They also can be known in principle by man and so again God's knowledge would be weaker than that of humans. Thirdly, the claim must therefore be concerned with indeterministic singular future events. Such a position is represented by Inwagen as is evident from the quotation in 10.1.2 although Inwagen also includes the first initial condition of the universe such that he excludes three types of events from God's plan: the first initial state of the universe, events occurring by "natural indeterminism" and human free will decisions.[6] To the first two points of Inwagen we shall make the following three comments, whereas with human free will decisions we shall be concerned in sections 11.3.3 and 15.3.5.

(a) First of all, to exclude the first initial state of the universe from God's plan is completely absurd. All theories of modern cosmology accepting a finite age of the universe, starting with some Big Bang, agree about the importance and pecularity of the first state; although it is not clear which things (constants, laws, etc.) have been already fixed together with the first state or very shortly before it ("shortly" means here time intervals in

6 Cf. Inwagen (1995) p. 54f

magnitudes close to the Planck time) the first state is decisive for the future states. To say therefore that it escapes God's plan, i.e. it is not known and not willed and not caused by God is rather ridiculous, since in this case God could not be the real creator of the universe.

(b) Secondly the question concerning natural indeterminism is concerned with all cases which have been discussed in detail in chapters 4., 6., and 8. As it is clear from the elaboration there, the occurrence of such events is random or chance-like relative to some parameters or properties but ordered and law-like relative to others; moreover "pure chance", "chance alone" and "blind chance" are journalistic slogans rather than scientific concepts. This means that for the law-like parameters even man can make some predictions. All the more God will know the sophisticated and hidden causes such that he then knows these future events w.r.t. its law-like parameters "in their causes" as Thomas Aquinas expresses himself.[7] On the other hand he will permit and entrust his creatures to cause and decide themselves in bringing about events. These events might be partially chance-like too. And insofar they are, God has not determined them in either way. But since knowing does not imply causing, God can know indeterminate contingent future events without determining them, since this is even possible for man:

> "You might be able to predict what you will do in a given situation even if you are free, in that situation, to do something else. If I know you well, I may be able to predict what action you will take in response to a certain set of conditions; it does not follow that you are not free with respect to that action."[8]

(c) Thirdly it has to be observed that it will be easy to know contingent future events for any observer who is spatially closer to the event than we are on earth. Thus a star explosion 1000 light years away we shall know only after 1000 years whereas an observer 5 light years away can predict it 995 years earlier. Therefore if God is omnipresent everywhere in the universe by his knowledge and by his power he can easily know all those contingent future events which we can possibly know only much later because the propagation of signals depends on the velocity of light on which his knowledge does not depend.

---

7 Cf. Aquinas (1981) I, 14,13. This point is elaborated in detail in Weingartner (2008a) sections 11.31 – 11.32.

8 Plantinga (1974) p.30

11.3.3 God's knowledge of contingent future events

The contingent future event might be indeterminate like a human free will decision or like other indeterminate events which are not yet determined to one like in a real yet undecided branch. The question whether God can know such contingent future events has already been discussed in some sense in ancient philosophy, but seriously and in detail since the Middle Ages. An extensive historical survey in two volumes has been given by W. L. Craig.[9] Aquinas defends God's foreknowledge of such events, because God has the possibility to know them in their actual states and not "as future", since he is outside time.[10] This question is rather complicated and cannot be elaborated here in detail. It has been defended in detail elsewhere that God knows also such contingent future events.[11] The defense consists there roughly of two parts.

(1) In the first part (ch. 10[12]) it is shown that neither knowledge nor truth can change the ontological status of a state of affairs. This is obvious if the ontological status is logical or mathematical necessity as with true propositions of logic or mathematics. It is still clear with all states of affairs which are determined by dynamical laws. But it is also shown to be correct if the state of affairs is contingent or future contingent. The main point is that the contingency of a state of affairs is not changed if someone knows that it occurs or that it will occur; and similar if it is said (at the time of occurring or before) that the respective proposition (representing the state of affairs) is true. In other words: From "it is true that p" where p is a contingent fact it does not follow "it is determined that p" (such that p would not be contingent anymore). What correctly follows is only: "it is true that p is contingent". Similarly from "it is known that p is the case" where p is a contingent fact it does not follow: "it is determined that p". What follows correctly is only: "it is known that p is the case and p is contingent" or "it is known that p is contingently, i.e. not determinately, the case". Therefore also God's knowledge or foreknowledge does not destroy the contingency or indeterminacy of man's free will decisions. This point is also supported by Dionysius and Thomas Aquinas:

---

9 Craig (1988) and Craig (1991).

10 Cf. Aquinas (1981) I, 14,13. (Ver) 2,12.

11 Weingartner (2008a) chs. 10 and 11.

12 Ibid.

> "On the contrary, Dionysius says that to corrupt nature is not the work of providence. But it is in the nature of some things to be contingent. Divine providence does not therefore impose any necessity upon things so as to destroy their contingency."[13]

(2) In the second part (ch. 11.) it is shown how God can have knowledge of contingent future events like human free will decisions. First of all it has to be realized that free actions or decisions of the human will (abbreviated as: $FADW$) are not states of affairs without any causes or laws although without compulsion from outside.[14] Thus we can assume that God knows all possibilities of compulsion hindering $FADW$. Further he will know all considerations of deliberation and planning of the human person for $FADW$. Moreover he will know all motives including ethical and moral reasons. Further he will know all the power of human persons for making $FADW$. And eventually he will know all respective counterfactuals of the form: if A would occur than the human person would choose B ... etc.[15]

Secondly, God might have a possibility to know contingent future states of affairs like human free will decisions in their actual states. That is, he would not know them as future.[16] If someone knows the occurrence of event e as future (for him, for x) then there must be a time interval between the time of his knowing (t_1) and the time when e occurs (t_2) where t_1 is earlier than t_2 ($t_1 < t_2$). But it is not the case that God knows something at some time, i.e. his knowledge has no time index.[17] Although he knows that some event e occurs at some time t (where the time index belongs to the event e) relative to a reference system of this world. Since God's knowing is not at some time he need not to know events of this world as past or future *for him*, even if they are past or future relative to a reference system (an observer) of this world.

---

13 Dionysius (Div.Nom.) 4,23. Aquinas (1981) I,22,4.

14 Cf. the detailed discussion of *free will* and *free will decision* in ch. 15 below.

15 God's knowledge of all the respective counterfactuals was defended by Molina who called it "scientia media". For a detailed discussion see Craig (1988) p. 169ff and Craig (1991) ch. 13. The claim of Craig that Molina was the first to point out that God knows counterfactuals is hardly tenable. At least at the time of Thomas Aquinas such questions were frequently discussed and similar views have been defended. Cf. Aquinas (1981) I, qu.14, articles 9, 12 and 13.

16 Thomas Aquinas has proposed this view as an additional explanation, especially for cases where "knowing the future events in their causes" fails. Cf. Aquinas (1981) I, 14,13 and (Ver) 2,12.

17 This has been defended in detail in ch.3 of Weingartner (2008a).

11.3.4 Results of chapter 11

Since it was shown in sections 11.3.1–11.3.3 that God knows everything concerning his creation and God's providence is concerned with creation it follows that everything what comes under God's providence is known by God.

T 11.1. *Everything that comes under God's providence is known by God.*

In more detail, this means:

T 11.2. *Since the universe belongs to God's providence, everything about the Universe – its laws, constants, states, initial conditions, events – is known by God.*

T 11.3. *Since the universe belongs to God's providence, everything that happens in the universe – be it past, present or future (relative to some reference system of the universe) – is known by God.*

11.4 Answer to the Objections

11.4.1 (to 11.1.1)

God's knowledge does not exclude contingent (indeterministic) states of affairs. The answer to this objection should be clear from 11.3.3 (1). The ontological status of the contingency of a state of affairs cannot be changed by the fact that someone knows that this state of affairs is happening or will happen. Nor can the status of contingency of a proposition be changed by correctly saying that this proposition is true. Therefore the third premise of the objection in 11.1.1 is not correct:

From "it is known at t_o that p will occur at $t_1 > t_o$ (p_{t_1})" it does not follow that p must obtain at t_1 where "must" is interpreted as some kind of necessity viz. not-contingency. What follows is only that p as a contingent (i.e. not necessary) fact will obtain at t_1. Similarly, if God knows that p_{t_1} (where $t_1 > t_o$, t_o = present), he knows that the contingent state of affairs p obtains at t_1. This also becomes clear from the fact that God's knowledge about any state of affairs is always complete. Thus if he would know only that p obtains at t_1 without knowing that p is a contingent state of affairs his knowledge would be incomplete what is impossible for God. From these considerations God's knowledge of present or future (relative to a reference system of the world) states of affairs does not exclude indeterministic or contingent states of affairs. Therefore the conclusion of objection 11.1.1 is not proved.

11.4.2 (to 11.1.2)

God's knowledge does not destroy free will decisions. In order to show the mistake in objection 11.1.2 we shall put the argument into symbolic form:

(1) $gK(aAp_{t_3}) \wedge aAFp_{t_3}$ — Assumption where $t_3 > t_0$ (t_0=present)
$aAp \ldots a$ acts (such) that p;
$aAFp \ldots a$ acts freely that p;

(2) $gKp \Rightarrow \Box gKp$ — defended in ch.2 of Weingartner (2008a)

(3) $gKp \Rightarrow p$ — defended in ch.1 of Weingartner (2008a)

(4) $gK(aAp_{t_3}) \Rightarrow \Box aAp_{t_3}$ — from (1), (2), (3) and Modal Lg

(5) $\Box aAp_{t_3} \rightarrow \neg aAFp_{t_3}$ — empirical premise

(6) $gK(aAp_{t_3}) \rightarrow \neg aAFp_{t_3}$ — from (4) and (5)

(7) $aAFp_{t_3} \rightarrow \neg gK(aAp_{t_3})$ — from (6)

(8) $\neg(gK(aAp_{t_3} \wedge aAFp_{t_3})$ — from (7)

Concerning this argument we shall ask two questions: (a) Is the argument valid, i.e. does the conclusion (7) and (8) as well as (6) logically follow from the premises (2), (3) and (5). It is easily seen that the answer is: Yes, provided that we use a well-known principle of Modal Logic which says: If $\Box p$ (*necessarily* p) and if $p \Rightarrow q$ (p *necessarily implies* q) then $\Box q$ (*necessarily* q). The second question (b) is the question whether the premises are true. Since only then the conclusion is proved to be true by this argument. But in this respect we find an important neglect: What kind of action is A in 'aAp_{t_3}'. The time index tells us that the result of the action will take place in the future (point of time t_3) relative to the present point of time t_0. But it does not tell us whether the action itself is contingent and hardly predictable or determined by dynamical laws and therefore strictly predictable. If the action is an action of free will then it is contingent and not determined by dynamical laws. And according to what has been said in 11.3.3 (1) and 11.4.1, knowledge cannot change the ontological status (contingency or free will action) of states of affairs (here of the free will action). Thus the epistemic operator 'K' cannot change the action operator 'A'. In order to correct the argument by correcting the premises we first have to complete premise (1) by changing 'A' (standing for any action, determined or free) to 'AF' (standing for a contingent action of free will). Then the corrected argument reads as follows:

(1') $gK(aAFp_{t_3})$

(2') = (2)

(3') = (3)

(4') $gK(aAFp_{t_3}) \rightarrow \Box aAFp_{t_3}$

Now we can easily see that premise (5) becomes false: "If necessarily person a acts freely that p_{t_3} then person a does not act freely that p_{t_3}." And so we cannot use premise (5) anymore. And hence conclusions (6) and (7) cannot be derived anymore. The whole argument then stops with conclusion (4'): If God knows that person a acts freely that p_{t_3} (where $t_3 > t_0$, t_0 = present) then necessarily person a acts freely that p_{t_3}. This corrects the argument and solves the respective difficulty concerning human freedom and God's knowledge of contingent future events.[18] Observe further that mixed modalities like $\Box\Diamond p$ (*necessarily possibly* p) or $\Diamond\Box p$ (*possibly necessarily* p) are well-known in Modal Logics. For example the principle $\Diamond p \rightarrow \Box\Diamond p$ is used as an axiom, which, when added to system T, leads to system S5. Although it will hold that $p \rightarrow \Box\Diamond p$, the opposite implication will not hold. We may therefore correct the argument in 11.1.2 also by instantiating premise (2) with the help of explicitely stating the contingency of that state of affairs p brought about by the action of free will of person A.

(2") $gK\Delta p_{t_3} \rightarrow \Box gK(\Delta p_{t_3})$ where $\Delta p \leftrightarrow_{def} \Diamond p \wedge \Diamond\neg p$

In this case the argument ends with (4"):

(4") $gK\Delta p_{t_3} \rightarrow \Box(\Delta p_{t_3}))$ where $t_3 > t_0$, t_0 = present; that is: If God knows that the contingent state of affairs p will obtain at $t_3 > t_o$ then necessarily the contingent state of affairs p will obtain at $t_3 > t_o$.

Also with this interpretation of the first premise the question of compatibility of contingent future states of affairs and knowledge of future states of affairs is resolved.

18 The argument discussed by Linda Zagzebski can also be corrected along these lines. Then her premise (7) is false and conclusion (8) is no longer derivable.

12 Whether everything that comes under God's providence is willed or permitted by God

12.1 Arguments Contra

12.1.1 First argument

Whatever is willed by God must be permitted by God. And consequently: Whatever is not permitted by him cannot be willed by him. But there seem to be events which are forbidden and not permitted by him like human actions violating his Ten Commandments. Such actions (events) are then neither permitted nor willed by him. But according to ch. 10 everything that happens (consequently also such actions) comes under God's providence.

Therefore, if what has been established in ch. 10 is correct, it cannot be true that everything that comes under God's providence is willed or permitted by God.

12.1.2 Second argument

If it follows from the Ten Commandments that action A (say lying) is forbidden, then action A is forbidden by God. And what is forbidden by God is not permitted by God and consequently also not willed by God. But the Ten Commandments and what follows from them certainly come under God's providence.

Therefore there is something which comes under God's providence but is neither permitted nor willed by God. And consequently it cannot be generally true that everything that comes under God's providence is willed or permitted by God.

12.2 Argument Pro

As Augustine says: Everything that happens is either willed or permitted by God.[1] From this it follows: If something comes under God's providence then it is either willed or permitted by God.

12.3 Proposed Answer

To have providence about something implies to take care of it. But nobody can take care of something if he is not related to it by his knowledge and by his will. It was shown in ch. 11 how God is related by his *knowledge* to things of creation that come under his providence. This chapter shows how God is related by his *will* to things (of creation) which come under his providence. It confirms condition (d) of definition Df 10.1 (ch. 10). It will be shown in the subsequent sections that everything that comes under God's providence is either willed or permitted by God.

However, it is not true that everything that comes under God's providence is willed by God. Since men's free will decisions, including immoral decisions and actions, come under God's providence, but they are not willed by God, but only permitted by him. The reason for that is that God is not all-willing, i.e. for some states of affairs (like immoral actions) he neither wills them to occur nor wills them not to occur but permits them to occur (cf. 12.3.2 below). This may also happen for some other states of affairs which happen by chance or randomly. Although he neither wills them to occur nor wills them not to occur he permits them to occur and insofar they still come under God's providence.

12.3.1 God permits order and teleological order

In chapters 4., 5. and 7. it has been shown that there is order and teleological order including values in non-living and in living things of this world (universe). As it has been explained in chs. 5. and 7. there are many different kinds of order

1 Augustine (1887) 95.

which are defined there by definitions Df 5.3-Df 5.5, Df 5.7, Df 5.9, Df 5.10 and Df 7.2-Df 7.7.

This order and teleological order in things of this world is permitted by God. To see this consider the following justification:

Assume that the order and teleological order defined and described in the above mentioned chapters is not even permitted by God. Then it would follow that it does not exist which is refuted by the facts. Therefore it must be at least permitted by God. More accurately this can be shown as follows: God permits that $p =_{df}$. it is not the case that God wills that *not-p* is the case, i.e. God does not prevent that p is the case. Therefore if God would not permit that p, then he would prevent it or then he would will that *not-p* is the case. But since his will must be always fulfilled (cf. 12.3.3 below), *not-p* would be the case, contrary to the facts. Therefore God must at least permit order and teleological order in things.

A formal proof would be as follows (where p represents the state of affairs that there is order and teleological order in non-living and living things of this world and g is defined as in 1.3.3):

Df 12.1. $gPp \leftrightarrow \neg gW\neg p$

1. $\neg gPp \rightarrow gW\neg p$ from Df 12.1
2. $gWp \rightarrow p$ God's will is always fulfilled (cf. 12.3.3)
3. $gW\neg p \rightarrow \neg p$ from 2. $\neg p/p$
4. p fact (established in chs. 4.,5.,7.)
5. $\neg gW\neg p$ from 1. and 4. by M.T.
6. gPp from 5. and 1.

Observe that if p represents a state of affairs of a human free will action, then God's will and permission have to be related to such states of affairs only indirectly via "it should be the case" or "it ought to be the case". Above in premise 1, not-permitting implies willing that "not", i.e. preventing. Applied to God's commands, not- permitting implies commanding that "not", i.e. forbidding (see section 12.4.1 below).

12.3.2 God is not all-willing

Observe that we cannot prove that God wills that there is order and teleological order in the universe (p) by the following demonstration:

1. Everything is subject to God's will; that is: for all p: either God wills that p is the case or God wills that *not-p* is the case. Symbolically:

$$AW\ (\forall p)(gWp \vee gW\neg p)$$

2. Since it has been proven that God permits that p (gPp) it cannot be true that God wills that *not-p* is the case. The latter is also contrary to facts.
3. Therefore it follows that God wills that p is the case (gWp).

Although 3. follows from 1. and 2., the argument is not a proof of 3., since premise 1. is false. 1. is the thesis (premise) of the all-willingness of God (AW). That this thesis must be false can be seen as follows. Since thesis 1. of the all-willing God holds for all states of affairs ($\forall p$), let p represent the state of affairs that some human person commits an immoral action (sin). Then if God wills that *not-p*, i.e. that the immoral action does not occur, then it would not occur (since his will is always fulfilled, see 12.3.3 below). But since this immoral action takes place this cannot be true and therefore it follows (by premise 1. above) that God wills that the immoral action occurs (p). From this it would also follow that God is inconsistent since he gave moral rules (for example the Ten Commandments) to men but would violate them by willing the occurrence of immoral actions. From these absurd consequences it follows that the thesis of the all-willing God must be false.[2] And as a consequence for occurring immoral human actions of free will it follows: God neither wills that they do occur nor that they do not occur; but God permits that they occur.

12.3.3 God's will is always fulfilled

The will of God is understood in such a way that his will is always fulfilled, i.e. never fails. This can be expressed as a principle in the following way: For any event e: if God wills that e occurs then e (in fact) occurs.

---

2 Observe that in all three „Abraham-religions" (Judaism, Christianity and Islam) there is an almighty and an omniscient God but nowhere an all-willing or all-causing God. For a detailed discussion of this erroneous thesis and its consequences cf. Weingartner (2003) section 6.4.

Or more generally for states of affairs: For any state of affairs p: if God wills that p is the case, then p is the case. Symbolically:

$$W\ (\forall p)(gWp \rightarrow p)$$

If this principle were not true, God would not be almighty; since he would will something which does not happen. This is often the case of man's imperfect will but it cannot be the case for God.

Observe that the opposite of the above principle cannot be true. It says: For any states of affairs p: if p is the case then God wills that p is the case. This is the thesis of (religious) fatalism: Whatever happens is willed by God. Symbolically:

$$F\ (\forall p)(p \rightarrow gWp)$$

That it cannot be true can be seen from its absurd consequences: since immoral actions (sins) happen they are willed by God. God would will then all terrible acts (as killing millions of people including mothers and children) of war criminals like Hitler, Stalin, Napoleon, Alexander, Nero, ... etc.

A further absurd consequence has been discussed by Peter Geach[3]: Since lies (of men) are a fact, God would will all lies and so also contradict his commandments and therefore since he is willing that lies occur one could not trust his revelations; the credibility in his revelation would be destroyed!

It can be shown that the thesis of all-willingness (AW) follows from the theses of (religious) fatalism (F):

1. F: $(\forall p)(p \rightarrow gWp)$
2. $\neg gWp \rightarrow \neg p$ — from 1. by contraposition
3. $\neg p \rightarrow gW\neg p$ — from 1. by $\neg p/p$
4. $\neg gWp \rightarrow gW\neg p$ — from 2. and 3.
5. $gWp \vee gW\neg p$ — from 4.
6. $(\forall p)(gWp \vee gW\neg p)$

On the other hand, the thesis of (religious) fatalism (F) follows only from both, the thesis W (God's will is always fulfilled) and AW (all-willingness):

1. W: $(\forall p)(gWp \rightarrow p)$

3 Geach (1977) p. 61f.

2. $AW: (\forall p)(gWp \vee gW\neg p)$
3. $gW\neg p \rightarrow \neg p$ from 1. $\neg p/p$
4. $\neg gWp \rightarrow gW\neg p$ from 2.
5. $\neg gWp \rightarrow \neg p$ from 3. and 4.
6. $p \rightarrow gWp$ from 5. by contraposition
7. $F: (\forall p)(p \rightarrow gWp)$

As we have seen, both F and AW are false because they lead to absurd consequences. The only true thesis is W. This is the thesis that God's will is always fulfilled.

However, there might be the objection that God wills that his commandments (for example the Ten Commandments) are obeyed. But they are not always obeyed. Thus his will does not seem to be always fulfilled. The answer to this objection is the following. Expressions like "God wills that man obeys his Ten Commandments" are not formulated in a correct way. Since according to W man would in fact obey his commandments; but this is not the case as we know. Therefore if God's will is applied to human actions of free will the correct formulation is that God wills that man *should* (*ought to*) obey his ten commandments, since God does not destroy the freedom of man. The same explanation holds for the expression "your will be done" in the *paternoster*: God's will *should* be done by man.

On the other hand, this does not hinder that in some cases God *wills* that the human person *wills* something and in these cases the decision is not a free will decision but may be based on some inclination which is genetically inborn or a result of environment conditions, or of education.

12.3.4 God wills order and teleological order

Assume that this is not the case w.r.t. order. Then this cannot mean that God wills that there is no order since this is against the facts (on the supposition that his will is always fulfilled). It must mean therefore, that either he does not will that there is no order or that he does not will that there is. The first was already established since God permits order (cf. 12.3.1) and Df 12.1 above). And this argument with respect to order can be repeated in an analogous way for teleological order. And that God does not will teleological order is also shown to be false subsequently.

The last thesis that God does not will that there is order can be shown to be false by the following reasons.

First, it would mean that all order and teleological order present in the universe God would only permit, but he would not will it. Secondly since it holds that whatever God causes he wills[4], it would follow that God does not (and did not) cause any order or teleological order in the universe. But this is absurd; even if we admit that some order and teleological order has been produced by creatures. But that the creator of the universe did not cause any order or teleological order whatsoever must be absurd and is incompatible with being the creator. As a creator he wills and also causes the dispositions which enable creatures to develop abilities for producing order themselves. Thus God does not create every order or teleological order directly. Order and teleological order are in his plan but he generously enables creatures to take over the execution of his plan by producing order and teleological order themselves.

12.3.5 God wills and permits chance and randomness

In chapters 6. and 8., it has been shown that there is chance and randomness in non-living and in living things of this world. In fact there are many different kinds of chance and randomness which is manifest from the definitions Df 6.1, Df 6.2, Df 6.4, Df 6.5, Df 6.7–Df 6.10 and Df 8.1–Df 8.4.

It will be substantiated subsequently that these kinds of chance and randomness are willed or permitted by God.

(1) God permits chance and randomness
   This is easy to prove along the lines of the proof in 12.3.1: Assume that the kinds of chance and randomness described and defined in the above mentioned chapters are not permitted by God. Since not-permitted p is equivalent to: willed that $not\text{-}p$ according to definition Df 12.1, it follows that under the above assumption, God wills that there is no chance or randomness. And since his will is always fulfilled it follows that there is no chance and ran-

4 This is also defended by Aquinas (1981) I, 19,4. Observe however that the opposite "whatever God wills he causes" does not hold in general: God wills his own goodness and his own existence but he cannot cause it. But it holds w.r.t. creation; and therefore, if his will is restricted to creation, the respective equivalence will hold.

domness. But this is contrary to facts as has been established in chs. 6. and 8. Therefore it follows that chance and randomness is permitted by God.

(2) God wills chance and randomness
This can be substantiated thus:

(a) If God has created nature then he has not ruled everything by dynamical laws since we know that a great part of physics, chemistry and biology obeys statistical laws but no dynamical laws. But statistical laws allow degrees of freedom and branching for the individual case (for example for the molecules in a gas). For those then there are kinds of chance and randomness according to definitions Df 6.4, Df 6.5 and Df 6.8–Df 6.10. Therefore if God wills that a part of physical, chemical and biological systems obey statistical laws then he also wills chance and randomness according to the definitions above.

(b) But from this it does not follow that God needs to engage his will into every state of affairs directly. Since he wills the cooperation of creatures (on different levels) and since he wills degrees of freedom and chance and randomness, by creating the world in this way, he can retain from interfering with his will in some such events. That is, he can leave them to occur by chance or to be caused or decided by creatures.

12.3.6 Result of chapter 12

T 12.1. *Everything that comes under God's providence is either willed or permitted by God.*

T 12.2. *God wills and permits order and teleological order in the universe.*

T 12.3. *God wills and permits chance and randomness in the universe.*

T 12.4. *God is neither all-willing nor all-causing.*

T 12.5. *God's will is always fulfilled.*

T 12.6. *For every state of affairs of the universe it holds: God wills or permits it.*

T 12.7. *For every occurring immoral human action of free will it holds: God neither wills that it does nor that it does not occur; God merely permits its occurrence (see 12.4.1 below).*

12.4 Answer to the Objections

12.4.1 (to 12.1.1 and 12.1.2)

It is necessary to make an important distinction concerning what is willed or forbidden by God w.r.t. his creation or creatures. There is a difference between what God wills to be the case, in the sense that he causes it to be the case on the one hand, and what God wills to be the case in the sense that it should (ought to be) the case on the other. Or shorter: there is a difference between what God causes to be the case and what God commands to be the case.

Analogously, there is a difference between what God forbids (or does not permit) to be the case, in the sense that he prevents it to be the case on the one hand, and what God forbids (or does not permit) to be the case in the sense that it should not be (ought not to be) the case on the other. Or shorter: there is a difference between what God prevents to be the case and what God commands not to be the case.

For example, God wills in the sense of "causes" the emergence of light (Gen. 1,2) and he forbids in the sense of "prevents" that the fundamental physical constants or the total amount of energy in the universe have a different value (from the one they actually have)[5].

Assume now that the states of affairs in question are free will decisions and actions of human beings. Since he has willed to create man with free will, he consequently wills not to interfere with man's free will decisions and actions. Therefore "God commands that p" is neither identical with "God wills (in the sense of causes)

5 According to our knowledge today the fundamental constants of physics especially the two dimensionless ones α and m_p/m_e had been fixed at the very beginning (Big Bang); they cannot be the result of an evolution. The same holds for the numerical value of the total amount of energy distributed in the universe. Thus, on the assumption of God as the creator of the universe, he has caused or prevented these states of affairs. Of course we might just say that he causes the actual values to be so.

that p" is nor with "God wills that some (all) human person(s) will (or act) that p". The latter holds because according to the principle W (God's will is always fulfilled) some (all) human persons would be forced to will (or act) accordingly. Symbolically:

God commands that $p \neq gWp$

$gComm(p) \neq \forall x_{\in H}\ gWxWp$

$\neq \forall x_{\in H}\ gWxAp$

$gComm(\neg p) \neq gW\neg p \neq \forall x_{\in H}\ gWxW\neg p$

$x_{\in H}$ ... x is human

xAp ... x acts in such a way that p occurs

xWp ... x wills that p

$xComm(p)$ ... x commands that p

Therefore we have to say: If p represents a state of affairs ruled as obligatory (as commanded) by the Ten Commandments, for example to believe in one God or to honor the parents, then God wills that all humans *should will* p and that all humans *should act* in such a way that p occurs.

And if p represents a state of affairs ruled as forbidden or not permitted by the Ten Commandments (but not prevented by God) as for example to lie or to steal, then God wills that all humans *should will* that not-p and that all humans *should act* in such a way that not-p occurs (or that p does not occur). Instead of saying "p represents a state of affairs ruled as obligatory or commanded by the Ten Commandments" we may just say "God commands that p" or abbreviated: $gComm(p)$. Analogously with forbidden or not permitted actions: $gComm(\neg p)$. Then the respective symbolic formulation is this:

12.4.1.1 $gComm(\neg p) \rightarrow gWxSW\neg p$

12.4.1.2 $gComm(\neg p) \rightarrow gWxSA\neg p$

$xSWp$ ... x should will that p

$xSAp$ ... x should act in such a way that p occurs

12.4.1.3 $gComm(\neg p) \rightarrow \forall x_{\in H} gWxSW\neg p$

12.4.1.4 $gComm(\neg p) \rightarrow \forall x_{\in H} gWxSA\neg p$

Observe that the latter two versions are the stronger forms to interpret a prohibition of the Ten Commandments. The weaker forms result if the negation sign is shifted before the operator W (wills that). The stronger consequence says: for all humans x, God wills that x should will that $not\text{-}p$ (or: x should act that $not\text{-}p$). The weaker consequence says: for all humans x, God wills that x should not will that p (or: x should not act that p). The stronger case aims at preventing that p (by willing and acting that $not\text{-}p$), the weaker case only at preventing the willing or the acting that p (by not willing and not acting that p):

12.4.1.5 $gComm(\neg p) \rightarrow \forall x{\in}H\, gWxS\neg Wp$

12.4.1.6 $gComm(\neg p) \rightarrow \forall x{\in}H\, gWxS\neg Ap$

After these considerations the answer to the objections 12.1.1 and 12.1.2 is the following: The expressions "forbidden by God" and "not permitted by God" (in the second premise of 12.1.1 and in the first premise of 12.1.2) have to be interpreted as "commanded not to occur by God" or "commanded by God not to be done". The reason is that the respective actions are human free will actions. And therefore "forbidden" or "not permitted" cannot mean "prevented" here since then God would take away the free will decision. Consequently we may say that there are two different meanings of *God's permission*. One is defined by Df 12.1: God permits$_1$ that $p =_{df}$ it is not the case that God will that $not\text{-}p$.

And according to this meaning it holds:

God does not permit$_1$ that $p =_{df}$ God wills that $not\text{-}p$
$=_{df}$ God prevents that p

The second meaning is:

God permits$_2$ that $p =_{df}$ it is not the case that God commends that $not\text{-}p$

And according to this meaning it holds:

God does not permit$_2$ that $p =_{df}$ God commends that $not\text{-}p$
$=_{df}$ God forbids that p

By principles 12.4.1.3 and 12.4.1.4 above $gComm(\neg p)$ implies for all humans x that $gWxSW\neg p$ (or: $gWxSA\neg p$) and this is not incompatible but compatible with $\neg gW\neg p$ viz. gPp (recall definition Df 12.1). That means that from: God commands that $not\text{-}p$ it follows (12.4.1.3 and 12.4.1.4) that God wills that all humans *should* will (act) to bring about $not\text{-}p$ and this is perfectly compatible with "God permits that p" or with "it is not the case that God wills that $not\text{-}p$" (the latter is equivalent to the former according to definition Df 12.1). It is also compatible with "God does not will that p" or with "God permits that $not\text{-}p$". Since if p is the occurrence of an immoral action then neither God wills that p nor God wills that not-p (he is not all-willing) but permits that p.

The consequences of the weaker forms 12.4.1.5 and 12.4.1.6 say that God wills that all humans *should* not will (act) to bring about p. They are also compatible with "God permits that p".

Therefore there is no hindrance that every human action which obeys or violates the Ten Commandments can come under God's providence, since it is at least permitted by God.

And consequently it is true as defended in 12.3.1–12.3.5 that everything that comes under God's providence is either willed or permitted by God.

13 Whether everything that comes under God's providence is caused by God or by creatures

13.1 Arguments Contra

13.1.1 First argument

There are several processes in non-living and in living systems that are processes of self-organization.

> "The characteristic feature of a self-organizing process is that a spatial pattern develops in an initially homogeneous tissue."[1]

Since such processes in fact happen, they come under God's providence as has been defended in chapter 10. But processes of self-organization seem not to be caused from outside, and thus they are neither caused by God nor by creatures.

Therefore not everything what comes under God's providence is caused by God or by creatures.

13.1.2 Second argument

There are several processes of natural selection in populations (POP) of living systems, where by natural selection we understand those interactions between members of POP and members of its environment Env (recall Df 5.2) which lead to a reduction of POP to a part of it.[2]

But processes of natural selection seem not to be caused from outside; and thus they seem neither caused by God nor by creatures.

Therefore not everything that comes under God's providence is caused by God or by creatures.

---

1 Cf. Maynard-Smith and Szathmary (1999) p. 231

2 Cf. Mahner and Bunge (2000) p. 320

13.1.3 Third argument

If everything that happens (concerning creation) comes under God's providence (ch. 10) then the whole universe must come under it. But if the universe is everlasting then it is not caused. And there are several present cosmological theories which defend an everlasting universe either as cyclic universe or as oscillating universe.[3]

Therefore if the universe is everlasting then not everything that comes under God's providence is caused by God or by creatures.

13.1.4 Fourth argument

If everything that happens concerning creation comes under God's providence (ch. 10) then the whole universe must come under it.

But if the universe is self-contained then it is not caused. The universe can be self-contained in one of the following three senses: (a) in the sense that it contains its own cause as a kind of singularity[4]; (b) in the sense that it does not need an initial state like in the cosmological model of Hartle and Hawking.[5] (c) in the sense that it contains its intelligent observer.[6]In all three cases the universe seems not to be caused by God or by creatures.

Therefore: Not everything what comes under God's providence is caused by God or by creatures.

13.2 Argument Pro

Even if many things inside the universe can be caused by creatures, several things at the beginning cannot be caused by creatures: that there is some matter at all, that this matter has already certain properties like atomic structure and obeys con-

3 Cf. Heller (2004)

4 There are rigorous proofs that this kind of singularity is unavoidable under very general conditions. Cf. Hawking and Ellis (1973) p. 266

5 Hartle and Hawking (1983)

6 Cf. Mittaelstaedt (1998) p. 116ff.

stants of nature and certain initial states (initial conditions). If we rule out an everlasting or a self-contained universe but accept the standard (Big Bang) theory then the properties and magnitudes of the universe at its earliest state must be caused from "outside", that is by God.

13.3 Proposed Answer

Everything that comes under God's providence is caused by God or by creatures. This can be defended along the following lines: First, it can be defended concerning the universe as a whole 13.3.1; secondly, w.r.t. the universe of order and chance 13.3.2; thirdly, concerning a universe in which self-organization, natural selection, development and evolution occur (13.3.3–13.3.7).

13.3.1 The universe as a whole

The universe as a whole must come under God's providence since every fact concerning the universe is something that happened or that happens. But according to ch. 10 everything that happens concerning creation (including what has already happened) comes under God's providence.

If God has created the universe he must have caused something. If he has caused anything he must have caused the beginning, which involves the existence of matter, its first state (the Big Bang) and the fundamental laws of nature together with the fundamental constants. This is necessary because (at least according to our knowledge today) both the fundamental laws of nature and the fundamental constants had to be fixed at the beginning, in a way such that they cannot be the result of an evolution. This also holds true for the existence of matter and for its first state.

> "The numerical values that nature has assigned to the fundamental constants, such as the charge of the electron, the mass of the proton, and the Newtonian gravitational constant, may be mysterious, but they are crucially relevant to the structure of the universe that we perceive … Had nature opted for a slightly different set of numbers, the world would be a very different place. Probably we would not be here to see it."[7]

---

7 Davis (1982) Preface

> "Several well-known physicists and astronomers, among them Carter, Dyson, Wheeler, Barrow, Tipler, Hoyle, to cite only a few have all made the point in recent publications – that our type of carbon-based life could only exist in a very special sort of universe and that if the laws of physics had been very slightly different we could not have existed."[8]

In case someone believes in an everlasting universe, at least the existence of matter would have been everlasting. But such models of universes are so far only consistent mathematical constructions without empirical support.[9]

On the other hand, the finite age of the universe according to the standard Big Bang model has strong experimental support. Especially the cosmic background radiation discovered by Penzias and Wilson offer strong evidence for the finite age of the universe.

13.3.2 The universe of order and chance

In chapters 5–8 two comprehensive facts have been established:

fact 1 It has been shown in chapters 5 and 7 that there is order and even teleological order in non-living and in living things of this universe.

fact 2 It has been shown in chapters 6 and 8 that there is chance and randomness in both non-living and living systems of this universe.

Moreover, in ch. 9 the following logical fact has been established: Logical Fact: fact 1 and fact 2 are compatible with God's providence; where compatibility was defined w.r.t. events (processes), properties, propositions and thoughts. If fact 1 is caused by creatures and fact 2 is implied in the sense of presupposed by creatures, i.e. by things of this world then one could guess that it might be caused and presupposed exclusively by self-organization or natural selection or development or evolution.

However, it will be shown in sections 13.3.3–13.3.8 that fact 1 and fact 2 are not exclusively caused by these four processes even if hereditariness, 13.3.9, is included.

8 Denton (1998) p. 16

9 One of the more well-known theories of that sort is the no-boundary theory of Hartle and Hawking (1983). Cf. 13.44 below. For an overview of such cosmological models see Heller (2004). The spatial finiteness of the universe is implied by the well corroborated Theory of General Relativity, cf. Hawking and Israel (1979).

13.3.3 Self-organization

> "Under self-organization we understand an emergence of a spatial pattern in an initially homogenous tissue of a non-living or living system without need of an asymmetric stimulus."[10]

Or more generally:

> "A system is self-organizing if it acquires a spatial, temporal or functional structure without specific interference from outside."[11]

Observe that the above characterizations do not claim that self-organization is a process without *any* influence from outside. The expressions "without specific interference from outside" or "without an asymmetric stimulus" do not rule out *any* cause from outside. In fact all known examples of self-organization show that some kind of energy supply is a necessary condition for the process. Thus for instance in the case of the patterns in fluid dynamics (Bénard-Instability) the fluid is heated; in case of a laser, a pumping mechanism supplies energy for the laser; in case of the polarization of the Fucus-embryos, light rays are needed from outside[12]; in case of the Belousov-Zhabotinsky reaction, the oscillating process (periodically from red to blue) relaxes more and more and leads to equilibrium, since the chemical energy for it is exhausted in a closed system[13].

There are several types of order (fact 1) which can be explained by self-organization. Many examples of emerging patterns have been systematically described by Haken[14]. Self-organization in living systems has been profoundly investigated by Stuart Kauffman. He focused on the *autonomous agent*, a self-reproducing molecular system, which is able to carry out one or more thermodynamic work cycles.[15] Many such types of order are also connected with chance and randomness (fact 2) in the sense that the emergence of order presupposes degrees of freedom or branching in nature.

On the other hand, there are many important types of order which cannot be explained by self- organization. First of all the three dimensional spatial order on the atomic level (recall section 5.3.1) then geometrical patterns in molecules, for example in fullerenes, the order of the periodic table of the elements, etc. The

---

10 Cf. Maynard-Smith and Szathmary (1999) p. 231

11 Cf. Haken (1988) p. 11

12 Cf. Maynard-Smith and Szathmary (1999) p. 231

13 Cf. Haken (1990) p.8

14 Haken (1990) and Haken and Wunderlin (1991)

15 Kauffman (2004) p.24 and Kauffman (2000)

same is true for types of chance like the degrees of freedom concerning chemical bindings or those concerning mutation rates.

13.3.4 Natural selection

We assume that every individual selection process consists of interactions between an individual living system ls and its environment $Env(ls)$, (cf. Df 5.2). Then 0-1 selection may be defined thus:

Df 13.1. 0-1 selection (Env, ls) = those interactions between ls and $Env(ls)$ which have a causal influence on the continuation of the existence of ls in relation to $Env(ls)$.

This definition can also be extended to populations. A more specific kind of selection can be defined thus:

Df 13.2. Let A(POP) be the aggregate (not set) of a population POP of differently adapted living systems (ls) of the same species with shared environment (Env). Further let N be the set of descendants of the ls of A(POP). Then: POP-selection = those interactions between the ls of A(POP) and their $Env(ls)$ which lead to a sorting (grading) of the descendants of the ls of A(POP), or in other words to a reduction of POP to a part of it.

Natural[16] selection presupposes chance (fact 2, 13.3.2) and in consequence variation; variation originates from environmental influences, from recombination of parental genes and from different types of mutation. Usually two well-known types of mutation are distinguished: those of recombination in the copying process and those caused by environment for example radiation (recall section 8.3.3). However there might be a further way of how variation originates: by "evolution genes". One type of such genes produces *generators* of genetic variation, the other produces *modulators* of the frequency of genetic variation occurring in a population of living systems.[17]

16 Definitions Df 13.1 and Df 13.2 are very similar to those of Mahner and Bunge (2000) p. 319 and 322.
17 Cf. Arber (2000)

From these considerations it follows that the emergence of new variations does not belong to natural selection but is presupposed by it and thus selection is not creative in this sense. Only on the basis of a multiplicity of variants selection favors certain phenotypes and eliminates others according to Df 13.1, Df 13.2.[18] Therefore all those types of order which are produced by the causal influence on the existence of ls (cf. Df 13.1) or by the sorting or grading of the descendants of the ls (cf. Df 13.2) can be explained by natural selection.

However, selection also has its limits. First, Darwin's hypothesis of a stepwise accumulation of useful variations ("gradualism") as a basis for selection is not generally satisfied. Secondly, selection fails in random landscapes. Thirdly, in equilibrium landscapes selection may run into an error catastrophe. Fourthly, "selection for cell types is limited not only by the abundance of local optima but, as complexity increases by the encroaching failure of selection to overcome the effects of mutation".[19]

Moreover, the fundamental laws of nature, the fundamental constants together with the existence of matter and its first state (recall 13.3.1 above), cannot be a product of natural selection. First of all, for the simple reason that if nothing exists (not even unstructured matter) there cannot be selection. And secondly, selection presupposes laws of nature and fundamental constants since they are necessary for the causal interactions between the living system and its environment which are, in turn, necessary for natural selection.

From these considerations it follows that not all types of order or teleological order can be explained by natural selection. And not all types of chance are implied or presupposed (as necessary conditions) by natural selection.

13.3.5 Development

Under a development D of a living system ls we understand a process of becoming of ls which is not directly or exclusively produced by the environment $Env(ls)$ of ls (cf. Df 5.9):

Df 13.3. D is a *development* of living system ls iff

(a) D is a process of becoming of ls (Df 5.9) and

(b) D is not directly or exclusively produced by the environment $Env(ls)$ of ls.

18 Cf. Mahner and Bunge (2000) p. 323

19 Kauffman (1993) p. 532 and Kauffman (1995) p. 183f.

More generally, we might define development also for systems in general (non-living or living): Replace "living system ls" by "system s" in the above definition:

Df 13.4. Like Df 13.3 where "living system ls" is replaced by "system s".

Development[20] is not a necessary condition for a non-living or a living system. Since development is defined relative to an interval of time via definition Df 5.9 of the process of becoming, some systems might not have development for some time. Thus where the growth of a crystal is a development this crystal might not develop further, i.e. it might not grow further, it might not change its shape further and it might not differentiate further. This is also true for several unicellular organisms.

Accordingly, three types of processes of development are usually distinguished:[21] *growth, morphogenesis* and *differentiation.*

A system undergoes a process of *growth* during the time interval $t_1 < t_2$ if its anabolism by assimilation of molecules from outside and by synthesis of molecules inside succeeds its respective catabolism during $t_1 < t_2$.

A system undergoes a process of *morphogenesis* during the time interval $t_1 < t_2$ if it receives a new shape or if one if its subsystems receive a new structure (recall Df 5.3 and Df 5.6) during the time $t_1 < t_2$.

A system undergoes a process of *differentiation* during the time interval $t_1 < t_2$ if the number of its subsystems (Df 5.6) and of its internal activities (Df 7.1, (ii)–(v)) increases. An example of a process of development which includes all these three types (growth, morphogenesis and differentiation) is the genesis of an embryo.

From the above definitions it can be seen that all types of processes of development are processes of becoming and are therefore processes of increasing order (Df 5.9 and Df 5.7).

Since they are not all deterministic they presuppose chance and degrees of freedom. Some of them might also be processes of increasing teleological order (Df 5.10) if the later state can be interpreted as a goal relative to the earlier state.

20 For the last definition cf. Mahner and Bunge (2000) p. 266
21 Cf. Mahner and Bunge (2000) p. 268ff.

On the other hand, we cannot say that every process with the result of a type of order is a development. This is so for the simple reason that the process of development in a non-living or living system already presupposes the existence of Ord_1, Ord_2 and Ord_3 in that system.

From this it follows that to say "the fullerene C60 developed from a lower carbon structure" or "the cell developed from..." are rather loose ways of speaking and do not make sense if they are not interpreted in a more precise sense according to the definitions given for development (Df 13.3, Df 13.4) above. This abbreviated way of speaking confuses "development" with some completely unspecific and uninformative concept of "transition from a state at t_1 to a state at t_2".

For a more precise and scientific way of speaking it is necessary to give informative definitions. And *development* according to definitions Df 13.3, Df 13.4 already presuppose the existence of Ord_3 as said above. From this it also follows that claims like "the world developed from ...", "life developed from ..." are mere metaphorical talks which are scientifically useless.

It further follows that there cannot be a "development" of the first state of the universe nor of matter, nor of the fundamental constants of nature.

13.3.6 Evolution

Under an evolution of a living system ls we understand a development of ls such that ls changes from one species to another or ls changes from one species to a variation of the same species.

Df 13.5. E is an *evolution* of living system ls iff

(a) E is a development of ls (Df 13.3) and

(b) either

  (i) there is a species A and A' such that ls belongs to species A at t_1 and to a variation A' of species A at t_2 or

  (ii) there is a species A and B such that ls belongs to species A at t_1 and to species B at t_2

Df 13.6. E is a POP-*evolution* of a population (POP) of different adapted living systems ls of the same species A in the same environment $Env(ls)$ iff

(a) E is a development of all ls belonging to POP

(b) there is a 0-1 selection (Df 13.1) of all ls belonging to POP

(c) there is a POP-selection (Df 13.2) of all ls belonging to POP

(d) there is an evolution (Df 13.5) of some of the ls belonging to POP

Observe[22] that according to the definitions above, evolution in general (Df 13.5) does not presuppose selection, but the evolution of a population does. Further the evolution of a population presupposes adaption; where better (worse) adaption or fitness means – as usual – better (worse) capability of reproduction. The capability of reproduction is usually assumed to be hereditarily dependent.[23]

In order to see more exactly the implications of evolution of a population POP of living system ls, we may list all the necessary conditions involved so far:

(1) transition of ls from species A at t_1 to a variation A' of species A at t_2 or transition of ls from species A at t_1 to an entirely different species B at t_2 (Df 13.5)

(2) adaption of ls (Df 13.6)

(3) 0-1 selection of all ls belonging to the population (Df 13.1)

(4) POP-selection of all ls belonging to the population (Df 13.2)
(3) and (4) imply in turn:

(5) variation of ls; (5) implies:

(6) mutation of ls

(7) development of ls (Df 13.3); this in turn implies:

(8) process of becoming of ls (Df 5.9)

(9) Ord_3 of ls (relative to ls') (Df 5.7)

(10) ls is an open system

(11) ls has lower entropy than ls'

(12) ls is a subsystem of ls'

(13) ls has Ord_2

22 Definitions Df 13.5, Df 13.6 are constructed in a similar way to those by Mahner and Bunge (2000) p. 306 and 308.
23 Cf. Brandon (1990)

(14) ls has structure

(15) some of the internal or external relations of ls obey special mathematical (arithmetical geometrical) relations

From this list one can immediately see that “definitions” like “evolution could be defined as any change in phenotypic distributions over generational time”[24] are rather useless, because they are much too wide: the change in phenotype distribution of a species that is becoming extinct would also be an evolution. In many disciplines and even in works of biology ‘evolution’ is just used as a synonym for ‘change’.[25]

Even formulations like “evolution by means of natural selection” or “evolution through natural selection” are either only metaphorical short-cuts or dangerous abbreviations since they suggest that natural selection is a sufficient condition for evolution. And this means to neglect a whole list of other necessary conditions.

13.3.7 Transition from species A to variation A'

Concerning (1) the transition from species A to a variation A' of species A is very well empirically confirmed by fossils, by fast variation in nature and by evolutionary experiments. This first transition is also called *micro-evolution*. One example is the different types of so-called “Darwin finches” which can be mutually crossed or hybridized; they spread probably from the west of South America to the Pacific Isles including Galapagos. Another example is the descent of dogs. The analysis of mitochondria DNA shows that all dog-breeds originate from the species wolf (and not from coyote or jackal); they were produced by mutual crossing. Experiments with guppy-populations are another example. An example of fast micro-evolution are the colored perches (cichlidae) in the East-African lakes: there are about 500 different species in the Lake Victora which developed within about 100.000 years[26], whereas the normal period for building subspecies is 2-

24 Brandon (1990) p. 5

25 Cf. Mahner and Bunge (2000) p. 302f. where they criticize such insufficient terminology.

26 This was shown by DNA sequence analysis by Meyer, see Salzburger and Meyer (2004) and Meyer et al. (1990).

3 millions of years. An even faster development seems to have happened in the Lake Malawi.[27]

Such transitions of *micro-evolution* from a species A to a variation of a species A' might often transcend what today is conventionally or more practically classified as a species. But on a more tolerant criterion all these variations could belong to the same species or type. Such a criterion is that of mutual crossing or hybridizing. This criterion goes back even to Aristotle. A modern but narrower version of this criterion is due to Ernst Mayr. It has the additional necessary condition of geographical barriers: Species exist because of sexual reproduction and are demarcated by geographical barriers.

Although it seems that most speciation events required a period of spacial isolation[28] a certain percentage (10–15%) of several species (for example birds) hybridize across the usual (and Mayr) demarcation of species.[29] Such results support the above more tolerant Aristotelean criterion: all descents which can be obtained by intercrossing or hybridizing belong to one huge species or type. An interesting modern proposal which uses this principle is that of "fundamental types" (Grundtypen) by Junker and Scherer.[30]

13.3.8 Transition from species A to species B

The second transition from a species A to an entirely different species B which is called *macro transition* or *macro evolution* has still its problems, although it is believed by most biologists of evolution.

(i) First of all (as it becomes evident already from 13.3.7 above) the concept and scientific demarcation of species is a problem that is only partially solved:

> "We conclude that, despite the intense interest of biologists in the 'species problem' for over two centuries the answers are not as clear as they should be."[31]

---

27 For further examples of microevolution see Kutschera (2008) p. 216ff. and Junker and Scherer (1998) p. 290ff.
28 Mayr (1942)
29 Meyer (2010)
30 Junker and Scherer (1998) p. 34ff. This proposal is also critically discussed by the authors concerning its advantages and weaknesses (p.45ff). It is especially difficult to execute enough hybridisation in order to get sufficient reasons for constructing a taxonomy.
31 Maynard-Smith and Szathmary (1999) p. 166

Moreover, it should be noted that for the greater part of biomass on Earth, for Prokaryotes the concept of species has never been defined. The theory of neo-Darwinism (modern synthesis) concentrated its research on species of Eukaryotes only.

(ii) Secondly, the transition from A to an entirely different species of higher order B – say from a reptile to a mammal – is a transition which requires a completely new plan or blueprint, i.e. such an evolutionary process must be a process from lower to (essentially) higher complexity. But there seems to be no general law to support such a transition:

> "On the theoretical side, there is no reason why evolution by natural selection should lead to an increase in complexity."[32]

Bacteria, for example seem to be no more complex today, than for several two thousand million years ago; similarly crocodiles for hundred millions of years.

The transition to higher complexity is usually explained in the Darwinian and Neo-Darwinian Theory as occurring gradually in very small steps. However there are also serious difficulties with this type of gradualism:

> "But we have now seen two alternative model "worlds" in which such gradualism fails. The first concerns maximally compressed programs. Because they are random ... Finding one of the few useful minimal programs requires searching the entire space – requiring unthinkably long times compared with the history of the universe even for modestly larger programs. Selection cannot achieve such maximally compressed programs."

The second concerns landscapes where the richness of epistatic couplings is very high:

> "locating the highest peak or one of the few highest peaks requires searching the entire space of possibilities. For modestly large genomes, this is simply impossible."[33]

(iii) Thirdly, the fossil record for a transition from A to an entirely different species B (for example from mammal-like reptiles to mammals) is still incomplete and the intermediate stages permit different hypotheses:

> "And of course, there must have been many intermediate stages in the transition that cannot be reconstructed for want of appropriate fossil representation of those partic-

32 Maynard-Smith and Szathmary (1999) p. 4

33 Kauffman (1995) p. 183. Recall section 8.3.2 and the respective untenable claims of the "chance hypothesis".

ular grades… The known fossils certainly do not themselves constitute an ancestral-descendant series."[34]

13.3.9 Heredity

It is of crucial importance whether adaption and fitness (item (2) of the list in 13.3.6) – here understood as usual by capability of reproduction – are interpreted hereditarily.[35] Although properly speaking only the first state of a zygote can be interpreted hereditary since then environmental influence enters.

If the state S_o at the time t_o is the state of the origin of a living system[36] ls we may define hereditary property P thus:

Df 13.7. Property P of ls is *hereditary* iff ls possesses P in state $S_o(t_o)$ of ls

Df 13.8. Property Q of ls is *non-hereditary* iff

(a) ls does not possess Q in state $S_o(t_o)$ of ls

(b) ls possesses Q in some state $S_1(t_1)$ of ls where $t_1 > t_o$.

Df 13.9. Let Q be a *non-hereditary* property of ls and $S_o(t_o)$ be the state of the origin of ls. Then: Property Q of ls is *hereditarily dependent* iff

(a) ls possesses Q in some state $S_1(t_1)$, where $t_1 > t_o$.

(b) Q is the result of a process of development (Df 13.3) where the initial state in the process of becoming is the state of origin of the living system

Df 13.10. Property Q is an *only-acquired* property of ls iff ls possesses Q at some $t_1 > t_o$ (i.e. after the state of the origin of ls) and Q is neither *hereditary* nor *hereditarily dependent.*

---

34 Kemp (2005) p. 88

35 Cf. Lewontin (1970), Brandon (1990) who claim the hereditariness of adaption and fitness and of degrees of it.

36 The state of the origin $S_o(t_o)$ of a living system ls can be the state of conception or in case of parthenogenesis the egg cell at the beginning of its development or (in case of asexual propagation) the moment of the separation of a daughter cell. The following definitions are similar to that of Mahner and Bunge (2000) p. 296f.

Df 13.11. Property Q is an *acquired* property of ls iff

(a) ls possesses Q in some state $S_2(t_2)$ where $t_2 > t_1 > t_o$

(b) Q is the result of a process of development with the initial state $S_1(t_1)$ when ls possesses property P

(c) P is *hereditarily dependent*

Concerning Df 13.7 observe that a property of ls is hereditary only if ls is not yet under the influence of the environment; environmental influences occur only at some (later) time after the origin state $S_o(t_o)$. Although t_o as a "cut" is of course a conceptual idealization.

Concerning Df 13.9 observe that *hereditarily dependent≠genetically dependent*. This is so, because there is epigenetic inheritance: although liver cells, kidney cells and skin cells behave differently they all contain the same genetic information; but the differences between them are not genetic but epigenetic.

> "Genetic change, in the sense of altered DNA sequence, is not required for the differentiation of somatic cells..."[37]

Concerning Df 13.11 observe that those properties, which are usually called *acquired*, are in an indirect way – via other properties – *hereditarily dependent*. Among them come all learned properties and abilities. Moreover *only-acquired* properties are rather negative, like an injury which is not due to an unskillfullness of the injured but, for example, due to unforeseeable environmental changes.

The inheritance of acquired properties is still controversial. Jablonka and Lamb worked out a model whereby epigenetic changes could be stably inherited through sexual reproduction without need for changes in the DNA sequence. Although such epigenetic changes exist and although they must be important for the development of the ls, it is not known how frequent they are and to what extent they can replace natural selection.[38]

Other important issues of the list of conditions concerning evolution in 13.3.6 have been already discussed in earlier sections: Selection (3), (4) was already discussed in 13.3.4 above. Mutation (6) which causes variation (5) was elaborated in section

---

37 Cf. Maynard-Smith and Szathmary (1999) p.10 and 247ff., Jablonka and Lamb (2005) p. 113f. and Mahner and Bunge (2000) p. 297f.
38 Cf. Note 37.

8.3.3. Development (7) was discussed in section 13.3.5 and process of becoming in section 5.3.4 and Ord_3 and Ord_2 in 5.3.3.

From sections 13.3.3–13.3.9 it became clear that not all types of order can be explained by the four processes of self-organization, natural selection, development and evolution. That means that the explanation with the help of all four types is incomplete w.r.t. several important facts or processes be they biological or other. The incompleteness of the Darwinian explanations is summarized in the following nine items by Peter Schuster in accordance with Maynard Smith and Szathmary:

> "Despite apparent success in the interpretation of optimization through variation and selection, the Darwinian principle is unable to provide descriptions for all phenomena observed in biological evolution. Among other problems *there are major evolutionary transitions*, which *escape an explanation by Darwin's concept*. These major transitions in evolution remind one of the ladder theory of the biosphere, since each transition opens access to a new hierarchical level. Such major transitions are:
>
> (i) the transition from independent RNA genes to an integrated genome,
>
> (ii) the *origin of the genetic code* as a prerequisite for the transition from an RNA world to a DNA(+RNA)+protein world,
>
> (iii) the *formation of the cell* with metabolism and compartment structure,
>
> (iv) the formation of the complex *eukaryotic cell* through endo-symbiosis of *two or more prokaryotes*,
>
> (v) the formation of *symbiosis* between species,
>
> (vi) the transition from *unicellular to multi-cellular organisms*,
>
> (vii) the transition from solitary animals to animal societies,
>
> (viii) the transition from animal societies to primitive human societies, and
>
> (ix) the development of the present human societies with language and writing.
>
> All major transitions share one common feature: They lead from a lower hierarchical level to the next higher and they are accompanied by an increase in complexity. In general competitors at the lower level are integrated into a synergetic unit characterized by cooperation of previously competing elements. A mechanism for such an integration called the 'catalytic hypercycle' was proposed already in the nineteen seventies.[39] Like a theme with variations the hypercycle is still the only model that describes transitions from lower to higher levels of complexity in mechanistic detail."[40]

39 Eigen and Schuster (1979)
40 P. Schuster (2004) p. 360f.

13.3.10 What cannot be caused by creatures (internal causes of the universe) on principal grounds must be caused by God and his providence

Do the different types of incompleteness discussed in sections 13.3.3 to 13.3.9 suggest that we need to introduce God like a *deus ex machina* as soon as there is a phenomenon which cannot be explained by today's science? The answer to this question is: No. Since this would reduce God to a stopgap. And the problem or phenomenon might be solved or explained by science later.

However there are two more general questions: (1) whether for any phenomenon or event of this world there is a cause within this world (1a); or expressed w.r.t. our scientific knowledge about the world: whether every phenomenon or event of this world can be explained with the help of both, other (usually earlier) events of this world and laws of this world (1b). And question (2): Whether there is a cause for the world as a whole inside the world (2a); or: whether there is an explanation of the world as a whole with the help of both, events of this world and laws of this world (2b).

If all these four questions could be answered with *Yes* then the question of ch. 13: Whether everything that comes under God's providence is caused by God or by creatures can be answered with *Yes*. This is so for logical reasons: If all events in the world, including all the facts of the world as a whole, were caused by creatures, i.e. by causes from inside the world, then the disjunction (caused by God or caused by creatures) would also be satisfied; since any disjunction is satisfied if one part is satisfied. And then (on logical grounds) the implication: "If it comes under God's providence then it is caused by God or by creatures" must be true.

However, this is not the solution to this question since in fact both questions (1) and (2) have to be answered with: No (see 13.3.10.2, 13.4.3 and 13.4.4 below).

If question (1) has to be answered with *No*, then there are some phenomena of this world for which there is no cause in this world or for which there is no explanation with laws and events of this world.

If question (2) has to be answered with *No*, then it is necessary to assume a cause for the world (as a whole) "outside" the world or give an explanation of the world as a whole with some principle which transcends all laws and events of this world.

It will be shown subsequently that both questions have to be answered with *No*. In support of that we shall give first two quotes from Wittgenstein which describe the situation very well:

> "So people stop short at natural laws as at something unassailable, as did the ancients at God and Fate. And they both are right and wrong. But the ancients were clearer, in so far as they recognized one clear terminus, whereas the modern system makes it appear as though everything were explained."[41]

> "The sense of the world must lie outside the world. In the world everything is as it is and happens as it does happen ... For all happening and being-so is accidental. What makes it non-accidental cannot lie *in* the world, for otherwise this would again be accidental. It must lie outside the world."[42]

13.3.10.1 Leibniz's answer

Leibniz reduced the above two (four) questions to one (two) more general questions with his Principle of Sufficient Reason:

(1'a) Whether for any phenomenon of this world including the world as a whole there is a cause

(1'b) Whether every truth about an event or phenomenon of this world or the world as a whole has its explanation by a proof.

And he answered (1'a) and (1'b) with Yes by his Principle of Sufficient Reason:

> "that nothing is without a reason, or that every truth has its a priori proof, drawn from the notion of the terms, although it is not always in our power to make this analysis."[43]

> "Generally, every true proposition (which is not identical true or true *per se*) can be proved a priori by the help of axioms, or propositions true *per se*, and by the help of definitions or ideas... It is certain, therefore, that all truths, even the most contingent, have an a priori proof, or some reason why they are rather than are not. And this is itself what people commonly say, that nothing happens without a cause, or that nothing is without a reason."[44]

The principle of sufficient reason can be formulated at least in three versions: (i) Nothing happens without a sufficient reason. (ii) Every true proposition has its a priori proof. (iii) Every true proposition is finitely or infinitely analytic. To understand the last version one has to know two things: First, Leibniz's understanding

41 Wittgenstein (1960) 6.372
42 Ibid. 6.41
43 Leibniz (1875–1890) Vol.2, p. 62
44 Leibniz (1875–1890) Vol 7, p. 300f

of analysis: Analysis is a process of logical inference using definitional replacement and determination of predicational containment. Second, Leibniz's view of two kinds of proof processes: In the area of truths of reason the proof-process is terminating after a finite number of steps, i.e. the proposition proved is finitely analytic. On the other hand, in the realm of contingent truths the proof-process is not terminating after a finite number of steps, i.e. the proposition is infinitely analytic. In both cases however, we have a genuine proof process intended as an inferential procedure of the most rigorous kind, i.e. a proof of a proposition within a deductive system.[45]

According to Leibniz, there are four great comprehensive areas of scientific research that can be built up according to the principle of rationalism and of *more geometrico* as axiomatic systems: logic and mathematics, metaphysics, physics, jurisprudence (including ethics). He thought that *in principle* these systems of truths are finitely axiomatisable, consistent and complete though for mankind the finite axiomatisability, the consistency, and the completeness are available only for logic, mathematics, and metaphysics but not for the other two areas since they include contingent truths.

According to Leibniz, only God knows the consistent and complete axiom systems of all domains, also of those including contingent truths. But his knowledge is not discursive, such that he derives theorems from axioms but comprehends all truths in one action of knowledge.[46]

Leibniz was correct that the completeness (including axiomatisability and consistency) is available for man w.r.t. First Order Predicate Logic (PL1).[47]

An axiom system representing a theory about a scientific domain D is called *complete* if every true statement of the scientific domain D is derivable from the axiom system. And analogously a set of causes C is complete w.r.t. a domain D, if every state (or event) in D is caused by some or other element of C, or (expressed methodologically): ... can be sufficiently explained by C.

Leibniz was also correct that Syllogistics, i.e. a monadic part of PL1 is decidable although PL1 is not.[48] But Leibniz was not correct w.r.t. mathematics, since already Peano arithmetic is not complete and not decidable. And so many domains of

45 For a detailed exposition see Weingartner (1983a) p. 166ff.
46 Cf. Aquinas (1981) I, 14,7.
47 The proof was given by Gödel in Gödel (1930).
48 Cf. Leibniz (1961) and Weingartner (1983a) p. 174ff.

higher mathematics are incomplete and not decidable.[49] And Leibniz was surely not correct for some comprehensive ontology, metaphysics or general theory of being if it is formulated in a rigorous axiomatic way.[50]

Leibniz's answer to the above questions (1'a) and (1'b) is as follows: For every phenomenon of this world including the world as a whole there is a sufficient reason (cause). For the whole world the sufficient reason can only be God; for parts of the world there are also reasons belonging to the world but only in the sense that they received their power of causality from God. For every truth (including truths about the world) there is an explanation by a proof. But man can find the proof only for logic (he was right about PL1 and Syllogistics) mathematics (here he was wrong) and metaphysics (here he was also wrong). But God knows the sufficient proofs for all truths, also for those domains in which contingent truths hinder man to be able to find the ultimate proof and the true axiom system.

13.3.10.2 Can the laws or theories of physics be complete?

It[51] should be emphasized first that results on completeness or incompleteness obtained in the field of logic and mathematics[52] cannot automatically be transmitted to physical laws since it is very questionable whether important necessary conditions for these results (like axiomatic construction, closure conditions, definability of the concept of provability within the system etc.) are available for a system of physical laws.

(1) It seemed that the picture of the world (universe) according to Laplace (cf. section 4.3.1 (c)) with laws of nature and one initial condition is complete w.r.t. the description of all states of the universe. But already Thomas Aquinas pointed out an incompleteness in such a world picture. Also for Leibniz all those theories of the universe which include contingent statements must be incomplete.

---

49 The proof was also given by Gödel in Gödel (1931). This does not rule out however that certain specific parts of mathematics can be decidable, as for example the theory of real closed fields and that of elementary geometry.
50 Cf. Bunge (1977).
51 For a detailed exposition of this question see Weingartner (1997) and Mittelstaedt and Weingartner (2005) ch. 11.1
52 Cf. note 47 and 49 above.

The laws of nature in the world picture of Laplace are dynamical laws. Several limitations concerning completeness of such laws have been discussed already in 4.3.1 (c). Further limitations come up if condition D4 (4.3.1 (c)) is not, or only partially, fulfilled: This is the case of *dynamical chaos* (cf. 4.4.2 above). An incompleteness arises here concerning both (a) the separation of adjacent conjugate points which grows exponentially and (b) the loss of information about the position of a point in an interval (0,1) after one iteration which also grows exponentially. An important consequence of that is an objective form of unpredictability w.r.t. events governed by dynamical laws.

(2) The incompleteness of statistical laws can be explained by the following two factors:

  (a) Statistical laws are incomplete because they don't describe individual processes; they describe huge ensembles but not the individual microstates. The resulting macrostate (for example a liter of air) is in fact an ambiguous thing consisting of quickly changing microstates. Moreover: the same macrostate can be realized by a huge number of microstates.

  (b) The incompleteness of statistical laws increases with the complexity of the system.
  Example: Imagine skiers on a big ski resort: first 10, then 100, then 1000, then 50.000 (this is the capability of cable cars and lifts per hour in a big ski resort in Austria). The loss of information about individual skiers and their traces and also about the whole state of all the skiers at a certain point of time increases with this number. Physically we have to replace 50.000 skiers by 10^{22} gas molecules in a liter of air.

Imagine now the number of hydrogen atoms of the universe (10^{80}) and the number of microstates of the molecules of the universe. This is a hint for understanding how big the incompleteness is.

(3) Further Types of Incompleteness: There are further types of incompleteness.

  (a) In quantum mechanics the physical laws of measurement do not allow to determine jointly all possible properties of a given system. This is so because of the Heisenberg uncertainty relations. In any contingent situation which is described by a state Z of system S only a subset P_Z of properties can be measured jointly on S.[53]

---

53 For more exact statements on this cf. Mittelstaedt and Weingartner (2005) p. 275ff. and 292ff.

(b) Then we mention the incompleteness discussed in the EPR-Gedanken-experiment. It concerns the incompleteness of quantum mechanics.[54]

(c) From a more general point of view the intended generality or invariance (symmetry) of laws of nature means extinguishing some specific difference or parameter and consequently producing some incompleteness. Examples:

(i) Permutational symmetry means that the laws remain the same if we interchange two particles of the same sort (say electrons, protons, neutrons, ... or photons, pi-mesons, gravitons ... according to the Fermi-Dirac or Bose-Einstein statistics). Thus laws are "incomplete" with respect to "individual" electrons.

(ii) Translation-symmetry in space extinguishes absolute place leading to a level of generality of three conservation principles of momentum.

(iii) Translation-symmetry of time leads to the conservation of energy and makes unobservable an absolute point of time, or a point of time as the beginning of the world.

(iv) Galilean invariance: Inertial systems are indistinguishable.

(v) Charge symmetry implies that the absolute sign of electric charge is unobservable.

(vi) Parity implies that right-left is indistinguishable.
As a biological example consider that some children are born with the heart on the right side which seems to show that the underlying biological law obeys parity and the dominating cases (heart on the left side) seems to be due to initial conditions (may be with an exponential building up effect) in the evolution.

The list could be continued with Lorentz invariance, invariance of General Relativity, with time-reversal symmetry, CPT-symmetry and Gauge symmetries. The consequence is clear and obvious: Symmetries (invariances) produce unobservables and extinguish differences thus destroying a certain type of completeness of the laws. That means that one cannot have both to a high degree: invariance (symmetry) and com-

54 Cf. the exposition in Mittelstaedt and Weingartner (2005) p. 290ff. and Mittaelstaedt (1998) p.85,88,100.

pleteness. Observe however that this point is closely connected with the understanding of a law and with the problem of distinguishing the law from the initial conditions.

(d) Incompleteness in Chemistry and Biology
Since the laws of physics are underlying laws for chemical and biological processes these processes inherit the respective types of incompleteness from the laws of physics. How the laws of physics underlie chemical and biological processes has been shown in detail by Prigogine, Haken and by Eigen and Schuster.[55]

Whereas these types of incompleteness, coming from physics, are of principal nature, there are also several specific types of incompleteness belonging to chemistry and biology, some of which may be at least partially removed by future research.

13.3.11 Result of chapter 13

(1) Not everything belonging to the universe including the universe itself can be caused by creatures, i.e. by things belonging to the universe.[56]

This is manifest first w.r.t. the world as a whole. It cannot be caused by some part of it as has been shown in 13.3.1, and it cannot be caused by an intelligence belonging to this world as will become clear in section 13.4.4 below.

Secondly, this is also true w.r.t. events, states or processes of this world: Not every event, state or process of this world can be caused by some other event, state or process of this world, since the events, states , processes as causes are incomplete in a principal sense; that means that it is not an incompleteness of a technical nature and it is not due to inexactness.

This is so especially with the four important processes of self-organization, natural selection, development and evolution as has been shown in sections 13.3.2–13.3.9. And in an analogous way the laws of nature together with state-

55 Prigogine (1977), Nicolis and Prigogine (1987), Haken (1983), Haken (1987), Eigen and Schuster (1979).

56 As has been mentioned already we restrict creatures to the universe, since we will not take into account other creatures like angels in this study. For an extensive treatment about angels see Aquinas (1981) I, qu. 50-65.

ments describing initial states or events are also incomplete in a principal sense as has been shown in sections 13.3.10.1 and 13.3.10.2.

(2) It might be asked whether it is necessary to assume additional sufficient causes in order to remove the incompleteness; or whether it is necessary to assume a cause of the world (universe) which is outside the world (universe).

Proposals which deny such a necessity are those of an everlasting universe and those of a self-contained universe. Since these proposals concern the objections 13.1.3 and 13.1.4 (at the beginning of this chapter) they will be treated in the answer to these objections (sections 13.4.3 and 13.4.4).

(3) On the other hand if we want to assume a cause or explanation[57] of the world as a whole and also for removing principal incompleteness it seems that God and his providence is needed for at least two of his activities and its effects:

(a) The creation of important features of the universe at its beginning: Fundamental laws of nature (cf. 10.3.2, 10.3.3, 13.3.1), fundamental constants of nature (cf. 10.3.2, 10.3.3, 13.3.1), 3 spatial +1 time dimension (cf. 5.3.1), the extremely precise fine tuning of fundamental magnitudes (cf. 7.4.2, 13.3.1), a great number of important coincidences (cf. 7.4.2, 13.3.1).

(b) The creation of creatures, with the help of the features in (a), which have the abilities to cause, invent, plan, develop, and evolve their own creatures and sometimes also institutions (factories) of production for their creatures.

T 13.1. *Not everything belonging to the universe including the universe itself can be caused by creatures, i.e. by things belonging to the universe.*

T 13.2. *The question whether the universe has a finite age or is everlasting is independent of the question whether it has a cause.*

T 13.3. *A universe finite in time is scientifically confirmed to a greater extent (cosmic background radiation, Standard Big Bang Theory) than an everlasting one (13.4.3).*

T 13.4. *The universe cannot contain its own cause as a singularity (13.4.4).*

57 Cf. Swinburne (2011) where God is defended as the simplest explanation of the universe.

T 13.5. *The universe cannot be self-contained in the sense of containing its intelligent observer or its intelligent cause (13.4.4).*

T 13.6. *God is needed as a cause and explanation of the fundamental laws of nature, of the fundamental constants of nature of the space time (3+1) dimension and of the extremely precise fine tuning and coincidences.*

T 13.7. *God is needed as a cause and explanation for the creation of creatures which have the ability to contribute to the development of the universe.*

13.4 Answer to the Objections

13.4.1 (to 13.1.1)

Processes of self-organization acquire a spatial, temporal or functional structure without *specific interference* from outside (cf. 13.3.3 above). But as has been said there this does not mean that there is no influence from outside, even if there is no influence which is specific for the special spatial, temporal or functional pattern or structure which emerges. Thus there is energy supply as a necessary cause for the process from outside.

13.4.2 (to 13.1.2)

As has been elaborated in section 13.3.4 the emergence of new variations does not belong to natural selection, but is presupposed by it. Thus variation is a necessary condition for natural selection. Variation is caused by environmental influences, by recombination of parental genes. These are different types of mutation caused by mistakes of copying (in recombination), by influences of environment, or by a special type of genes called *evolution genes*. Therefore natural selection needs several causes, as necessary conditions, from outside.

13.4.3 (to 13.1.3) Everlasting universe

The Greek philosophers were the first to propose that the world (universe) is everlasting.[58] The doctrine of Aristotle, for example, proposed that prime matter was everlasting; although he taught that God's activity was to give to prime matter a *form* on different levels or stages. God, in this case (as outside the universe) is still a cause for giving the form i.e. the essence, but not a creator of prime matter, not out of anything pre-existing.

Another proposal also originating from antiquity is the theory of the cyclic universe. This means that the universe, or better a state of it, repeats itself after a finite period of time, even if this period of time may be very long. In the 20th century there are two theories which correspond to these two proposals.

The first – everlasting universe – corresponds to Einstein's earlier proposal of 1917 for a static everlasting universe. It is a solution of his field equations which is static, i.e. not changing in time.[59] But this proposal was soon refuted by more and more data (red shift, cosmological background radiation) which confirm the expansion of the universe.

A way out of such consequences by keeping the everlasting universe is the idea of the eternal or everlasting return or of the cyclic universe. Several modern cosmological models correspond to this second proposal.[60] One is Gödel's solution (of 1949) to Einstein's field equations of his Theory of General Relativity. This solution assumes closed time-like curves (i.e. closed histories of some particles or of some observers). And therefore it violates the so-called *chronology condition*[61] which states that non-space-like geodesics (time-like geodesics and null geodesics) are not closed. The chronology condition guarantees a "stable causality condition" which is stressed by Hawking and Ellis:

> "This shows that in physically realistic solutions the causality and chronology conditions are equivalent."[62]

58 Since eternity does only have presence but no past and no future, it is more adequate to say the world (universe) might be everlasting (or omnitemporal) because "everlasting" allows past, present and future.
59 Cf. Einstein (1917)
60 For an overview cf. Heller (2004).
61 For some details see Mittelstaedt and Weingartner (2005) p. 169, 219 and 244.
62 Hawking and Ellis (1973) p. 192.

Causality (in the usual understanding i.e. that the cause must be earlier than the effect since the propagation of the causal effect can occur at most with the velocity light) would break down and one could travel into one's own past, if the chronology condition were not satisfied. For these reasons, and for others, like the impossibility of defining a universal concept of cosmic time[63] Gödel's 1949-solution (one among many possible) seems inadequate in the physical or realistic sense. However Gödel (in 1952) gave another solution of Einstein's Field Equation which is physically adequate in the sense that it satisfies the chronology condition and implies an expanding universe.

A somewhat weaker form of the idea of the *everlasting return* is the so-called *Oscillating Universe*. This means that each expanding phase of its evolution (which takes place now) is followed by a contracting phase and so on. However, this theory is very questionable because it is inconsistent with the *singularity theorems*, which have been proved by Penrose and Hawking.[64] According to these theorems there has to be a real singularity at the beginning of each expanding phase, i.e. there is no continuous history or identifiability through time of particles or observers.

If we look at the history of philosophy we see that the cyclic theory of the universe as a proposal for dispending from a cause was already criticized by Basilius (*330): Although we cannot specify a point of beginning or a point of end in a cyclic process, like in the orbits of planets or stars, we can always ask who invented the circle or the orbit with all its properties and functions.[65]

Concerning the question whether the world (universe) is everlasting or whether it has a finite age, Thomas Aquinas tried to show that neither position is provable from laws of nature. His reason was very simple: universal laws abstract from hic (particular point in space) and nunc (particular point of time).[66] In modern terms: time symmetric laws cannot designate or select a beginning in time or a first event:

> "Thus the time displacement invariance, properly formulated, reads: the correlations between events depend only on the time intervals between those events; they do not depend on the time when the first of them takes place."[67]

---

63 Cf. Mittelstaedt (2008) p.129ff.

64 Cf. Penrose (1979) and Hawking and Ellis (1973)

65 Cf. Basilius (1886) (Hexaemeron) 3; Migne MPG 9A

66 Aquinas (1981) I, 46,2. Cf. Mittelstaedt and Weingartner (2005) p. 69f.

67 Wigner (1967) p. 31 or Wigner (1995) p. 314. What is meant here is time-displacement-symmetry, i.e. a law connects a state S_1 of the world with a later state S_2 of the world but does not

Nevertheless, the cosmic background radiation is an important support of the Standard Big Bang Theory according to which the universe has a finite age.

Moreover, the question whether the world is finite in time (has a finite age) or is everlasting is independent of the question whether it has a cause. Also an everlasting universe, if contingent or just factual, may need a necessary cause which lies "outside". Therefore the everlasting universe is only to postpone the question whether it is caused. And consequently God can be its cause "from outside". And thus the universe can come under God's providence.

13.4.4 (to 13.1.4) Self-contained universe

(1) Can the world (universe) be "self-contained" in the sense that it contains its own cause?

Within the framework of cosmological models, i.e. global solutions of Einstein's field equations (of his Theory of General Relativity) that describe an expanding universe, the time-like trajectories (presupposing that they satisfy the chronology condition, i.e. that they are not closed) considered as chains of causes and effects can be traced back to a point where all time-like trajectories coincide. One could propose this event to be considered as the "first cause" of the universe contained in the universe itself. This however is not possible since this event is a singularity that must be excluded from space time of the universe for mathematical reasons. There are rigorous mathematical proofs that this kind of singularity is unavoidable under very general conditions.[68] But if this singularity has to be excluded from space time of the universe it cannot be contained in the universe.

This result, however, does not automatically invalidate the search for every *first cause* contained in the universe. The reason is that in the neighborhood of the singularity General Relativity is not entirely correct and has to be replaced by Quantum Gravity (a theory that combines General Relativity with Quantum Mechanics). Within the framework of this theory the creation of matter can consistently be described by pair production that is induced by fluctuations

tell us whether there is a first or a last state. This question cannot even be decided by Laplace's deterministic world picture. Cf. Mittelstaedt and Weingartner (2005) p. 146 and 151.

68 Hawking and Ellis (1973) p.266.

of a Riemannian vacuum.[69] It seems first that one could continue the search for a *first cause* and ask for a cause of the vacuum fluctuations. However, a single cause, sufficient for these vacuum fluctuations, cannot be assumed in this theory because the distribution of the fluctuations which are governed by a statistical law do not help here.

This means that any search for a first cause of the universe which belongs to the universe must end here. In other words, there is no first cause belonging to the evolution of the universe.

If in such a connection it is claimed that there is a creation of universes or of matter from *Nothing*, one has to observe, that the term “*Nothing*” has to be understood in a relative sense: It does not mean “creation of matter not out of anything”, but “from *Nothing*” w.r.t. the model, i.e. in this case “*Nothing*” means that of which the cosmological model says nothing about.

(2) Can the world (universe) be “self-contained” in the sense that it does not need an initial state S_1 as the cause for a later state S_2?

In this sense the cosmological model of Hartle and Hawking is self-contained.[70] If we go back in the history of the universe we finally arrive at the Planck scale.[71] In this area and beyond, classical physics loses its validity and has to be replaced by Quantum Gravity. Assuming that the universe is spatially closed, its history beyond the Planck scale is not a “history” in the usual understanding since there is not the usual time flow, but an imaginary time $t = itc(i = \sqrt{-1})$. This eliminates the different roles of space and time and leads to a purely geometrical description in order to avoid the Big Bang. Consequently, according to his model, the universe has no temporal beginning and no boundary in the sense of an initial state.

69 Cf. Vilenkin (1982) and Mittelstaedt and Weingartner (2005) p.245.

70 Hartle and Hawking (1983), Hawking (1988). This proposal was also called the „no boundary“ approach by Hawking himself: “The boundary condition of the universe is that it has no boundary”, ibid. p. 144. To avoid misunderstanding it should be mentioned that the “no boundary” approach does not mean: no boundary at all. For example, the geometries needed presuppose certain regularities which are determined by boundary conditions concerning the radius of the 3-sphere and the scalar field.

71 The Planck scale consists of the Planck length ($l_{pl} = 1,62 \cdot 10^{-33} cm$) the Planck time ($t_{pl} = 5,4 \cdot 10^{-44} sec$) and the Planck mass ($m_{pl} = 2,18 \cdot 10^{-5} g$).

Independent of general doubts about the unnatural disappearance of the difference between space and time coordinates (with all its consequences) and the somewhat tricky introduction of imaginary time, Hawking's and Hartle's theory will have to be judged by tests in the future.[72] As Hawking himself says quite critically:

> "I'd like to emphasize that this idea that time and space should be finite without boundary is just a *proposal*: it cannot be deduced from some other principle. Like any other scientific theory, it may initially be put forward for aesthetic or metaphysical reasons, but the real test is whether it makes predictions that agree with observation."[73]

After this critical passage it is quite astonishing that Hawking claims that "the idea that space and time may form a closed surface without boundary also has profound implications for the role of God in the affairs of the universe." And further:

> "So long as the universe had a beginning (B), we could suppose it had a creator (C). But if the universe is really completely self-contained, having no boundary or edge (S), it would have neither beginning nor end ($\neg B$): it would simply be. What place, then for a creator? (C? *or* $\neg C$?)."[74]

A short comment is necessary here:
If the last passage is supposed to be an argument with the conclusion $\neg C$ (i.e. there is no creator) it would be fallacious. Since $B \rightarrow C, S \rightarrow \neg B, S$ therefore: $\neg C$ is a logical fallacy.

From the premises $B \rightarrow C, S \rightarrow \neg B$, and S one cannot draw any conclusion about C (or $\neg C$). The conclusion $\neg C$ would follow if we had instead of $B \rightarrow C, C \rightarrow B$; but then – despite the question of the truth of S – this premise $C \rightarrow B$ is questionable too because, as we pointed out above (13.4.3) a creator is compatible also with a creation which does not have a certain age or beginning. This shows that also great scientists sometimes produce invalid arguments if they surpass their scientific domain.

---

72 A strange consequence of an earlier proposal of Hawking (1988) was that the arrow of time would reverse at the maximum of expansion of the universe. Later (1994) some of his pupils (Lyons, Page, Laflamme) found solutions which avoid consequences like that. The contracting phase has no reversal of time and entropy and irregularities increase in the expanding and contracting phases. There are also other recent theories of the inflationary universe without a beginning in time which do not use imaginary time. Cf. for example Linde (1990). But also here Basilius' question is not answered. And Wittgenstein would say: these modern systems make it appear as though everything were explained.

73 Hawking (1988) p. 144

74 Ibid. p. 149. The letters in brackets are mine.

Also a rather strong claim is made at the end of the book:

> "However, if we do discover a complete theory ... then we shall ... be able to take part in the discussion of the question of why it is that we and the universe exist. If we find the answer to that, it would be the ultimate triumph of human reason – for then we would know the mind of God."[75]

This claim is entirely different from the one cited above. In fact both claims seem to be somewhat inconsistent in the sense that the latter presupposes God (with mind), whereas the former does not only not presuppose one, but suggests not to have a "place" for him in a universe without boundaries (forgetting the fact that in the main religions God is transcendent with respect to the universe).

However, one could interpret the two different passages also consistently in the sense that the first says that the creator of the universe cannot be found in the universe (cannot be part of it) and the second says that the creator (God) must be outside the universe as an explanation that and why the universe (and we) exist. The point that an intelligent creator cannot be part of his creation will be discussed in the following paragraph.

(3) Can the world (universe) be "self-contained" in the sense that it contains its intelligent observer or creator?

If there is a cause for the world (universe), then this cause must be intelligent. We can even assume it must be omniscient w.r.t. the facts of the world, i.e. it must have a complete knowledge of the world (universe). Can such an intelligent cause of the world (universe) be contained in the universe? To answer this question the following facts, which can be proved rigorously, are relevant.

An *internal observer* of a physical object system cannot distinguish all states of the object system. The knowledge that he can obtain about the object system is *incomplete*.[76] Hence the quantum mechanical measurement process provides only incomplete information about the quantum physical reality. However, if the object system S is a part of the physical reality, the incomplete information of the internal observer about the system can be made complete

75 Hawking (1988), p. 185.

76 For a detailed examination of the „Internal Observer" cf. Mittaelstaedt (1998) section 5.3, p. 116ff. Cf. also Popper (1950) part II.

by an external apparatus plus observer. But if the object system S is the entire universe, the incompleteness of the internal observer's knowledge cannot be removed. This holds also for Quantum Cosmology. However, it must be emphasized that this deficiency of information is not a particular disadvantage of quantum mechanics, since there are rigorous arguments[77] that any theory which is concerned with the *entire* universe leads to similar restrictions of measurability and observability. Hence, one should rather speak of the incompleteness of any cosmology. As a consequence, it follows that every internal observer or internal intelligent cause cannot have complete knowledge of the universe. Therefore an intelligent cause that has complete knowledge of the universe must not belong to the universe; it must be outside the universe.

Also Laplace's intelligence (cf. section 4.3.1) cannot be part of the universe; it has to be immaterial and has to be outside the universe. As has been shown in section 4.3.1 above there are at least four types of incompleteness, (i)–(iv), contained in this deterministic and mechanistic world view. A further kind of incompleteness seems to be a consequence of the Theory of Relativity; it is analogous to the case of the "internal observer". An observer O, localized in a finite space time region $STR(O)$, depends on measuring rods, clocks and signals concerning his results. This means for real signals, that they cannot be faster than the velocity of light in vacuum. From this, essential restrictions follow for O. First, the observer O can have knowledge of the following two classes of phenomena: (1) of those which are in his past light cone and (2) of those future events which he can predict with the help of (1) plus dynamical laws. If however he wants to observe at time t an object A which is (at time t) far away from $STR(O)$ then O can know of A only properties belonging to this part of the word line of A which lie in the respective past light cone of O. Of all other properties he cannot prove that they belong to A or that they don't. Can O complete his knowledge? Assuming $STR(O)$ is a Minkowski Space Time Region, O may wait until the event occurs in his past light cone. Although at this moment there will be new events of which he has no knowledge so far. But the situation aggravates if we allow accelerated observers; then there are spacetime regions the events of which will never (at no observer time of O) occur in the past light cone of O. Still more problematic is the case of generally including gravitation (according to General Relativity). Then there will be space time regions which never (at no observer time of O) can be covered by

77 Cf. Breuer (1995) and Breuer (1996)

the causal past of O (even if O moves on geodesically force-free lines). Statements about objects in such regions are then principally not decidable for O.

Thus, also a cosmological observer ("internal" concerning the universe) cannot have complete knowledge of the events of the universe, independently of how intelligent he would be. And therefore: An intelligent being that has complete knowledge about the universe cannot belong to the universe, but must be "outside" the universe.

After all these considerations we can answer the above question (3) in the negative: The world (universe) cannot be "self-contained" in the sense that it contains its intelligent observer. An intelligent observer or creator who has a complete knowledge of the entire universe must not belong to the universe; he must be "outside" the universe.

As a summary concerning the question of a self-contained universe, we may say that such a universe does neither disprove God as a cause not belonging to the universe nor God's providence of the universe. This is so because w.r.t. (1) the universe cannot contain its own cause as a singularity. Further, w.r.t. (2) because a self-contained universe in the sense of "no-boundary" of Hartle and Hawking is really just a proposal without any predictions that agree with observation and with rather strange consequences about the unnatural disappearance of the difference between space and time. Moreover w.r.t. (3) the universe cannot be self-contained in the sense of containing its intelligent observer or its intelligent cause. Since any internal observer or internal intelligent cause is incomplete in an essential sense w.r.t. the facts and effects of the universe.

14 Whether everything that comes under God's providence is directed to some goal or integrated into a network of goals

14.1 Arguments Contra

14.1.1 First argument

As has been shown in 13.3.1 the whole universe must come under God's providence. But the whole universe does not seem to be directed to some goal; nor does it seem to be integrated into a network of goals. A reason for that is the so called heath death and the entropy flow leading to a complete equilibrium or stagnation.

Therefore not everything that comes under God's providence is directed to some goal or integrated into a network of goals.

14.1.2 Second argument

According to ch. 10 things without consciousness also come under God's providence. But it seems that only living things with consciousness can be directed to some goal or integrated into a network of goals, since they can direct themselves towards goals or integrate themselves into some network of goals.

Therefore not everything that comes under God's providence is directed to some goal or integrated into some network of goals.

14.1.3 Third argument

According to ch. 10 everything that happens in the universe comes under God's providence. Thus, since many things that happen in the universe happen according to evolution, those things that happen according to evolution must come under God's providence. But as the founding fathers of the modern theory of evolution say, evolution does not show a "persistence towards a predetermined goal"[1] and "is devoid of purpose".[2] Moreover an "inherent tendency for evolution ... towards a discernible goal"[3] would contradict "the fundamental unpredictability and creativity for novelties of evolution".[4]

Therefore: Under the true assumption that some things happen according to evolution, not everything that comes under God's providence is directed to some goal.

14.2 Argument Pro

As Aquinas says:

> "It is necessary that the type of the order of things towards their end should pre-exist in the divine mind: and the type of things ordered towards an end is, properly speaking, providence."[5]

Therefore it seems that everything that comes under God's providence is directed to some goal or integrated into a network of goals.

14.3 Proposed Answer

Everything that comes under God's providence is directed to some goal or is integrated into a network of goals. A short argument in support is this:

Everything that comes under God's providence is planned by God. Everything that is planned by God is directed to some goal or integrated into some network of goals; since planning something means to direct, (subordinate or integrate) something to (under, into) some goal (network of goals).

Therefore: Everything that comes under God's providence is directed to some goal or integrated into a network of goals.

1 Huxley (1974) p. 497
2 Stebbins (1982) p. 4
3 Simpson (1949) p. 32
4 Dobzhansky (1968) p. 165
5 Aquinas (1981) I, 22,1.

In addition to that there is also the following argument in support of the thesis: Every goal-directed process comes under God's providence. The argument is this: It has been shown in ch. 5 that there is teleological order in non-living things; and it has been shown in ch. 7 that there is teleological order in living things (ls). As the final state of any process of teleological order is a goal relative to its initial state, all processes of teleological order are goal-directed processes. Since according to ch. 10 everything that happens in creation or among creatures comes under God's providence, it follows that every goal-directed process (that happens) comes under God's providence.

It will be shown subsequently that not every biological process is teleological, i.e. directed to some goal. Whether one biological or non-biological process is teleological depends on whether the respective process contributes to some *basic good* or whether it is a process of *becoming* in which the final state is a goal. If this condition is satisfied, the process is teleological or possesses a teleological order (14.3.1, 14.3.2). However, even if the single process is not teleological, the biological or non-biological system to which it belongs might possess teleological order: That all living systems possess teleological order was shown in section 7.3.2 above. That some non-living systems possess teleological order was established in section 5.3.5 above. Yet subsequently it will be shown that all non-living systems are teleological (possess teleological order) in a weaker sense than living systems. Furthermore it will be shown that all living systems can be integrated into a network of goals, some in a stronger and some in a weaker sense (14.3.3). Moreover it will be shown that all non-living systems can be integrated into a network of goals either locally or globally (14.3.4). Finally, we shall give a number of reasons for assuming that all obtaining states of affairs can be integrated into a network of goals (14.3.5 and 14.3.7).

All these facts about teleological order (directedness to some goal) and about the integration into a network of goals are (past, present or future) facts belonging to creation and therefore belong to God's providence.

14.3.1 Are biological processes teleological?

Under a biological process we understand here just a process of a living system ls.

In accordance with the definition of teleological order Df 5.10 we should ask more accurately: Do biological processes i.e. processes of living things possess a teleological order? The answer to this question cannot be *Yes* unconditionally. It depends on a very important condition, i.e. on the condition whether the biological process supports some basic good (basic value) in the sense of Df 7.4 or is *valuable* to ls according to Df 7.6. That means it depends on the condition that the biological process supports life or health (+ life) of a living system (or a society of ls) or of the continuation or conservation of the species of ls. Thus the answer is this:

Df 14.1. A biological process B of ls is teleological (or possesses teleological order) iff

(a) B supports life or health + life of ls or a society of ls or

(b) B contributes to the continuation of the species-history of ls or to the conservation of the species of ls.

Ayala expresses a somewhat similar idea with the help of what he calls a "criterion of utility":

> "A feature of a system will be teleological in the sense of internal teleology if the feature has utility for the system in which it exists and if such utility explains the presence of the feature in the system".[6]

From definition Df 14.1 it is clear that not every biological process is teleological. This is also manifest from the considerations in sections 6.3.7 and 8.3.6 about chance and randomness w.r.t. goals or teleological order.

On the other hand, what holds for some process of an ls does not necessarily hold for the ls as a whole: According to definition Df 7.1 every ls possesses metabolism, self-regulation, propagation and adaption. Since these are defining properties of every ls they are in a good sense essential properties of every ls. But all these four properties are processes of becoming (Df 5.9) and their final states are relative goals (Df 5.15). Therefore it follows that every ls is teleological in this sense, although not every process of an ls (biological process) is teleological. Since every ls is teleological it follows that every ls is directed to some goal. Further every ls (or better: every fact concerning ls) comes under God's providence according to ch. 10 and also every process comes under God's providence. Thus for every ls and for those processes which are teleological it holds that both: they come under God's providence and they are directed to some goal.

6 Ayala (1970) p.13. Cf. Ayala (2010).

14.3.2 Are non-biological processes teleological?

By a non-biological process we understand here a process of a non-living system. For example the growth of a crystal is a non-biological process. Under non-living systems we understand natural systems. Concrete artifacts like concrete tables or chairs or computers and also conceptual objects like numbers or hypothesis are excluded. In our terminology (i.e. according to definition Df 5.10) we should ask: Do non-biological processes possess a teleological order? This depends on the question whether the non-biological process is just some kind of change from state S_1 or state S_2 or if it is a process of becoming (cf. Definition Df 5.9). Only in the latter case a non-biological process possesses teleological order. And in this case its final (or later) state is a relative goal w.r.t. the initial or earlier state according to definition Df 5.10. In the former case (just change from state S_1 to state S_2) we cannot speak of teleological order nor can we interpret the final state as a goal.

Df 14.2. A non-biological process C is teleological (or possesses teleological order) iff

(a) C is a process of becoming (Df 5.9)

(b) the final state of C is a relative goal w.r.t. its initial state (Df 5.10)

Concerning the question whether every non-living system is teleological, we have to distinguish a stronger sense of *teleological* which pertains to living systems (ls) and a weaker sense which may be attributed to non-living systems. The stronger sense has its reason in definition Df 7.1 of ls which states that every ls has metabolism, self-regulation, propagation and adaption, i.e. these are all properties (or processes) possessing teleological order. Moreover, these properties are defining (or essential) properties of every ls.

However, a non-living system does not have such properties or processes. We might call a non-living system teleological in a weaker sense however, if some of its processes or properties are teleological, because they are processes of becoming and their final states can be interpreted as goals of their initial states.

Df 14.3. A non-living system is teleological (or possesses teleological order) iff some of its processes are teleological (possess teleological order) according to definition Df 14.2.

Since every non-living system possesses some process (or property) of teleological order we may say that in this weaker sense every non-biological system is teleological. But this does not hold for non-biological processes, as it is clear from the beginning of 14.3.2: Only some of them are teleological, others are not.

Since every non-biological system might be called teleological in the above weaker sense, it is also directed to some goal in this weaker sense. And therefore such systems – or better: all facts about them – come under God's providence (ch. 10) and are directed to some goal.

It should be clear from section 5.3.4 and 5.3.7 that teleology (teleological order, teleological process, teleological system) might sometimes be what Barrow and Tipler called *determinate natural teleology*.[7] This is the case when the final state is achieved according to dynamical laws as a uniquely determined from the initial state, rather independently of environmental influences. The growth of a crystal or the development of an egg into a chick may be appropriate examples. Yet in most cases of teleological processes, the underlying process of becoming is not or only partially guided by dynamical laws, but by statistical laws i.e. *indeterminate natural teleology*. This means that the final state is not uniquely determined from the initial state, but is just one of several possible final states, although one where some property is relatively maximized or optimized.

14.3.3 Can all living systems be integrated into a network of goals extrinsic to the living system?

In order to answer this question we have to distinguish between goals which belong to the ls (or intrinsic goals w.r.t. the ls) and goals outside the ls (or extrinsic goals w.r.t. the ls). And those goals into which a ls can be incorporated, are those outside the ls.

For example, according to definition Df 14.1 a biological process which supports life or health (+ life) of a ls supports an intrinsic goal of ls, viz. a goal which belongs to ls. On the other hand a biological process which contributes to the continuation of the species-history of ls or to the conservation of the species of ls, contributes to an extrinsic goal of ls, viz. a goal which is outside the ls. With the help of this distinction we can say in that sense a ls is incorporated into a network of goals:

7 following Ayala (1970), Dobzhansky et al. (1977), cf. Barrow and Tipler (1986) p. 134.

Df 14.4. A living system ls is integrated into a network of goals iff

(a) there is some teleological process Tl of ls

(b) there is some extrinsic goal Gl outside ls such that Tl contributes to the realization of Gl

(c) Gl is interrelated to other extrinsic goals outside ls

Examples 1 A cell is integrated into a network of goals of the greater organism or ls to which it belongs. With its teleological processes the cell contributes to the realization of goals of the whole organism. Similarly an organ w.r.t. the organism to which it belongs or an individual plant, animal, man w.r.t. its plant-society, population or society. In more general terms any ls w.r.t. goals of its activity-space which is that part of the environment on which ls acts (recall Df 5.2(a)). A special case in this respect is the symbiosis of two ls, ls_1 and ls_2 such that ls_1 realizes some important goals of ls_2 which are extrinsic to ls_1 and vice versa.

Examples 2 A parasite is a living system ls_1 whose environment necessary for its survival is a greater living system ls_2 (the host of ls_1). But we can hardly say that the parasite with its teleological processes contributes to the realization of the goals of its host. He might kill the host (and thereby kill itself). Still we might say in a more indirect way the parasite with its teleological processes contributes to the species history and to the conservation of the species of those parasitic animals. In some cases it may be difficult to distinguish between the parasitical case and symbiosis: the huge number of bacteria in the human digestive system is such an example. In this case the bacteria also contribute to a human goal (health). When animals eat other animals, such teleological processes serve, first their survival, but in a more indirect way contribute to the history of the species and to the conservation of the species.

Examples 3 A cancer cell possesses teleological processes which are defining properties for a ls and is therefore a teleological system (cf. definition Df 7.1 and 14.3.1). But it can hardly be said that the teleological processes of a cancer cell contribute to goals of the animal or man having such cells. On the contrary, they destroy the living system in which they are embedded. There is however at least one ls which is such that the (teleological processes of the) cancer cell contribute(s) to the realization of its goals: the framework of other cancer cells around the original cancer cell (presupposing a state with at least two cancer cells). In a similar way this holds for certain bacteria or viruses (conjoined with cells, otherwise they are no ls) which either destroy or seriously damage the attacked ls.

Examples 4 There are bacteria which cause infections of the attacked ls and to that extent they violate extrinsic goals of that ls. On the other hand their attack may be overcome and lead to a strengthening of the immune system of the ls in question. This is so with every vaccination process. In this case despite the violation of some goals extrinsic to the bacterium of that ls, the bacterium contributes to the realization of some other goals of ls (immunization against certain illnesses).

Examples 5 There will be always some non-teleological processes of ls which neither contribute to the realization of extrinsic goals of ls nor to intrinsic goals of ls. One may think of particular atomic chemical reactions which are neutral to either intrinsic or extrinsic goals like particular movements of electrons or photons. As particular changes of microstates they cannot contribute as such to a macrostate which is a statistical outcome of a huge number of microstates.

Examples 6 There will always be some goals of some scientists which can be realized by any of the teleological processes of any ls: they contribute to the possibility of doing research and satisfying interests of scientists. But we do not include these kinds of examples because we want to find out whether independently of man's interests and goals ls can be integrated into a network of goals.

Examples 7 Independently of examples 6 there are many teleological processes Tl of ls possessing consciousness, especially men, such that Tl contributes to the realization of some extrinsic goal outside ls: for example a bird builds its nest or a person contributes to the welfare of his family, of his ill friend, of his society … etc.

According to definition Df 14.4 the question of 14.3.3 can be answered positively if the three conditions (a), (b), (c) are satisfied for every living system ls. It is easily seen that this is the case for condition (a). Every living system possesses at least four important teleological processes: metabolism, self-regulation, propagation and adaption.

Moreover, it is also not difficult to see that condition (c) is satisfied for every living system. Every goal extrinsic to some ls is connected to other extrinsic goals and consequently, there is a certain interdependency of these goals and therefore we can speak of a network. Thus if a cell contributes to the nutrition of an ls (to which it belongs) the nutrition is connected with growth and with propagation. It is similar with other extrinsic goals: the strengthening of the immune system contains many interrelated goals (Examples 4). Also, the conservation of a species (Examples 2) involves several extrinsic goals. Even in the case of Examples 3 there seem to be several goals connected with each other concerning the growth and development of cancer in ls (which are extrinsic goals of the cancer cell).

But is condition (b) satisfied generally? It is easily seen that condition (b) is satisfied by examples 1. Also in the case of Examples 4, condition (b) is satisfied because some extrinsic goals are realized at least as side-effects (like the strengthening of the immune system). Examples 5 are compatible since for the incorporation into a network of goals only teleological processes count. Concerning Examples 2 we can at least say that the parasites and bacteria contribute to their species history with their teleological processes. Thus even if they do not contribute to the realization of goals of other living systems, they contribute at least to their own species. If the same can be said about Examples 3 then the question of 14.3.3 can be answered positively. But in any case we should make the following distinction: Extrinsic goals in a wider sense are those which go beyond the realization of the species history and conservation of the species (but include these). Extrinsic goals in the narrower (minimum) sense are those which only realize the history and conservation of the species.

According to this distinction the question of 14.3.3 can be answered positively in the following way: All living systems can be integrated into a network of goals extrinsic to the living system: some in a stronger sense as they contribute (with their teleological processes) – globally – to the realization of a wide range of extrinsic goals which go beyond their species' history and conservation of their species. Some others in a narrow sense – more locally – as they contribute to the realization of the minimum range of extrinsic goals, which are the species' history and the conservation of their species only.

However, the demarcation of a species is scientifically justified[8] only concerning eucaryotes. Concerning procaryotes (like bacteria and archaea) this demarcation is not so clear.

Nevertheless, the definition of living system applies also to procaryotes. And therefore their teleological processes contribute at least to the conservation and history of their group; and this then is the minimum extrinsic goal.

To conclude, we can say: Since all living systems can be integrated into a network of goals either in a stronger or in a weaker sense this fact must come under God's providence according to ch. 10, Df 10.1 (f).

14.3.4 Can all non-living systems be integrated into a network of goals?

According to section 14.3.2 every non-living system is teleological in the sense that it possesses some teleological processes. According to definition Df 14.4 a living system is integrated into a network of goals if it satisfies three conditions. Condition (a) is also fulfilled by non-living systems as is clear from 14.3.2. If there are extrinsic goals at all, there will be always more extrinsic goals so that they will also be interrelated, which satisfies condition (c). But is condition (b) satisfied for non-living systems? Do their teleological processes or just their properties contribute to the realization of some extrinsic goals outside the non-living system in question?

We shall again consider real examples as a help for deciding this question.

Examples 1 The growth of a crystal is a process of becoming of which the final form (according to the crystal system) can be conceived as goal w.r.t. earlier states. In this sense the growth of a crystal is a teleological process. Further examples of that sort are ice crystals on the window, the growth of the ice-cover on the surface of a lake, or the crystallisation process out of melting metals.

Examples 2 The magnetization process is a process of becoming of which the final state can be considered as a goal w.r.t. earlier states, since it is a state of higher order (cf. definitions Df 5.9,Df 5.10). If we consider now the magnetization of the iron in the inner center

8 Even in the case of eucaryotes there is an ongoing debate about how exactly to demarcate a species. Cf. Schluter (2009) Sobel et al. (2010) and Mahner and Bunge (2000) p.251 ff.

of the earth, then we know that it causes the magnetic dipol and the magnetic field of the earth. In the inner center (between 5100 and 6360 km) the iron is solid and responsible for the geomagnetism. This geomagnetism and its magnetic field contribute to the realization of several extrinsic goals such as the orientation of animals like migrant birds.

Examples 3 Water and its properties contribute to the realization of carbon-based life on earth:

> "Water gives every appearance of being uniquely fit for the type of carbon-based life that exists on earth. Every one of its chemical and physical properties seems maximally fit not only for microscopic life but also for large warm-blooded organisms such as mammals, as well as for the generation and maintenance of a stable chemical and physical environment on the surface of the earth."[9]

Thus the properties of water contribute to the realization of a lot of extrinsic goals connected with carbon-based life.

According to the above considerations we can formulate definition Df 14.5 for non-living systems, which is analogous to definition Df 14.4.

Df 14.5. A non-living system nls is integrated into a network of goals iff

(a) there is some teleological process or property p of nls

(b) there is some goal Gl outside nls such that p contributes to the realization of Gl

(c) Gl is interrelated to other extrinsic goals outside nls.

It can be seen from the examples that many non-living systems satisfy definition Df 14.5. For other non-living systems it depends whether they – to some extent – are necessary for the existence of other non-living systems which are in turn necessary for carbon-based life on earth. In this sense then they also serve extrinsic goals, not locally as isolated systems but globally by contributing indirectly to the realization of some goal Gl. That means that non-living systems can also be integrated into a network of goals on a global scale. Furthermore it follows that this fact comes under God's providence according to definition Df 10.1(f) of ch. 10.

9 Denton (1998) p. 19

14.3.5 Can all obtaining states of affairs be integrated into a network of goals?

At first glance this appears impossible. Why should every single small fact have some sort of connection to a goal? For example, why should a single movement of an atom or molecule in a gas be incorporated into a network of goals? Or a collapse of a galaxy? Or a mutation in the DNA? Or in general: any chance-like event?

However, subsequently it will be shown that – according to our present knowledge of the universe – it seems likely that every state of affairs of the universe can be integrated into a network of goals. This will be done in the following steps. First, a definition will be given which says what it means that some states of affairs are integrated into a network of goals. Since this definition uses the term *teleological explanation*, it will also be described what a *teleological explanation* is. Thirdly, several reasons will be given to support the hypothesis that every state of affairs of the universe can be integrated into a network of goals.

Df 14.6. p can be integrated into a network of goals iff

(a) p represents a state of affairs in this world (universe)

(b) p is true

(c) p is the conclusion of a *teleological explanation*

Observe that (a) says that p cannot be just any proposition, but has to be a proposition stating some fact about the universe U (cf. definition Df 11.1, ch. 11).

Importantly, p cannot be a proposition (theorem) of logic or of mathematics, for in this case it is neither concerned with creation (the universe) nor with providence – provided of course that we understand *theorem of mathematics* in a most general sense and not as specified mathematical or geometrical structure of the universe. The latter we count to the laws of the universe.

Concerning (c) we have to say what we understand by a *teleological explanation*: In a *teleological explanation* one explains facts with the help of values and goals.[10] The facts are represented by the conclusion, the values and goals are contained in the premises:

10 Cf. Weingartner (1984) and Weingartner (2008b)

1. State $s_f(t_f)$ is the goal of some process of becoming or development (Cf. definitions Df 5.15, Df 7.8, Df 13.3)
2. For state $s_f(t_f)$ to obtain, it is necessary that the earlier states $s_1(t_1), s_2(t_2) \dots s_n(t_n)$ obtain. In order to be a valid explanation, premise 2 is insufficient. It has to be a general law-like statement of the following form: If state $s_f(t_f)$ obtains then always (dynamical law) or in most cases (statistical law) the earlier states $s_1(t_1), s_2(t_2) \dots s_n(t_n)$ obtain.
3. State $s_f(t_f)$ – the goal – obtains.
4. Therefore: the states $s_1(t_1), s_2(t_2) \dots s_n(t_n)$ obtain.

This argument is called *teleological argument*, because it explains a fact with the help of a value or goal. In the simplest case, the fact can consist of only one state $s_1(t_1)$, but usually it consists of all the necessary means to reach the goal. Subsequently, we shall give three examples for teleological explanations used in science.

14.3.5.1 Carbon-based life

1. The realization of Carbon-Based Life (CBL) is the goal of the process of becoming and development on earth.
2. If CBL is realized as a goal, then a certain series of specific physical and chemical facts and parameters obtain.
3. CBL was realized as a goal.
4. Therefore: A certain series of specific physical and chemical facts and parameters obtain. It should be clear from this, that the numerous physical and chemical facts and parameters leading to the state of the earth today can be integrated into a network of goals, which can be expressed in an abbreviated way as *carbon-based life*.

14.3.5.2 Evolutionarily stable strategy

Evolutionarily stable strategies develop in animal populations. Introduced by Maynard Smith[11], they can be concerned with different types of learning processes leading to a reproductively stable effect. This process can be viewed as a development leading to a specific goal: the evolutionarily stable strategy. The following example is taken from two types of members in an animal population (of higher animals).

Assume we explain the proportion of injuring champions (IC) to cooperative champions (CC) in a population with the help of the goal to realize an evolutionarily stable strategy (ESS)[12].

1. If ESS is realized as a goal, then the average expectation value for IC equals that for CC.
2. Assume the following initial conditions:
   Winner: $+50$ Loser: 0
   Injury: -100 Losing energy and time: -10
3. If the average expectation value for IC equals that for CC and if the above initial conditions (2.) are satisfied, then the proportion of the number $[IC]$ of IC in the population to the number $[CC]$ of CC in the population is $7:5$.
4. Teleological Hypothesis: ESS is realized as a goal.
5. Therefore: $[IC]:[CC]=7:5$

This second example shows that a certain proportion of injuring and cooperative members of an animal population can be integrated into a network of goals which can be described as evolutionarily stable (stabilized) strategy.

14.3.5.3 Queen Elizabeth I's goal

Queen Elizabeth I's aim was neither to offend the Anglican Church nor the Roman Catholic Church (p) in respect to certain circumstances f. These circumstances

11 Maynard-Smith (1982) and Maynard-Smith and Szathmary (1999). Cf. Nowak (2006)
12 The example is due to Wickler and Seibt (1987) p.57ff.

f have been described by the historian Maitland[13]. Elizabeth, when she had to proclaim her title, was

> "confronted with the alternative either of acknowledging with the late Mary (who became queen after Henry VIII) the ecclesiastical supremacy of the Pope or of voiding the Marian statutes and breaking with Rome as her father had done. Either alternative was fraught with grave perils, because the alignment of political and military forces both at home and abroad which favored each alternative was unsettled. Maitland therefore argued that in order to avoid committing herself to either alternative for the moment, Elizabeth employed an ambiguous formulation in the proclamation of her title: a formulation which could be made compatible with any decision she might eventually make."[14]

Queen Elizabeth believed that – given the field (of circumstances) f – a necessary condition for not offending either the Anglican Church or the Roman Catholic Church (p) was to employ an ambiguous formulation in the proclamation of her title (q) and she also believed that she was able to do this. The ambiguity of the formulation consisted in putting "etc." in the title instead of continuing with "only supreme head on Earth of the Church of England called Anglicana Ecclesia" (or the like as her father). Further, Elizabeth preferred p (i.e. not to offend either of the churches) to $non - q$ (i.e. to not being ambiguous or in other words to give a clear and unabbreviated formulation, which is definite in one way or another) in respect to (the circumstances) f.

This example can be brought into the following valid teleological argument:

(1) If p is a goal for x in the field f and x believes that q is a necessary condition for p in f and that x is able to bring it about that q and x prefers p to $non - q$ in the field f , then x acts in such a way that q obtains.

(2) p is a goal for (the person) a (instance of 'x') in f, a believes that q is a necessary condition for p in f and that a is able to bring it about that q and further a prefers p to $non - q$ in f.

(3) Therefore: a acts in such a way that q (obtains).

Through the fact that it is an instance of *modus ponens* + universal instantiation, it is obvious that the above argument is logically valid. It is also easy to see that the argument is teleological in the following sense: the conclusion expresses a fact while the premises contain a value statement in the sense that something is said to be a goal (a relatively highest value) with respect to necessary means for

13 Maitland (1911)

14 Cf. Nagel (1971), p. 552. Nagel discusses this example as a case of historical explanation.

reaching that goal. This means that the argument explains facts with the help of values, i.e. with the help of aims and goals.

The example of Queen Elizabeth I may be generalized by the following argument: if politicians have to announce something publicly and if – according to their beliefs (their estimation) – using unambiguous language would offend at least one influential group of people and if they prefer to use ambiguous language over such an offence, then politicians always (or in most cases) use ambiguous language. Also, this conclusion i.e. that the politician uses ambiguous language, expresses a fact which is explained by the premises which consist of both factual statements and value statements: that the politician announces something publicly and that he has certain beliefs and estimations are factual statements. The value statement is hidden, sometimes it is not even mentioned, but presupposed: the politician prefers to use ambiguous language over an offence against influential people. His aim is not to offend or even to please people.

This last example demonstrates more clearly that the explained fact – Elizabeth used ambiguous language – is integrated not into a single goal, but into a network of interrelated goals: not to offend one of the two churches, to escape both Henry VIII's decision and that of Maria Stuart, to prefer (to deem higher) these actions over the disadvantage of proclaiming her title in an ambiguous way … etc.

14.3.5.4 Children's understanding of goals

The last example of Queen Elizabeth I illustrates a well-known fact: that adult humans have goals, mobilize means of which they believe that they are necessary for achieving these goals, recognize and understand the goals of others, and integrate their own actions as well as those of others into a network of goals. Recent research proves that even very small children's behavior shows that they have goals and are able to recognize and understand the goals of others (adults). One study, for example, showed that 6- and 10-month-old infants evaluate individuals as appealing or aversive: infants prefer an individual who helps others to one who hinders others. (Hamlin et al.) Other studies show that infants can recognize the structure of human actions (*action parsing*) in the sense that they grasp its beginning through its realization of the goal (Bird, Baldwin). Moreover, infants, from about 15 months on, are able to understand the goals of adults even if they fail to fulfill them (Meltzoff, Brooks; Csibra et al.). Furthermore, infants' skills of shared intentionality (for example, playing a cooperative game to achieve a common goal) develop gradually during the first 14 months of life (Tomasello et al.).[15]

A more mature and sophisticated understanding of the intentions of others is present if the child recognizes that the other person has a false belief concerning how to reach his goal. There have been well confirmed series of the so-called false-belief tests since its invention by Wimmer and Perner in 1983. Children of about 4 years of age are able to manage this test. In recent studies, it has been shown that several other tasks can be managed at about the same age: understanding synonymy, some degree of understanding class inclusion, attributing different sortal-labels or classifying predicates to the same individual (usually labeled by the misleading expression "alternative naming"), or undertstanding arguments using identity premises.[16]

Based on infants' looking time, some studies claim that 15-months-old infants manage non-verbal false-belief tasks. These experiments use the violation-of-expectation method, which has frequently been used to investigate infants' understanding of the goals of others.[17] However, the interpretation of the looking times creates additional problems concnerning the reliability of such experiments. Other studies rely on the looking direction, which seems more reliable. Independently of such more sophisticated problems concerning specific tests, it seems to be an overwhelming result that at a very young age already, children are able to grasp the goals and intentions of other human beings.

Summarizing section 14.3.5, we might say that the definition of integrating states of affairs (in particular certain means as specific circumstances) into a network of goals and the definition of teleological explanation (together with the three examples) show how it is possible that states of affairs can be integrated into a network of goals. In addition, the previous section has shown that even small children are able to integrate actions of adults into some kind of goal.In the following sections we will give reasons that show that this could in fact be the case on a global scale.

---

15 Hamlin et al. (2007); Baird and Baldwin (2001); Meltzoff and Brooks (2001); Csibra et al. (2003); Tomasello et al. (2005).

16 Wimmer and Perner (1983); Perner (1991); Haring (2013); Haring and Weingartner (2014a).

17 Onishi and Baillargeon (2005). See also the references in footnote 15.

14.3.6 Functional explanation

By a functional explanation one usually understands, an explanation which subordinates the existence of a part of a system under the whole system by describing its function in it. These are different types of functions[18]. We may roughly distinguish *proper functions* from *accidental functions*, however this distinction is not entirely clear. Thus a proper function is that of the eye to see, of the ear to hear and of the hand to grasp. But to shake hands is an accidental function of the hand, to support glasses is an accidental function of the ears and flirting one of the eyes.

One type of function we might characterize as some subset of the sum of all internal or external processes of a living system, which contribute to the realization of one of the conditions of living systems in definition Df 7.1. Another type of function is that where such processes contribute to higher values of the living system (cf. definitions Df 7.7 and Df 7.9).

Further types of functions can be defined with the help of adaption.[19] In general, a functional explanation is a teleological explanation which explains facts with the help of functions. But functional explanations are usually only applied to living systems (not to non-living systems). Both types of explanations use the realizations of certain properties or states of the living system, which are in some way goals of that living system.

14.3.7 Reasons for integration into a network of goals

(1) A first reason is the extraordinary fine-tuning of the cosmos and of the biosphere on earth. Here are some of the numerous examples:

> "If one regards the Planck time as the initial moment when the subsequent cosmic dynamics were determined, it is necessary to suppose that nature chose ρ to differ from ρ_{crit} by no more than one part in 10^{60} . . . ".[20]

> "There is indeed no other candidate fluid which is remotely competitive with water as the medium for carbon-based life. If water did not exist, it would have to be invented.

---

18 Mahner and Bunge (2000) p. 159, distinguish five types.

19 For a detailed discussion of different types of functions, see Mahner and Bunge (2000) ch.4.5.

20 Davis (1982) p.89. Cf. Barrow and Tipler (1986) p. 411 and 375. ρ_{crit} is the largest density the universe can possess and still expand for all future time.

In the many mutually adaptive properties of this most remarkable of all fluids, we are brought dramatically face-to-face with an extraordinary body of evidence of precisely the sort we would expect on the hypothesis that the laws of nature are uniquely fit for our own type of carbon-based life as it exists on earth."[21]

"Hoyle realized that this remarkable chain of coincidences – the unusual stability of beryllium, the existence of an advantageous resonance level in C^{12} and the non-existence of a disadvantageous level in O^{16} – were necessary, and remarkably fine-tuned, conditions of our own existence and indeed the existence of any carbon-based life in the universe."[22]

"Any universe hospitable to life – what we might call a *biophilic universe* – has to be 'adjusted' in a particular way. The prerequisites for any life of the kind we know about – long-lived stable stars, stable atoms such as carbon, oxygen and silicon, able to combine into complex molecules, etc – are sensitive to the physical laws and to the size, expansion rate and contents of the universe. Indeed, even for the most open-minded science fiction writer, 'life' or 'intelligence' requires the emergence of some generic complex structures: it can't exist in a homogenous universe, not in a universe containing only a few dozen particles. Many recipes would lead to stillborn universes with no atoms, no chemistry, and no planets; or to universes too short-lived or too empty to allow anything to evolve beyond sterile uniformity … Even a universe as large as ours could be very boring: it could contain just black holes, or inert dark matter, and not atoms at all. Even if it had the same ingredients as ours, it could be expanding so fast that no stars or galaxies had time to form; or it could be so turbulent that all the material formed vast black holes rather than stars or galaxies – an inclement environment for life. And our universe is also special in having three spatial dimensions. A four dimensional world would be unstable; in two dimensions, nothing complex could exist.

The distinctive and special-seeming recipe characterising our universe seems to me a fundamental mystery that should not be brushed aside merely as a brute fact."[23]

"Our amazement grows further when we not that not only is the radiant energy in this tiny region [from ultraviolet to infrared] the *only radiation of utility to life* but that radiant energy in most other regions of the spectrum is *either lethal* or *profoundly damaging* … So the sun not only puts out all its radiant energy in the tiny band of utility to life but virtually *none, in those regions of the spectrum which are harmful to life …*

Now this is a remarkable enough coincidence in itself. But there are further coincidences to consider. To be of any utility to life, the radiation of the sun has to reach the surface of the earth. To do so it must pass through the atmosphere. Necessarily, any atmosphere surrounding a terraqueous planet containing carbon-based life is bound to contain some carbon dioxide gas, water vapor, at least some nitrogen, and for ad-

---

21 Denton (1998) p.46

22 Barrow and Tipler (1986) p.253. The disadvantageous process would be $C^{12} + He^4 \rightarrow O^{16}$ where all the carbon were rapidly burnt to O^{16}.

23 Rees (2003) p.376f.

vanced highly active life forms considerable concentrations of oxygen. It is difficult to see how the actual concentrations of these gases could be very different from what they are in any atmosphere supporting a carbon-based biosphere (see discussion in chapter 6). At the temperature range that exists at the earth's surface, there is bound to be water vapor in considerable amounts in the atmosphere.

The fact that the atmospheric gases oxygen, nitrogen, carbon dioxide, and water vapour transmit 80 percent of the sun's radiation in the visible and near infrared and allow it to reach the earth's surface is another coincidence of enormous significance ... If the atmosphere had contained gases or other substances which absorbed strongly visible light, then no life-giving light would have reached the surface of the earth ...

Despite these three remarkable coincidences, life would still not be possible without a fourth coincidence – the fact that liquid water is highly transparent to visible light."[24]

"... man is not only a unique animal, but the end product of a completely unique evolutionary pathway, the elements of which are traceable at least to the beginnings of the Cenozoic. We find, then, that the evolution of cognition is the product of a variety of influences and preadaptive capacities, the absence of any one of which would have completely negated the process, and most of which are unique attributes of primates and/or hominids."[25]

"... the case of the evolution of eyes is [indeed] of decisive importance in the argument about the evolution of intelligence. The crucial point is that the evolution of eyes is not at all that improbable. In fact whenever eyes were of any selective advantage in the animal kingdom, they evolved. Salvini-Plawen and myself have shown that eyes have evolved no less than at least 40 times independently in the animal kingdom. Hence a highly complicated organ can evolve independently, if such evolution is at all probable.

Let us apply this case to the evolution of intelligence. We know that the particular kind of life (system of macromolecules) that exists on Earth can produce intelligence ... We can now ask what was the probability of this system producing intelligence (remembering the same system was able to produce eyes no less than 40 times). We have two large super-kingdoms of life on Earth, the prokaryote evolutionary lines each of which could lead theoretically to intelligence. In actual fact none of the thousands of lines among the prokaryotes came anywhere near it. There are 4 kingdoms among the eukaryotes, each again with thousands or ten thousands of evolutionary lineages. But in three of these kingdoms, the protists, fungi and plants, no trace of intelligence evolved. This leaves the kingdom of Animalia to which we belong. It consists of about 25 major branches, the so-called phyla, indeed if we include extinct phyla, more than 30 of them. Again, only one of them developed real intelligence, the chordates. There are numerous Classes in the chordates, I would guess more than 50 of them, but only one of them (the mammals) developed real intelligence, as in Man. The mammals consist of 20-odd orders, only one of them, the primates, acquiring intelligence, and among the well over

24 Denton (1998) p.53ff.
25 Lovejoy (1981) p.326

> 100 species of primates only one, Man, has the kind of intelligence that would permit [the development of advanced technology]. Hence, in contrast to eyes, an evolution of intelligence is not probable."[26]

We could go on with examples of this sort. Numerous examples for purposeful fine-tuning are collected in Barrow and Tipler (1986), Denton (1998), Davis (1982) and Rees (2001).

They all show that these facts are not only closely interrelated, but are incorporated into a network of goals where one of them might be the development of the human species. In the next section, this kind of integration into a network of goals is investigated with respect to God's providence.

(2) A second reason is that what cannot be integrated into a local goal might be integrated into a global (network of) goal(s).

> "It is otherwise with one who has care of a particular thing, and one whose providence is universal, because a particular provider excludes all defects from what is subject to his care as far as he can; whereas, one who provides universally allows some little defect to remain, lest the good of the whole should be hindered. Hence, corruption and defects in natural things are said to be contrary to some particular nature; yet they are in keeping with the plan of universal nature; inasmuch as the defect in one thing yields to the good of another, or even to the universal good: for the corruption of one is the generation of another, and through this it is that a species is kept in existence. Since God, then, provides universally for all being, it belongs to His providence to permit certain defects in particular effects, that the perfect good of the universe may not be hindered, for if all evil were prevented, much good would be absent from the universe."[27]

We might further consider the following analogy:
As a master builder employs different kinds of workers for executing his plans, God employs different kinds of creatures for executing his plan (providence) concerning creation (concerning the universe). Some workers (creatures) are more talented to help him carry out his plan. But he also employs less talented workers, whose help is not as effective and whose ability to learn is slower, even if they might be helped by the more talented workers. He might even have some workers who try to hinder his plan or to work against it. However, much more than a clever master builder, God is able to have the saboteurs serve the global goal, if not also some local goals and good work-

26 Letter from Ernst Mayr to FJT dated December 23, 1982. Cited in Barrow and Tipler (1986) p.132f.
27 Aquinas (1981) I, 22,2 ad 2.

ers, such that the plan of his providence is finally satisfied. Observe that the "workers" in this analogy might serve as a symbol for any non-living or living system (including man) involved in a developmental or in an evolutionary process of the universe.

As Peter Thomas Geach and Kurt Gödel put it:

> "God is the Supreme Grand Master who has everything under his control. Some of the players are consciously helping his plan, others are trying to hinder it; whatever the finite players do, God's plan will be executed."[28]

> "God created things in such a way that they themselves can create something."[29]

14.3.8 Result of chapter 14

T 14.1. *Every living system ls is teleological, although not every process of a ls is teleological. (14.3.1)*

T 14.2. *Every non-living system nls is teleological in the weaker sense that nls possesses some process (or property) of teleological order; even though not every non-biological (non-living) process is teleological (14.3.2)*

T 14.3. *All living systems can be integrated into a network of goals extrinsic to the living system: some in a stronger sense, some others in a weaker sense (14.3.3).*

T 14.4. *All non-living systems can be integrated into a network of goals extrinsic to the non-living system either directly and locally or indirectly and globally (14.3.4).*

T 14.5. *It seems very likely that all obtaining states of affairs can be integrated into a network of goals if not locally than globally (14.3.5). The reasons for Theorem 14.5 are given in 14.3.7.*

These arguments make it clear how every obtaining state of affairs can belong to God's providence.

---

28 Geach (1977) p.58.

29 Gödel MAX PHIL 4X.

14.4 Answer to the Objections

14.4.1 (to 14.1.1)

As has been shown in sections 13.3.9–13.3.11 and 13.4.4 (3) causes and explanations which concern the whole universe, but belong to the universe or use the laws of the universe (+ initial and boundary conditions) are necessarily incomplete.[30] This is also connected with the fact that a unique cosmological time (or unique simultaneity) cannot be attributed to the whole universe.[31] And in a similar way it is also not possible to predict the future states of the universe far away from its present states. Modern cosmology tells us that the whole universe is not a thermodynamical system with the inevitable consequence of heat-death due to gaining equilibrium or that of cold-death due to unlimited expansion. The present expansion might also lead to contraction and high energy-density after a finite period of time.[32] It is similar to the case of the *internal observer* (cf. 13.4.4 (3)): Like the knowledge of an observer, belonging to the universe must be incomplete about the universe, causes too, belonging to the universe, must be incomplete. And in an analogous way, goals and networks of goals belonging to the universe must be incomplete w.r.t. the whole universe.

In this sense Wittgenstein says:

> "The sense of the world must lie outside the world."[33]

Since God is outside time and outside the universe there is no hindrance that he can know everything about the universe, i.e. he can have complete knowledge about the universe, that is about his creation. And therefore there is also no hindrance that he can know all the goals and networks of goals (all the teleology) belonging to the universe. And all this comes under his providence. Moreover, he might have a goal or network of goals for the universe as a whole in form of a plan. This global plan then equally belongs to his providence.

---

30 See especially section 13.3.11 above.
31 Cf. Mittelstaedt (2008) and Mittelstaedt (2009)
32 Hawking and Ellis (1973)
33 Wittgenstein (1960) 4.61. See full quotation in 13.3.9 above.

14.4.2 (to 14.1.2)

It is correct that living things with consciousness can direct themselves towards goals or integrate themselves into a network of goals. But it has been shown in 14.3.1 that all living systems (including those without consciousness) are teleological i.e. directed towards some goal, because their essential features are all teleological. Although not all biological processes belonging to them are teleological.

Moreover, all living systems can be integrated into a network of goals extrinsic to that living system either in a wider sense (when the extrinsic goal lies outside the species) or in a narrower sense (when the goal lies inside the species or inside a special group of living things (cf. 14.3.3).

14.4.3 (to 14.1.3)

That the argument in 14.1.3 is logically valid can be shown thus:

1. $(\exists p)EVp$ — $EVp \ldots p$ happens according to evolution
2. $\forall p(EV(p) \rightarrow p \in Tg's(Prov))$ — (see section 1.3.3)
3. $(\forall p)(EV(p) \rightarrow \neg Tel(p))$ — $Tel(p) \ldots p$ is directed to some goal
4. $EV(p_1)$ — 1 Existential Instantiation
5. $EV(p_1) \rightarrow p_1 \in Tg's(Prov)$ — 2 Universal Instantiation
6. $p_1 \in Tg's(Prov)$ — 4, 5 MP.
7. $EV(p_1) \rightarrow \neg Tel(p_1)$ — 3 Universal Instantiation
8. $\neg Tel(p_1)$ — 4, 7 M.P.
9. $p_1 \in Tg's(Prov) \wedge \neg Tel(p_1)$ — 6, 8
10. $(\exists p)(p \in Tg's(Prov) \wedge \neg Tel(p))$ — 9 Existential Generalization
11. $\neg(\forall p)(p \in Tg's(Prov) \rightarrow Tel(p))$ — from 10

Since the argument in 14.1.3 is valid, we have to check the premises: Premise 1 is certainly an empirically true premise: Some things (events, processes) happen according to evolution. Premise 2 says that everything which happens according to evolution comes under God's providence. This follows from what has been defended in ch. 10 that everything that happens in the universe comes under God's providence. Since premise 2 follows from a stronger premise which has been justified in detail in ch. 10 we shall not give it up, before we have accurately investigated the remaining premise 3. Although it is claimed by famous representatives of the Synthetic Theory it will be shown that it contains several confusing issues:

(1) These authors when denying teleology in evolution do not give a single precise definition of *goal directed process* or of *teleological process* or of *process possessing teleological order*. However without precise definitions the claims are very vague and full of ambiguities.

(2) One confusing idea is that teleology implies predictability, since teleology is interpreted as predetermination. From the definition of teleological order (Df 5.10) and from the definition of teleological process (Df 14.1) it can be seen that such an interpretation is completely unjustified: the definition Df 5.10 uses the definition of *process of becoming* which contains the concept of *entropy*. That the conditions for a process being teleological do neither imply predictability nor predetermination should also be clear from the examples (1) – (4) of section 14.3.3 above. Moreover there is a second confusion involved here: That predictability implies determinism or dynamical deterministic laws and vice versa. But neither is the case in general, as will be shown in section 15.3.2 below.

(3) As Soontiens points out correctly, a frequently occurring ambiguity is that of *chance* understood as contrary to intention and purposiveness on the one hand and *chance* as contrary to lawfulness i.e. contingency on the other.[34] Since chance is usually connected with unpredictability and teleology is wrongly connected with predetermination, or in general with determinism, (by several authors of the Synthetic Theory) they see an incompatibility of chance in evolution with teleology (cf. the quotation by Dobzhansky in section 14.1.3). But as it was shown in chs. 6 and 8 all types of chance can be defined only relative to a certain type of order and some also relative to teleological order (recall definitions Df 6.9–Df 6.11 of ch. 6 and Df 8.5 of ch. 8). Moreover, it should be clear from chs. 6 and 8 that chance and order are present and compatible in one living system and this is the normal case. As is clear from chapters 7, 8 and 13, all processes of evolution like development,

34 Soontiens (1991) p. 135

variation, mutation, metabolism ... etc. possess components of chance and randomness on the one hand and order, determination and teleological order on the other.

From points (1)–(3) above, it follows that the claim of premise 3 (of the argument in 14.1.3) that evolution is either incompatible with teleology or does not show teleology is not correct. Therefore the conclusion of this argument is not proved.

15 Whether nature's order and God's providence are compatible with free will

15.1 Arguments Contra

15.1.1 First argument

Only if nature's order is globally indeterministic nature's order is compatible with free will. But nature's order cannot be globally indeterministic, since the huge domains of Classical Mechanics, Electrodynamics and Special Relativity obey dynamical-deterministic laws satisfying conditions D1 and D2 of ch. 4.

Therefore: nature's order is not compatible with free will.

15.1.2 Second argument

If nature's order in all higher-level brain processes is deterministic then such an order is not compatible with free will. But according to many neuroscientists[1] all higher-level brain processes are deterministic.

Therefore: nature's order is not compatible with free will.

15.1.3 Third argument

God's providence has no exception, i.e. it applies to every event of creation (of the universe). Therefore: Whenever something (some event) of this universe occurs then God's Providence and consequently his knowledge (cf. ch. 11) is concerned with it.

If God is omniscient he will know – before it happens – that a human person chooses A rather than *not-*A. And in this sense such a choice seems to be determined but not free.

Therefore: God's providence seems to be incompatible with free will decisions.

1 Cf. Prinz (2004), Singer (2004), Roth (2001)

15.1.4 Fourth argument

According to ch. 13, what comes under God's providence is either caused by God or caused by creatures. If human actions are caused by God or are caused by creatures they cannot be free will actions. Therefore: God's providence cannot be compatible with free will.

15.1.5 Fifth argument

Free will decisions are contingent events. According to the definition of contingency it holds: Event (state of affairs) p occurs contingently $=_{df}$ it is possible that p occurs and it is possible that p does not occur. Thus if it is contingent that God cares through his providence that p occurs, then it is possible that he cares that p occurs and it is possible that he does not care that p occurs. But in this case his providence is undecided w.r.t. the occurrence of p. And if this is the case then his providence is imperfect. But we have to assume that God is completely perfect. Therefore his providence cannot be undecided. And consequently (by negating the definiens of the above definition) it either is impossible that he cares that p occurs or it is necessary that he cares that p occurs. But in the first case there is no providence about (the occurrence of) free will decisions and in the second case this kind of necessity seems to be incompatible with free will decisions.

Therefore: Either there is no providence about free will decisions or the respective providence is incompatible with free will decisions.

15.1.6 Sixth argument

If not everything in the universe comes under God's providence (or God's plan) then free will decisions might not come under it. As Inwagen says there are three types of states of affairs that are not a part of God's plan; one of them is free will decision.

> "Our revised definition of God's plan is: God's plan consists of the totality of all His decrees other than reactive decrees. If this is the correct picture of God's relation to the created world and His plan for it, there would seem to be, within such a world, at least three possible

> sources of chance, or events or states of affairs that are not a part of God's plan: the free will of rational creatures, natural indeterminism, and the initial state of the created world."[2]

Therefore: There does not seem providence (God's plan) about free will decisions.

15.2 Argument Pro

On the assumption that God is the creator of the universe and that God has created man with free will it would be inconsistent if his providence would destroy man's free will.

Therefore: Since God cannot be inconsistent his providence must be compatible with his creation, i.e. with his creating man with free will.

15.3 Proposed Answer

The question whether nature's order and God's providence are compatible with free will presupposes that there is free will. Otherwise this question would be empty and the answer rather trivial. Therefore, in order to deal with this question in an adequate way we have first to show that there is free will since this is not a generally accepted assumption. Then secondly it will be shown that nature's order and God's providence are compatible with free will.

The first part will be divided into two parts. First certain hindrances for the existence of free will have to be removed. This is done by giving definitions for determinism and indeterminism and by showing that global or universal determinism cannot be true (15.3.1). Then five types of confusions are unmasked, which concern determinism, indeterminism, causality and predictability (15.3.2). Further, attacks against free will from *neuronal determinism* are critically discussed (15.3.3). After removing such hindrances it will be shown that there are different *degrees of freedom* on different levels of the brain, beginning from the atomic level via the level of channels and synapses up to the cellular and neuronal level as the building blocks of the nervous system (15.3.4). Finally a definition of free will and one of

2 Inwagen (1995) p.53f.

free will decision is offered and its details are discussed (15.3.5). Without a precise definition of free will (and free will decision) the question of compatibility of nature's order and God's providence with free will cannot be answered in a more accurate way. From this discussion it will be evident that there is free will and free will decision in the defined sense. Only after establishing that fact the question of compatibility will be discussed in detail and it will be answered in a positive way (15.3.6 and 15.3.7).

15.3.1 Determinism and indeterminism

Df 15.1. A physical, chemical, biological or psychological system with states $S_i(t_i)$ obeying a dynamical law L is *deterministic* (det_1) iff the following three conditions are satisfied:

(a) For any (future) state $S_2(t_2), t_2 > t_0$, there is a (past) state $S_1(t_1), t_1 < t_0$, such that from the proposition describing $S_1(t_1)$ plus the law of nature L (in the form of a differential equation) the proposition describing $S_2(t_2)$ is derivable.

(b) For any (past) state $S_1(t_1), t_1 < t_0$, there is a future state $S_2(t_2), t_2 > t_0$, such that from the proposition describing $S_2(t_2)$ plus the law of nature L (in the form of a differential equation) the proposition describing $S_1(t_1)$ is derivable.

(c) The dynamical law is understood in such a way that it satisfies conditions D1, D2 and D4 (in some cases also D3) of ch. 4.

The second condition (b) holds also because dynamical laws are time-reversal symmetric. Df 15.1 is a more detailed formulation of D1.[3] An important consequence of the above definition Df 15.1 is this:

T 15.1. *The same initial (or past) states lead with the same dynamical law to the same successor (or future) states.*

Df 15.2. *Determinism* (Det_1) is the doctrine that a certain physical, chemical, biological or psychological system (or in general: any system, the whole universe) is deterministic according to Df 15.1. Df 15.2 expresses the global determinism de-

3 For more details cf. Mittelstaedt and Weingartner (2005) p. 150 and Weingartner (2008c).

scribed by Laplace in ch.2 of his Essai philosophique sur les probabilités of 1814. Laplace assumed (wrongly) that D4 is always satisfied.

Df 15.3. An event (or state) e is *determined* iff e is a later state S_2 (t_2) of a physical, chemical, biological or psychological system which is a definite function of earlier states $S_i(t_i)$ of that system (according to Df 15.1).

Observe that Theorem 15.1 is weaker than (i.e. does not imply) Df 15.1. This is so because Theorem 15.1 does not require that there is a definite state $S_i(t_i)$ at every point of time t_i (time to be understood as continuous). For Theorem 15.1 it suffices that at certain selected points of time two identical states lead to the same successor states. And these successor states are definite functions of certain earlier states. Accordingly we can define a weaker kind of deterministic system and determinism thus:

Df 15.4. A physical, chemical, biological or psychological system is *deterministic* (det_2) iff the same initial (or past) states lead with the same dynamical law to the same successor (or future) states.

Df 15.5. *Determinism* (Det_2) is the doctrine that a certain physical, chemical or biological system (or in general any system, also the whole universe) is deterministic (det_2) according to Df 15.4.

There are physical, chemical, biological and psychological systems which satisfy Df 15.4 but do not satisfy D3 and D4 (ch.4). The systems in question are systems which show chaotic behavior or systems in chaotic motion. Chaotic motion is non-periodic and non-recurrent, although the underlying laws are dynamical laws which are time-reversible. Therefore this kind of chaotic behavior is called dynamical chaos or deterministic chaos. But we have to observe it is deterministic in a weaker sense since conditions D3 and D4 (ch. 4) are not satisfied and Df 15.1 is only satisfied in a partial sense. Moreover, because of several additional properties – most important, the sensitive dependence on initial conditions measured by a positive Liapunov exponent or more general by the Kolmogorov entropy – predictability is not satisfied.[4]

4 For more details see Mittelstaedt and Weingartner (2005) p. 152 ff. and 257 ff., H.G. Schuster (1989), Weingartner (1996). Besides dynamical chaos there are other types of chaos like quantum chaos and cosmological chaos which have different properties.

Df 15.6. A physical, chemical, biological or psychological system is *indeterministic* ($indet_1$) iff it satisfies the conditions S1, S2, S3 and S4 of ch.4.

Observe that an indeterministic system is not lawless. On the contrary an interdeterministic system ($indet_1$) obeys statistical laws. What is undetermined, or what has degrees of freedom is the singular state or event or process.[5] Accordingly we may define undetermined event.

Df 15.7. An event or state e is *undetermined* iff e is a later state $S_2(t_2)$ of a physical (chemical, biological or psychological) system which is not a definite function of earlier states $S_i(t_i)$ of that system.

Df 15.8. *Indeterminism* ($Indet_1$) is the doctrine that a certain physical, chemical, biological or psychological system (or in general any system, also the whole universe) is indeterministic ($indet_1$) according to definition Df 15.6.

From definition Df 15.7 it follows that an undetermined state or event is not strictly predictable, although it may be predictable with a certain degree of probability.

Df 15.9. An event or state e is *undetermined* ($indet_2$) iff e is not strictly predictable, i.e. with probability = 1, but only with a lower degree of probability.

Observe that unpredictability can have other reasons than what is expressed in the definitions of Df 15.7. For example the future states or events of chaotic motion are not strictly predictable, although they are a definite function of certain earlier states, since they obey dynamical laws.

15.3.2 Confusions concerning determinism, causality and prediction

(1) The first wide-spread confusion is that, generally, causality implies determinism and consequently (by contraposition): non-determinism implies non-causality. There are many counterexamples to such a position: A quantum jump of an electron from a lower level of energy E_1 to a higher level of

5 Cf. section 4.3.2 (and 6.3.4) above and the quotation of Schrödinger.

energy E_2 does not have a trajectory from E_1 to E_2 in the sense of D1 or Df 15.1 and is therefore not a determined event, but an undetermined one (Df 15.7). But as the Compton-Effect or the Light-Electric Effect by Einstein show such effects have causes: light of high frequency. Systems obeying statistical laws satisfy conditions S1–S4 of ch.4. But it can be shown that also statistical laws represent some causal relations although they are of different type as those represented by dynamical laws.[6] On a higher level: a free will decision is undetermined but can have causes as motives and reasons and has been decided by the respective person.

(2) A second wide-spread confusion is that, generally, determinism implies predictability and consequently (by contraposition): unpredictability implies indeterminism. The important counterexample to this confusion is dynamical chaos. Chaotic motion is unpredictable in an objective sense but it is deterministic at least in the sense of Df 15.4 since it satisfies D1 and D2, obeying dynamical laws. The loss of predictability depends on the level of integrability of the chaotic system: predictability is only partially available on the levels of KAM-integrability but not available for strong chaos.[7]

(3) A third confusion is that, generally, predictability implies determinism and consequently (by contraposition): indeterminism implies unpredictability. Also this claim is wrong: In a photon split beam experiment for an individual system it is objectively undetermined whether the photon has the property A or the counter property $non\text{-}A$. However in spite of the objective indeterminacy of each individual system, for a sufficiently large ensemble of photons we have a strict law which leads to strict predictions concerning the behavior of the large ensemble. Observe that here the individual subsystem is undetermined but the whole system containing a huge number of individual subsystems obeys statistical laws with strict predictability (for the whole system). This is even the normal case for fundamental laws of nature in the statistical sense independently whether initial states lead to branching successor states or very different initial states lead to an equilibrium state. Observe further that the above counterexample to confusion (3) does not contradict Df 15.9. Since the undeterminacy is concerned with the individual system but the predictability is concerned with the whole ensemble. Confusion (3) talks in general terms about indeterminism and unpredictability as it is usual with confusions. It overlooks condition S2 (ch. 4) for statistical laws which says

6 Cf. Mittelstaedt and Weingartner (2005) p. 233 f.

7 For more details cf. Mittelstaedt and Weingartner (2005) p. 262 f.

that important properties of the whole system do not hold for its individual parts.

Confusions (2) and (3) are even sometimes fused into an equivalence or definition saying: predictability iff determinism and unpredictability iff inderterminism. The counterexamples show that these implications do not hold generally even if they can be true for some specific cases.

(4) A fourth confusion is that, generally, causality implies predictability and consequently (by contraposition): unpredictability implies non-causality. A counterexample is again chaotic motion in the sense of dynamical chaos. Since dynamical chaos satisfies conditions D1 and D2 (and Df 15.5) it obeys dynamical laws which represent a basic (classical) type of causality. Another counterexample on a higher level is free will decision which is (at least usually) unpredictable but not non-causal, since it can have causes in the sense of motives and reasons and in the sense that it has been decided by the respective person.

(5) A fifth rather wide-spread confusion is that causality = mono-causality in the sense that for the effect E there is one unique cause C which is both necessary and sufficient for E. Such a situation very rarely occurs in reality. The idea may originate from some naive interpretation of simple examples of Classical Mechanics where one ball $B1$ bumps against another $B2$. But on a closer look one can understand immediately that the bump of B1 is not a necessary condition for the movement of $B2$. It is also only sufficient together with a whole series of other conditions being fulfilled. Also for judging a murder there is often a time consuming investigation whether the facts of the case are sufficient; moreover they are usually not (the only) necessary. The grandparents are causes as necessary conditions for their grandchildren, but of course not sufficient ones. According to Laplace (and Classical Mechanics) one past state is necessary and sufficient together with the dynamical law for a later state. More precisely according to Special Relativity (Minkowski spacetime) all the events of the whole past light cone are necessary and sufficient for the events of the future light cone. The classical picture of Laplace is however satisfied more accurately only for a two-body system, say the sun and one planet. But for the three (or more)-body system it is only approximately satisfied. And this is so independently of how accurate the measurement of the initial conditions

is possible.[8] In most cases of everyday life and of science (concerning physical, chemical, biological and psychological systems) what we call causes are factors which are neither necessary nor sufficient. Consider a vessel A with water which is filled by several pipes coming from several vessels $B, C, D, \ldots$ (in a position higher than that of A). We may ask the question what is the cause for the red color of the water in vessel A. It can be that the water of one of the vessels B, C, $D \ldots$ was colored, or that the water of more than one was colored, even with different colors but that led finally to the color result in the water of vessel A. But as one can see from this example the "causes" are neither necessary nor sufficient conditions. On a higher level a free will decision can have many different causes in the sense of inclinations, motives, deliberations, reasons ... etc. which are neither necessary nor sufficient conditions.

15.3.3 Attacks on men's free will decision: *Neuronal Determinism*

Although it should be clear from today's physics that a mechanistic interpretation of all phenomena with the help of exclusively dynamical-deterministic laws (à la Laplace) is untenable, (recall sections 6.3.1 of *extreme positions* and 15.3.1, 15.3.2 above), several neuro-scientists and philosophers behave as if a great part of physics which developed since the 19th century did not exist. Here are some quotations of such extreme views:

> "For me it is not understandable that somebody doing empirical science could believe that free non-determined action is conceivable"[9]

> "For every psychological effect ... there exists a set of causes, or antecedent conditions, that uniquely lead to that effect."[10]

> "The process of evaluation [leading to a decision] is based ... on neuronal processes and therefore follows deterministic laws of nature."[11]

> "There is no doubt that also higher-level processes in our brain which are responsible for our behavior are deterministic."[12]

8 Cf. Prigogine (1977) II, 1. For further wrong assumptions connected with Laplace's determinism cf. Falkenburg (2012).
9 Prinz (2004) p. 22
10 Bargh and Ferguson (2000) p.925
11 Singer (2004) p. 52
12 Roth (2001) p. 447

> "The initiation of the freely voluntary act appears to begin in the brain unconsciously, well before the person consciously knows he wants to act!"[13]

A short comment to these quotations is as follows:

(1) The claim of Prinz seems to say: In the domain of empirical sciences there are only determined events, processes or actions describable by dynamical-deterministic laws and non-determined events, processes or actions are not even conceivable. If this is the claim of Prinz then such a claim is of course rather ridiculous and it only shows that Prinz missed one and a half century of physics and a century of chemistry, biology and cosmology. All the phenomena of thermodynamics, radiation, friction, diffusion, osmosis, electric transport, of measurement in quantum mechanics, of the formation and destruction of stars and galaxies ... etc. do not obey dynamical-deterministic laws but are describable successfully by statistical laws. All these phenomena are therefore counterexamples to Prinz's claim. Moreover confusion (1), (2) and (4) may be also assumed by Prinz's claim.

(2) The quotation of Bargh and Ferguson claims a determinism à la Laplace for psychological events (antecedent conditions lead uniquely to the effect – provided the existence of dynamical deterministic laws which these authors forgot to mention). It is therefore a claim included in that of Prinz, now restricted to psychological events. More accurately it says that a psychological event is an effect uniquely determined by earlier events; more generally according to Minkowski space time and Special Relativity the events in the past light cone determine uniquely the effect at present. But there is not a single differential equation describing a trajectory which would lead to a unique solution for a psychological event. Such claims are therefore scientifically useless. They seem to be motivated by a non-scientific background consisting of a mechanistic-deterministic world-view. And the consequences of such a view are not compatible with the results of contemporary physics (recall the *extreme positions* of ch. 6 and the confusions of section 15.3.2 above).

(3) The quotations of Singer and Roth claim also determinism but now for neuronal and for brain processes. The comment to that is the same as the comments given to Prinz and Bargh and Ferguson. Moreover it is not clear what Singer understands by "deterministic law of nature". If we take the usual understanding then what is meant are dynamical laws. Then the claim seems to be that the cellular level or neuron level (order of magnitude $\approx 10^{-4}m$) of

---

13 Libet (2002) p. 555

(the human) nervous system is governed by dynamical laws (may be even in the sense of Laplace). Such a claim is untenable for several reasons:

(a) It forgets that information and evaluation processes by nervous systems occur at least at seven levels of complexity simultaneously. And the lowest quantum mechanical level is certainly not just governed by dynamical laws.

(b) In this sense it neglects the lower level of ionic channels and synapses (order of magnitude $\approx 10^{-7}m$) concerning which "any recording method will show that synapses in the central nervous system are noisy and stochastic."[14]

(c) The claim can hardly be true even just for the cellular level: All processes which use the semipermeable membrans of the cell like osmosis, diffusion and metabolism obey statistical laws (not dynamical laws). The same holds for electric transport of information in axons and dendrites. In conclusion we may say that the claims that only dynamical-deterministic laws viz. Classical Physics (or Classical Mechanics à la Laplace) represent the real structure of neuronal processes is completely untenable: Eccles (1990), Squires (1988) and Stapp (1993) and Stapp (1991) gave several reasons for the fact that conscious processes of the brain would be hardly explainable if the brain would work on the basis of Classical Physics.

(4) Libet found out that there is a so-called "readiness-potential" about 550 ms before the movement of an arm or a finger while the conscious voluntary act (to move the arms or finger) appears only about 200 ms before moving. From this fact some concluded that "not the conscious voluntary act decided, but the brain."[15]
As Walter points out correctly Libet's results are by far not sufficient to derive such a conclusion.[16]

From a logical point of view it can be easily seen that such "conclusions" are of course not valid logical consequences from the facts Libet found out but just logical fallacies. Libet himself however is much more modest and critical. On the one hand he underlines the role of the unconscious for the preparation and initiation of conscious and voluntary actions, on the other hand he first

14 de Schutter (2001) p. 387
15 Roth (2004) p. 73
16 Cf. Walter (2009) p. 15ff

acknowledges a kind of correcting function, which he calls Veto-function of the human will with which an action can be completed or suppressed and hindered; and secondly a kind of controlling or steering function over psychic mechanisms. In this sense free will is not an illusion.[17]

What is missing in most of these discussions is the point that movements of a finger are voluntary acts on a rather primitive level. Much better examples for free will decisions are some of the traditional and perennial examples, like that of Plato: the decision of the steersman to navigate the ship into a different direction.

(5) Haldane's Argument
That *neuronal determinism* leads to absurdity can be shown by Haldane's argument and by a revised form of it. Haldane's argument was used by Haldane to refute materialism and materialistic determinism:

> "If materialism is true, it seems to me that we cannot know that it is true. If my opinions are the result of the chemical processes going on in my brain, they are determined by the laws of chemistry, not of logic."[18]

As Popper points out this argument has a long history. He quotes Epicurus:

> "He who says that all things happen of necessity cannot criticize another who says that not all things happen of necessity. For he has to admit that his saying also happened of necessity."[19]

Since the laws of physics and chemistry need not be in conflict with the laws of logic, as it is evident from a correct working computer, the second part of Haldane's argument has to be revised. This was pointed out by Popper. The main point is that if there is a mistake – brains and also computers make mistakes – one needs standards *outside* or in some sense independent of the brain or computer to correct them:

> "Standards of validity, which are *not* embodied or incarnated in World 1[=materialistic world] objects"[20].

An argument similar to that of Haldane was used already by Thomas Aquinas:

---

17 Cf. Libet (2005) p. 183 and 197. See also Walter (2009) p. 16f. For further critical discussion see Bennett and Hacker (2003) p. 228 ff. and Falkenburg (2012).
18 Haldane (1937) p. 157 and Haldane (1930) p. 209
19 Epicurus, Aphorism 40 of the Vatican Collection.
20 Popper and Eccles (1985) p. 77

> "For it is clear that by means of the intellect man can have knowledge of all corporeal things. Now whatever knows certain things cannot have any of them in its own nature... if the intellectual principle contained the nature of a body it would be unable to know all bodies."[21]

All these types of arguments of Haldane, Epicurus, Popper and Thomas Aquinas are concerned with a special type of incompleteness which is also involved in the problem of the so-called "Internal Observer" of a quantum mechanical (or more generally: physical) system. To include the measuring apparatus or the observer or the intelligent knower into the physical system – as a part which can be described solely by properties of the system – implies that even the intelligent knower can have only incomplete knowledge of the system. This has been elaborated in detail in section 13.4.4 (3) above and should not be repeated here.

15.3.4 Degrees of freedom on different levels

As has been mentioned already in section 15.3.3 the human brain is a complex multi-level system. It is generally assumed that information processing by nervous system occurs at seven levels of complexity simultaneously.[22]

(1) *Molecular processes*
They occur on the scale $10^{-10}m$ and refer to chemical interactions among thousands of proteins. Many of them are specific to neurons and neuronal processes. Concerning this level the following results about quantum mechanics are important:

(a) Quantum Mechanics is only partially a dynamical deterministic theory and partially a statistical one with degrees of freedom for the single case. The simplest situation is given if the physical system S – an atom, a nucleus or an electron – is prepared in a pure state given by a vector ψ. Generally this state is time dependent and the dynamical law that describes the temporal development of this state $\psi(t)$ is given by the Schrödinger equation. At first sight one could get therefore the impression that quantum mechanics is a deterministic theory in the same sense as classical mechanics. There is however a most important difference.

21 Aquinas (1981) I, 75,2
22 Cf. de Schutter (2001) p. 381 and Falkenburg (2012).

The state $\psi(t)$ represents the set Σ_t of jointly measurable properties that at time t pertain to the system and this set Σ_t of "objective" properties is always smaller than the set Σ of all possible properties. Moreover since $\psi(t)$ is time dependent so is Σ_t and this means that the dynamical law may become useless if at a later time $t_1 > t$ the respective observable for t is no longer an objective property.[23] If a certain property P is not objective w.r.t. system S then nothing can be said about whether P pertains to S or not. However irrespective of the correctness of this statement, the property P can be "measured". In such a measurement process we cannot determine the result in the single case but we can predict its probability. This strictly reduced kind of causality was called *statistical causality* by Pauli.[24] We find therefore that in quantum mechanics there are two restrictions of the concept of dynamical deterministic causality. Either we have the incomplete causality of the Schrödinger dynamics, which is applicable only for a few time frames, or we consider dynamical measurement processes and find a causality that is only statistically applicable and not relevant in a single case. As to the general properties of the causality relation we find that the causality represented by the dynamical law of the Schrödinger equation is continuous and the cause is earlier than the effect. By contrast, statistical causality is not continuous, but also here the cause is earlier than the effect.

(b) Concerning degrees of freedom on the quantum level an important result has been proved by Conway and Kochen:

> "If the experimenter can freely choose the directions in which to orient his apparatus in a certain measurement, then the particles response (to be pedantic – the universe's response near the particle) is not determined by the entire previous history of the universe."[25]

As axioms for the proof they use three axioms (called SPIN, TWIN and MIN) about $spin_1$ particles. The above result is based on the following theorem which is called "strong free will theorem" by Conway and Kochen:

> "The axioms SPIN, TWIN and MIN imply that the response of a $spin_1$ particle to a triple experiment is free – that is to say, is not a function of properties of that part

23 Cf. Mittelstaedt and Weingartner (2005) p. 246 ff
24 Cf. Laurikainen (1988) p. 32f
25 Conway and Kochen (2009) p. 226. Cf. also Reznikoff (2010)

of the universe that is earlier than this response with respect to any given inertial frame."[26]

Independently of how one wants to interpret this result, what it shows unambiguously once more (i.e. in addition to a) above) is that on the molecular level – i.e. the lowest level of information processing by nervous systems – not everything obeys dynamical deterministic laws, but rather statistical laws with degrees of freedom for the singular case:

> "At many levels the brain employs mechanisms which are stochastic at the microscopic scale."[27]

This is so because molecular structures can only be represented correctly within the frame of quantum mechanics:

> "What is the role of quantum mechanics in biology? Quantum mechanics provides the basis of chemistry in two fundamental aspects: (i) molecular structures can only be understood within the frame of quantum mechanics and (ii) the empirically established chemical reaction kinetics found its deeper explanations in quantum mechanical collision theory."[28]

Although Schuster is quite critical by defending that free will in the sense of rational choice and conscious self-control is something completely different from the free will according to the quantum mechanical "free will theorem", he stresses the following points of importance for phenomena in biology:

> "Quantum mechanics … is invisibly incorporated into biological models as it is in the conventional approach to chemical reactions. There are exceptions where direct applications of quantum physics are indispensable for understanding phenomena in biology, the three most important of them are: (i) interaction of electromagnetic radiation with matter as it occurs, for example, in photosynthesis or in vision, (ii) electron transport, for example, in the redox chain, and (iii) proton transfer through tunnelling."[29]

In a similar sense Eccles stresses the fact that from identical initial conditions in identical dynamical situations different final states may result. This shows the reality of degrees of freedom or of real branching, specifically w.r.t. the exocytose where the probability of its occurrence can be

26 Conway and Kochen (2009) p. 228
27 Cf. de Schutter (2001) p. 386 and below.
28 P. Schuster (2009) p. 9
29 P. Schuster (2009) p. 9

increased by mental intention.[30]

In conclusion, we may say that the degrees of freedom on the molecular level must certainly be necessary conditions for the higher level activities of the brain and for the mental processes, but they are certainly not sufficient conditions for these processes.

(2) *Level of channels and synapses on the scale* $10^{-7}m$

Channels are membrane structures. They allow for the passage of ions through membranes, usually cell membranes. Ionic channels are voltage-gated. And it is generally known that electric transport does not obey deterministic laws, but statistical laws which allow degrees of freedom for the singular cases:

> "At many levels the brain employs mechanisms which are stochastic at the microscopic scale. For example active properties are based on the aggregate behavior of thousands of stochastically gated voltage-dependent ion channels ... While one needs specific recording methods to study the stochasticity of ionic channels, any recording method will show that synapses in the central nervous system are noisy and stochastic. Their probability of transmission can be as low as 10% and spontaneous release (i.e. not caused by a spike in the presynaptic neuron) is so frequent that it is often used to study synaptic properties."[31]

The fact of branching with a huge number of possible alternatives is stressed by the following quotation:

> "The probability for an action-potential pulse to release a vesicle at a cortical synapse appears to be about 50%. If, in some small time window (say a fraction of a millisecond), N synapses receive action-potential pulses then there will be 2^N *alternative* possible configurations of vesicle releases, each with a roughly equal probability."[32]

Moreover passage through membranes and transport of neurotransmitter molecules involve processes of diffusion and osmosis which are typical for obeying statistical laws.

(3) *Cellular or neuron level on the scale* $10^{-4}m$

The element of nervous systems is the neuron. It receives input on its dendrite and may generate a spike transmitted to other neurons via its axon. Recent electrophysiological investigations have shown that dendrites are rather active which restricts and corrects the so-called *passive cable theory* and its predictions concerning synaptic attenuation over distance. However both, active

---

30 Eccles (1994) ch. 9.5. This chapter contains also a discussion of Libet's experiments.

31 de Schutter (2001) p. 386f.

32 Stapp (1993) p. 152

and passive descriptions of the dendrite are often based on too simplified one dimensional assumptions like the one that the current, inside the dendrite, flows only along its main axis. This neglects the effect of electrical fields on diffusion of charged ions; moreover the interactions of currents in neighborhood dendrites across extracellular space require three dimensional investigations. But diffusion, electric transport and interaction through membranes and across extracellular space cannot be described sufficiently by dynamical deterministic laws. Real branching is essential there. In conclusion we may say that these facts support once more what has been said already in section 15.3.3: It is impossible that only dynamical deterministic laws can represent the real structure of neuronal processes. The more general reason for that is that these processes are very specific *processes of becoming* in the sense of Prigogine.[33] And such processes involve a change of entropy and require statistical laws in an essential sense: since all these neuronal and cellular processes are irreversible they are asymmetric w.r.t. time.[34]

These facts open degrees of freedom and possibilities of branching for the real neuronal processes. The above considerations show already that there is no exclusive determinism on the fundamental levels of the human brain which could be responsible for a strict deterministic behavior of "free will decisions". As everywhere in reality: the human brain also represents a cooperation of dynamical and statistical laws.

15.3.5 Definition of *free will* and of *free will decision*

15.3.5.1 Presuppositions of free will

A first consideration concerning *free will* shows that any kind of freedom or *being free* has to be relativized to a specific domain. It does not make sense to claim or require freedom w.r.t. every domain. Thus I am free to go shopping or to go to a concert or to make a trip to the mountains. But I am not free to dive 20 m, or I am not free to memorize a telephone book.

33 Cf. Prigogine (1977) chs. VI and IX. Cf. section 5.3.4 above.

34 Observe that dynamical-deterministic laws are time-reversible symmetric. Cf. Weingartner (2008c)

We start with two rough concepts of being free physically (FP) and being free psychically (FPs), where $FP(x,d)$, $FPs(x,d)$ say that person x is physically free (psychically free) concerning the domain or range d.

Df 15.10. $FP(x,d)$ iff there is no serious restriction (as for example illness) for x in the range d of bodily capacity and actual performance.

Df 15.11. $FPs(x,d)$ iff there is no serious restriction (as for example mental illness) for x in the range d of psychic (mental) capacity and actual performance.

For the definition of *free will* we have to presuppose, certainly that the respective person is psychically or mentally free. To generally require that the person is also physically free seems to be too strong, since we have to accept that also physically handicapped people can have free will if they are psychically (mentally) free. Using definitions Df 15.10,Df 15.11 we may define physical and psychical compulsion on person x by distinguishing external and internal physical and psychical compulsion. We say that person x is under external, internal physical compulsion in the domain d – $CPe(x,d)$, $CPi(x,d)$ – and person x is under external, internal psychic compulsion in the domain d – $Cpse(x,d)$, $CPsi(x,d)$, and we define these notions as follows:

Df 15.12. $CPe(x,d)$ iff CPe is a restriction or constraint of the physical (bodily) capacity or of the respective actual performance of x in d, caused by the environment of x and contrary to the inclination of x in d.

Examples: extreme weather conditions, handcuffs, surprise attack, etc.

Df 15.13. $CPi(x,d)$ iff CPi is a restriction or constraint of the physical (bodily) capacity or of the respective actual performance of x in d, caused by bodily defects of x and contrary to the inclination of x in d.

Examples: Physically handicapped people, injured people, physical illness, etc.

Df 15.14. $Cpse(x,d)$ iff $Cpse$ is a restriction or constraint of the psychic (mental) capacity or of the respective actual performance of x in d, caused by the environment of x and contrary to the inclination of x in d.

Examples: the applications of drugs for weakening political prisoners, any hindrance (from outside) contrary to the (inclination of the) will of the respective person, etc.

Df 15.15. $CPsi(x, d)$ iff $CPsi$ is a restriction or constraint of the psychic (mental) capacity or of the respective actual performance of x in d, caused by mental defects of x and contrary to the inclination of x in d.

Examples: compulsive act, compulsive psychosis, compulsive neurosis, obsession, obsessive ideas, etc.

15.3.5.2 Definition of 'free will'

Concerning the definition of *free will* we shall relativize this concept further to states of affairs belonging to some domain d. This seems reasonable since we want to say (among other things) that a person x can will and can realize a certain state of affairs p ($xCanWp$, $xCanRealize\ p$) such that p lies in the domain d. Therefore we shall define the complex concept: *person x is free or has free will w.r.t. the state of affairs p in the domain d.*

Df 15.16. $FW(x, p, d)$ iff the following conditions are satisfied:

(1)

(1a) $FPs(x, d)$

(1b) Not: $CPse(x, d)$ and not: $CPsi(x, d)$

(2)

(2a) $xCanWp$

(2b) Both $xCanW\neg p$ and $xCan\neg Wp$ hold, provided that the state of affairs p is not the realization of:

(i) a basic good (value) (cf. Df 7.4) or

(ii) the state of ultimate happiness

(3) If the state of affairs p is a goal for x then: $xCanWp$ and $xCanRealize\ p$

(4) If p is a goal for x and if there are means $q_1 \ldots q_n$ which support the realization of p, then for some q_i: $xCanWq_i$ and $xCanRealize\ q_i$

(5) If p is forbidden or if p is permitted (or obligatory) then:
$xCanWp$ and $xCanRealize\ p$

(6) If xWp and $xRealizes\ p$, then x causes that p (is the case) and x knows that x causes that p

(7) The (complex) state of affairs (xWp and $xRealizes\ p$) at t is not a definite function of an earlier state of affairs at $t < t_o$

Commentary on definition Df 15.16:

1. Domain of d
   The domain of d is here understood as a domain of states of affairs which satisfy the following restrictions:
   (i) it is consistent
   (ii) it is outside the domain of logic and of mathematics
   (iii) it is outside the domain of laws of nature, but it is consistent with this domain
   (iv) it is outside the domain of fundamental constants of nature, but it is consistent with this domain.

2. Conditions on 'x can will that p' ('$xCanWp$')
   The expression '$xCanWp$'('x can will that p is the case') is understood in the sense that it satisfies the following conditions:
   (i) p belongs to the restricted domain of d
   (ii) p is consistent
   (iii) p is consistent with everything that x necessarily wills

   Concerning (ii) we should remark that it is impossible to will a contradictory state of affairs. This is so at least if the contradiction is obvious, evident or apparent. Thus I cannot will both to study and not to study. However there are situations where the inconsistency is hidden. In such a case it is possible that someone wills that p and wills that q without knowing that from q it logically follows that $non\text{-}p$. But as soon as this consequence is known to him he cannot will anymore both p and q. For such cases then we could weaken condition (ii) to: p is apparently consistent.

   Concerning (iii) it is important to realize that what someone *can will* has to be consistent (compatible) with what he necessarily wills. For example if p

is the state of realization of a basic good (survival, health) then, the human will is necessarily inclined to it (cf. Df 7.2–Df 7.4). Thus the will of person x is necessarily inclined to the survival of x and to the health of x. Since there is a necessary inclination we cannot speak of *free will* w.r.t. basic goods (cf. (i) of Df 15.16 above). And since the necessary inclination is strong it follows that in most cases humans will strive for the realization of basic goods. This fact is a statistical generality or in other words: that humans strive for the realization of basic goods obeys a statistical law. However since statistical laws rule large ensembles (in this case: the majority of humans) they allow degrees of freedom for the individual case (for single persons). Thus there may be some exceptions, and in fact there are: hunger-strikes, death from starvation, martyrdom, etc. In general to renounce of basic goods in order to achieve a higher or ultimate good; or to accept basic evil (cf. Df 7.5) in order to achieve a higher or ultimate good. Sometimes these exceptional cases are connected with criminal motives and criminal actions as in the case of September 11, or cases of religious fanaticism.

But what is the higher or ultimate good for which the basic goods are sacrificed or the basic evils are put up with? According to Aristotle and several medieval scholars, like Thomas Aquinas, it is a kind of ultimate good or ultimate happiness. According to them the underlying principle is that every human action is done for some good purpose, which is superior and ultimate beyond all sacrificed goods and all evils put up with, in order to achieve this last good. This ultimate good they called *happiness*. And to this the human will is necessarily inclined such that there is no free will concerning this kind of ultimate happiness. Consequently it is not possible that $xCanW\neg p$ or that $xCan\neg Wp$ if p is the state of affairs of ultimate happiness. The exceptions discussed above concerning basic goods are no more applicable concerning ultimate happiness. Whereas in the first case basic goods can be renounced in order to achieve a higher or ultimate good, the goal of ultimate happiness cannot be renounced in order to achieve a still higher good since there is none. This explains the clause (ii) as an alternative to (i) in (2b) of Df 15.16: For most cases clause (i) suffices, because basic values are necessarily willed. In the exceptional cases it can be that someone does not will and does not reach some basic value, but in this case he puts up with this basic evil in order to achieve an ultimate good, i.e. ultimate happiness. In this sense, someone who commits suicide is also not objectionable for although suicide means sacrificing the basic good of being alive, he thinks that to end his bad life will make him 'happier' than to continue living it.[35]

3. Conditions (3)–(7)
   Condition (3) says that x can will and can realize some state of affairs p which is a goal for x. Under these states of affairs there might be some basic goods. Even if the will of x is necessarily inclined to these and x does not have *free will* concerning basic goods x certainly can will them and can realize them.

   However, there are many other goods that are goals for x, concerning which, x has free will. Since x can choose this goal or that goal.

   The fact that x experiences with certainty that x can choose with respect to conditions (3), (4) and (5) is a natural support of the existence of free choice and not a sign for suspicion. Since the main hindrances like global determinism and the main confusions have been removed in sections 15.3.1–15.3.4, the claim that free will and free choice is an illusion is similar to claims of the extreme skeptic or the extreme idealist, for example, "there is no reliable sense perception", "there is no genuine knowledge", "there is no reliable reflection or introspection" or "the world (including myself) is my dream".

   First, the last three extreme positions have been refuted already by Augustine with his "fallor ergo sum" (I am deceived (mistaken), therefore I am) and by Descartes with his "cogito ergo sum" (I think, therefore I am). Secondly, as Swinburne says, it is a mark of rationality to believe that things are as they seem to be, in the absence of counter- evidence.[36] And those hindrances which have been claimed as counter-evidence have been removed already in sections 15.3.1–15.3.4. Thirdly, such views of skepticism or idealism have the following properties in common which shows their absurdity:

   a) They replace or confuse the exceptions with (by) the rule, i.e. the few cases with most of the cases. And they don't realize that the exceptional cases of error can be controlled to a considerable degree. Though it is known that there is error in thinking and that there is sense illusion and that there are dreams, today's science, technology and medicine is built on neither of them.

---

35 The improvement of an earlier version of this section (2) is due to critical remarks by Sivlia Haring. Cf. Weingartner and Haring (2014).

36 Swinburne (1998) p. 105

b) They deny and refuse the most accessible, the obvious and the matter of course.

c) They are presupposing implicitly that man is constructed in such a bad way that he has always to deny and refuse that which is to him most obvious and most easily accessible by experience.

The weakness of such a position is expressed very well by Pascal in his Pensées:

> "Il faut savoir douter où il faut, assurer où il faut, en se soumettant où il faut. Qui ne fait ainsi n'entend pas la force de la raison. Il y a qui faillent contre ces trois principles, ou en assurant tout comme démonstratif, manque de se connaître en démonstration, ou en doutant de tout, manque de savoir où il faut se soumettre, ou en se soumettant en tout, manque de savoir où il faut juger."[37]

Condition (4) says that x *has free will concerning the means* which support the realization of a goal. To 'support' can be interpreted as being a sufficient condition for reaching a goal or as being a necessary condition for reaching a goal. These are two strong senses of 'support'. But a mean for a goal might be neither necessary nor sufficient, but still supporting the realization of the goal in a weaker sense.

Condition (5) says that x can will and that x can realize forbidden or permitted and obligatory actions; or in other words: concerning morally bad or good actions (including neutral actions) x can will them and bring them about. What is forbidden or permitted or obligatory may be ruled in this way by

(i) the promulgated ethical (moral) standards of some human society

(ii) the *Human Rights* which are based on an international agreement of many societies w.r.t.ethical (moral) standards

(iii) the rules of God (like the Ten Commandments)

(iv) a combination of these three.

37 Pascal (1963) §268 (170): One needs to doubt, where necessary, to make sure where necessary, to submit where necessary. Who does not do so neglects the force of reason. There are some who offend against these three principles: who claim that everything is provable, because they do not understand what a proof is – or doubt everything, because they don't know where it is necessary to submit – or submit to everything, because they don't know where it is necessary to judge (author's translation).

Condition (6) says: if the person x wills that p is the case and realizes p in the sense that x acts in such a way as to bring about that p is the case, then x causes p and x knows that x causes that p is the case. This is important since it implies the responsibility of the person's actions in connection with the evidence, viz. his (her) knowledge, that the decision was in the person's power and that he (she) caused the action. This will become more explicit from the next definition which is concerned with committing a free will decision.

Condition (7) says that there is no dynamical–deterministic law which leads from some earlier state of affairs at $t < t_o$ to the later state of affairs (xWp and $xRealizes\ p$) at t_o. In other words an action of free will described by "x wills that p and x realizes that p" is not determined by earlier events and dynamical laws. However there may be statistical laws which allow degrees of freedom for particular cases since conditions D1 and D2 are not satisfied for statistical laws as S1 and S2 say (recall ch. 4).

15.3.5.3 Definition of 'free will decision'

The following definition concerns a *free will decision*. We say that a person x is committing a *free will decision* represented by the state of affairs p within the domain d abbreviated as $FWD(x, p, d)$ iff the conditions listed in Df 15.17 are satisfied:

Df 15.17. $FWD(x, p, d)$ iff

(1) $FW(x, p, d)$

(2) x uses deliberation and planning with the help of reason. This includes:

   (i) Council about goals

   (ii) Council about the means for reaching the respective goal

   (iii) Council about moral goodness or badness of means and goals

(3) x knows that x has responsibility for *his (her)* actions and decisions; x knows that – especially in connection with the evidence x has about the fact that the decision was in *his (her)* power – that it was *he (she)* who caused the action.

15.3.6 Compatibility of nature's order and free will

In order to show the compatibility of nature's order with free will, we have to look at the different types of order which have been defined in chs. 5 and 7. Ord_1 in the sense of structure (Df 5.3) and Ord_2 in the sense of structure plus special arithmetical and geometrical relations (Df 5.5) cannot be incompatible with free will. This can be seen easily from some realizations of nature: Clouds or dunes with special patterns, snowflakes, living cells, neurons and synapses are realizations of Ord_1 and Ord_2. All the respective relations of the parts of these systems have degrees of freedom not only at the atomic level – this is established by Quantum mechanics – but also on higher levels – this is manifest from chemical bindings. Since there is no overall determinism, there are some statistical laws on every level, permitting degrees of freedom for the individual instances of the respective relations (linkage, internal, external cf. Df 5.3). If we raise to Ord_3 (Df 5.7) we see no essential difference. On the contrary, the conditions (iii, open system) and (iv, low entropy) are unambiguous signs that statistical laws are involved. And this implies degrees of freedom for the individual case. Since it was shown in ch. 7 that living systems possess all three types of order (Ord_1, Ord_2, Ord_3) the degrees of freedom hold also for all living systems. Moreover it was shown in section 15.3.4 that there are degrees of freedom on all different levels of the human brain.

Concerning teleological order and goals it has to be remembered first that according to definitions Df 5.15 and Df 7.8 goals are compatible with laws of nature and with constants of nature. Thus nature's order as it is governed by laws of nature and by constants of nature cannot be incompatible with any teleological order incorporated in nature.

However let us ask whether those goals and means which may be chosen by free will (cf. Df 15.16, (3) and (5)) can be incompatible with nature's order. We have to consider three possibilities:

(1) The choice is in accordance with nature's order. This is the case, for example, if somebody chooses his (her) profession in accordance with his (her) strong interest and abilities. Then the strong interests and the abilities are the means that support the achievement of the goal.

(2) The choice is permitted by nature's order. This is the case if somebody chooses a job in such a way that his (her) abilities and interests allow him (her) to perform the job in an acceptable way, although there is no strong support from his (her) abilities and interests for this job.

(3) The choice is against nature's order. This can be so in two ways: (a) First in the sense that the action cannot be performed or the goal cannot be reached. As for example if somebody wants to jump three meters high. (b) Secondly in the sense that the action can be performed but with bad consequences. For example if somebody chooses a job for which he (she) is completely unable and because of bad experience gives up the job later.

Considering the three cases we can say that the only case where there *seems* to be an incompatibility between nature's order and free will is case (3)(a). But in fact there is no conflict since in the case of choosing a goal which cannot be realized according to laws of nature, there is no free will (condition (3) of definition Df 15.16 is not satisfied).

15.3.7 Compatibility of providence and free will

In order to show the compatibility of providence with free will we have to look at the definition Df 10.1 of providence in section 10.3.1 and at the definition Df 15.16 of free will in section 15.3.5. More accurately we shall go through the different necessary conditions which are part of the *definientia* of these definitions.

Before we do that we have to make a short comment on the two definitions Df 15.10 and Df 15.11 concerning being free physically and psychically: the definientia state two facts: that there is no serious restriction in the domain of bodily capacity and that there is no serious restriction in the domain of mental (psychic) capacity. If these states of affairs obtain, the respective person is free physically and psychically. These facts are complemented by the condition that the respective person is not under compulsion, at least not under (external or internal) psychic compulsion (cf. Df 15.12–Df 15.15). To be free physically or psychically is, however, not a case of free will or of a free will decision. The second (being psychically or mentally free) is a presupposition of free will and free will decision.

Concerning providence there cannot be any incompatibility with the facts (states of affairs) of being physically or psychically free. Since according to chapter 9 everything what coexists (with the exception of contradictory thoughts) is compatible. And any two facts (where the one concerns a person being physically or mentally free and the other concerns facts about God's plan) are compatible because they are represented by true propositions, and true propositions cannot be incompatible. However the facts of being physically or psychically free might be considered also w.r.t. good and evil. Thus to be physically handicapped or being mentally ill can be called a serious evil for the respective person. And in most cases this kind of evil is not due to the suffering persons themselves. Therefore there seems to be a conflict with providence in so far providence is God's plan which directs things to their ends. This problem however will be dealt with in the next chapter 16 for two reasons: First, because this chapter is about free will and free will decision, but being physically or mentally free or handicapped is not a matter of free will or free will decision. Secondly, because chapter 16 deals explicitly with God's providence w.r.t. evil.

We shall now compare necessary conditions of God's providence with necessary conditions of free will.

15.3.7.1 God's knowledge and free will

According to Df 10.1 (c) God's providence about any state of affairs p implies God's knowledge about p (cf. ch. 11). Can this be in conflict with free will, or more accurately, with some of the necessary conditions of free will listed in the definiens of definition Df 15.16?

God's knowledge cannot be incompatible with conditions (1a)–(7). This can be seen as follows: All conditions (1a)–(7) state facts about human beings. Under the condition that God is the creator of the universe including human beings[38] we have to assume that he knows everything (which is the case) about his creation. Furthermore, this follows from perfect knowledge which we attribute to him. Perfect knowledge implies complete knowledge; that means that everything that is the case (that is true) is known by God.[39] More specifically God will know that humans have no free will concerning the state of ultimate happiness to which they all are inclined. They also have no free will concerning basic goods except in some exceptional situations where they accept the loss of basic goods for some ultimate or transcendent good. Similarly he will know that humans have free will w.r.t. goals and their respective means.

38 Observe that from this it does not follow that there is no evolution. As has been shown in ch. 13 creatures are contributors to the creation in the sense of being causal contributors to the evolution of the universe, because God is not all-causing and wills the cooperation of the creatures in the development of the world.

39 For God's knowledge see Weingartner (2008a).

One of the most important necessary conditions for free will is moral freedom, such that men can will and realize not only what is obligatory and what is permitted, but also what is forbidden. This is also underlined by all great religions: that men can will and act against the commandments and rules of God and that God knows that and permits that. There is also no conflict in this, that God knows everything that men knows, in this case particularly that men knows that he causes those actions concerning which he has free will. And finally God's knowledge is complete w.r.t. condition (7) as a necessary requisite for free will.

Finally, it was shown in sections 11.3.3 and 11.4.2 that God's knowledge of future contingent events including human free will decisions does not destroy the freedom of such (future) decisions. Therefore it is compatible with free will and with free will decisions.

Summarizing, we can say: If conditions (1a)–(7) are true statements about human free will and since it holds that everything that God knows is true, there cannot be any incompatibility between God's knowledge (as a necessary condition of God's providence) and free will.

15.3.7.2 Men's free will and God's will or permission

According to Df 10.1 (d) God's providence about any state of affairs p implies that God wills that p or God permits that p (cf. ch. 12). Concerning God's will (as a necessary condition of his providence) there could seem to be a conflict with men's free will. Because God's will is always fulfilled. But we know that men, because of their free will and free will decisions, do not always obey God's will as it is expressed in his Ten Commandments for example.

It has been shown in section 12.3.3 that this problem can be solved by a distinction: Since God does not force men in the domain where they have free will, one has to distinguish *willing that* p *is the case* from *willing that* p *should be the case*. And thus, if men's free will and his actions of free will are concerned, then God wills that men should (or ought to) obey his rules and in particular his 10 commandments. Therefore God's providence w.r.t. his will is not incompatible with men's free will.

Concerning God's permission (as a necessary condition of his providence) it is clear from section 12.3.5 that God permits chance and randomness. And from this it follows that he also permits the degrees of freedom underlying human free will and free will decisions. Therefore his providence concerning permission cannot be incompatible with free will and free will decisions.

15.3.7.3 Men's free will and the causation by God or by creatures

According to Df 10.1 (e) God's providence about any state of affairs p implies that God causes that p or creatures cause that p. Can this be in conflict with free will? Or more accurately: Can it be in conflict with some of the necessary conditions of free will listed in the definiens of definition Df 15.16 or with the respective presuppositions in definitions Df 15.10 and Df 15.11?

1. If we assume that actions of human free will come under God's providence and everything that comes under God's providence is either caused by God or caused by creatures (cf. ch. 13) then actions of human free will are caused either by God or by creatures. But then, it seems, there cannot be free will. Since there would be an incompatibility, first concerning the presuppositions for free will (cf. Df 15.10 andDf 15.11): If a human action is caused by God or by creatures then this means compulsion, either physical or psychical (cf. Df 15.12–Df 15.15). And if there is at least psychical compulsion there cannot be free will. Secondly, causation from outside (by God or by creatures) is incompatible with $FW(x, p, d)$ conditions (2) – (5) if God or some creature would cause that $non\text{-}p$ is the case. Thirdly, causation from outside could also violate condition (7) of Df 15.16, the validity of which is necessary for free will.

2. To solve this difficulty we have first to observe that an action of free will or a free will decision is not a non-causal process. On the contrary, the respective agent or person is aware or knows that he himself is the cause of his actions of willing and deciding; provided these actions of willing are not inclinations towards basic goods or towards ultimate happiness. Since w.r.t. those, men doesn't have free will.

3. Therefore there is no conflict with causation in general, but only with causation from outside in the sense of compulsion. Concerning the thesis of ch. 13 there need not be a conflict either. Because it says that everything that comes under God's providence (including actions of free will) are caused by God or by creatures. And since the agent or the person who performs an action of free will is a creature nothing hinders that this person causes this action. There would be an incompatibility only if another creature (person) B would cause the action of creature (person) A. There would also be an incompatibility if

some other living or non-living thing (more general: an earlier state) would be the sufficient cause for that action of willing and deciding (more general: for that later state). But this is ruled out by condition (7) of Df 15.16.

4. There could be another incompatibility if God would directly cause an action of free will or a free will decision; where "directly" means here: not by incorporating an earlier state as a cause, since this is forbidden by condition (7) of Df 15.16.

5. If God is almighty then it seems he could cancel or at least suspend for a short time men's property to perform actions of free will or free will decisions. But this would be incompatible with his giving this property to men. Is there a possibility that God could move men's will in such a way that

   (1) person x *has free will* or is *executing a free will decision* in the sense of Df 15.17 and

   (2) God's moving men's will would not contradict (1)? Thomas Aquinas thinks that there is. His main point is that God is able to move men's will from *inside* in such a way that man changes its inclination. In this case there is no compulsion from outside but the respective person directs his own will to another goal or makes another decision in such a way that definitions Df 15.16 and Df 15.17 are satisfied and specifically condition (6) of Df 15.16 is fulfilled:

   > "A thing moved by another is forced if moved against its proper inclination; but if it is moved by another giving to it the proper inclination, it is not forced; as when a heavy body is made to move downwards by that which produced it, then it is not forced. In the like manner God, while moving the will, does not force it, because He gives the will its own proper inclination."[40]

---

40 Aquinas (1981) I, 105, 5 and 1. The English Translation (by the Fathers of the English Dominican Province) translates the latin expressions "contra inclinationem propriam", "propriam inclinationem" as "natural inclination". This is wrong and misleading. Since Thomas Aquinas uses "natural" only in connection with belonging to the nature and essence. Although "natural" would be appropriate concerning the heavy body it is not appropriate in general, and not in particular as applied to free will. Since "natural inclination" concerning will would be restricted to natural or basic goods or to ultimate happiness, i.e. to those goods concerning which man has no free will but "inclination by nature". Therefore "propriam inclinationem" has to be translated as "proper inclination" as we did above.

15.3.7.4 Men's free will and the direction to some goal

According to Df 10.1 (f) God's providence about any state of affairs p implies that God directs p towards some goal or integrates p into a network of goals.

Concerning God's direction of some state of affairs p towards some goal, there could be a conflict if p is an action of free will w.r.t. goals (cf. Df 15.16 (3)).

(1) Observe first, that this goal could not be a basic good or a state of ultimate happiness, since concerning these goals man does not have free will and there is no hindrance that God's providence can direct men's will to such goals.

(2) Secondly, observe further, that a global goal or a network of goals can be reached or realized even if there is much freedom for the subordinated local goods. Thus a big river reaches the ocean, although the many branches of affluxes have lots of freedom for their directions (routes). Similarly a certain goal or a network of goals can be realized, despite the freedom for singular persons in choosing local goals. And some local goals can even be in the opposite direction of the global goal. As an example compare the master builder who has different workers, more or less gifted ones and even perhaps some saboteurs. As a clever master builder he will still reach his final (global) goal, the building of a house or hospital, for example, even with difficult delays and detours, if some of the local goals of the workers can be subordinated under the global goal or network of goals, even if the subordination is difficult. In a similar way God, by his providence, can reach global goals or networks of goals despite permitting freedom for local goals of cooperating or not cooperating creatures.

(3) Thirdly recall Aquinas's point that God may direct the will of a person from inside; i.e. not against its proper inclination but with its proper inclination towards a certain goal and in such a way that this action is still a free will action obeying the definition Df 15.16.

15.3.8 Conclusion

It has been shown in sections 15.3.7.1–15.3.7.4 that man's free will and free will decisions are compatible with the different components of God's providence concerning free will and free will decisions: with his knowledge of them (15.3.7.1) with his will or permission of them (15.3.7.2), with his or creatures' causation (15.3.7.3) and finally with his direction of human actions towards some goal or their integration into a network of goals (15.3.7.4).

15.3.9 Result of chapter 15

T 15.2. *There are several physical, chemical, biological or psychological systems which are deterministic (Df 15.1).*

T 15.3. *There are several physical, chemical, biological or psychological systems which are indeterministic. (Df 15.6)*

T 15.4. *Both determined and undetermined events and processes can occur in one and the same physical, chemical, biological or psychological system. Since most such systems are usually mixed and neither purely deterministic nor purely indeterministic.*

T 15.5. *Determinism, causality and predictability do not necessarily go together; see the confusions in 15.3.2.*

T 15.6. Neuronal Determinism *is untenable since:*

(i) *it neglects a great part of modern physics*

(ii) *it is inconsistent with the quantum mechanical basis of the molecular structure of the brain*

(iii) *it is incompatible with the interaction of electromagnetic radiation, with electron transport, with proton transfer through tunneling, all occurring in the brain, since none of them obey exclusively dynamical deterministic laws.*

T 15.7. *Free will of human persons presupposes that there is no serious restriction (for example illness) for the person – with the exception of being only bodily handicapped – in both his/her bodily capacity and actual performance and psychic (mental) capacity and actual performance.*

T 15.8. *There is* free will *of human persons in the sense of Df 15.16.*

T 15.9. *There is* free will decision *of human persons in the sense of Df 15.17.*

T 15.10. *Man's* free will *and* free will decision *are compatible with nature's order and God's providence and with the following components of the latter: with his knowledge, with his permission, with his or creatures' causation, with his integration of them into a network of goals.*

15.4 Answer to the Objections

15.4.1 (to 15.1.1)

As it is plain from chs. 4 to 8 nature's order is neither globally deterministic as Laplace thought nor globally indeterministic. It is correct that the domains of Classical Mechanics, Electrodynamics and Special Relativity obey dynamical-deterministic laws. But the domain of Thermodynamics and Statistical Mechanics, the huge domains of irreversible processes (or better: processes with extremely improbable recurrence) to which most processes of living organisms belong obey statistical-indeterministic laws like the law of entropy. Granted even that several subdomains of biological systems are describable by dynamical laws.[41] For the possibility of free will and for its compatibility with nature's order it is not necessary that nature's order is globally indeterministic. It suffices that there are huge domains, especially concerning living organisms and their behavior, which are governed by statistical laws.

15.4.2 (to 15.1.2)

The answer to this objection has been given in sections 15.3.3 and 15.3.4. The claims of some neuroscientists like Prinz, Singer and Roth seem to ignore half of physics and are inconsistent with the laws in microphysics to which the micro-level of the human brain belongs.

41 Cf. Nowak (2006).

15.4.3 (to 15.1.3)

The answer to this objection has been given already in section 11.3.3 (1) knowledge in general (and also God's knowledge in particular) cannot change the ontological status of a state of affairs (in this case: the contingency of a free will action). Thus knowledge alone (i.e. without will) does not cause. God causes with his will, but since he is not all-causing and has created men with the power of free will, he need not interfere in men's free will actions. If p represents the state of affairs of an action or decision of free will then God neither wills that p occurs nor wills that p does not occur, but permits p to occur.[42]

15.4.4 (to 15.1.4)

The answer to this question is clear from definition Df 15.16 condition (6) and from section 15.3.7.3: The person who performs the action or decision of free will causes that action and is aware and even knows that it is he (she) that causes it. Since this person is also a creature there is no conflict with the thesis of ch. 13 that whatever (including actions of free will) comes under God's providence is either caused by God or caused by creatures.

15.4.5 (to 15.1.5)

A short answer to the objection of 15.1.5 is this: From "it is necessary that God cares (with his providence) that p (a contingent action of free will) occurs" it does not follow that "p occurs necessarily". In order to give an accurate and detailed answer we have to put the argument into symbolic form: The first premise says that there are contingent events or states of affairs (Δp). The third premise is the definition of contingency (which we find already in Aristotle as the more complete one of his two definitions). The fourth premise is just an instance or application of the definition of contingency: If it is contingent that God cares (by his providence) that p occurs ($\Delta gCPp$) then it is possible that he cares that p ($\Diamond gCPg$) and possible that he does not care that p ($\Diamond \neg gCPp$). The further two premises are that then his providence is undecided and consequently imperfect. By denying God's

42 For further details to this problem see sections 11.3.3, 11.4.1, 11.4.2 above and Weingartner (2008a) chs.10 and 11.

imperfectness the consequent part of the third premise is negated (by modus tollens) which results in the disjunction: either it is impossible that God cares about p or it is necessary. In symbolic form the argument is this:

1. $(\exists p)\Delta p$ premise
2. Δp Existential instantiation
3. $\Delta p \leftrightarrow \Diamond p \wedge \Diamond\neg p$ definition
4. $\Delta(gCPp) \leftrightarrow (\Diamond(gCPp) \wedge \Diamond\neg(gCPp))$ instantiation 3.
5. $\Delta(gCPp) \rightarrow (\Diamond(gCPp) \wedge \Diamond\neg(gCPp))$ from 4.
6. $(\Diamond(gCPp) \wedge \Diamond\neg(gCPp)) \rightarrow$ God's providence is undecided premise
7. God's providence is undecided $\rightarrow$ God's providence is imperfect premise
8. Not: God's providence is imperfect premise
9. Not: God's providence is undecided from 7., 8.
10. $\neg(\Diamond(gCPg) \wedge \Diamond\neg(gCPp))$ from 6., 9.
11. $\neg\Diamond(gCPp) \vee \Box(gCPp)$ from 10.
12. $\Diamond(gCPp)$ established in chapter 1 together with chs. 4, 5 and 7
13. $\Box(gCPp)$

It can be easily seen that this argument (in symbolic form) is valid, and also that the premises are acceptable. The mistake occurs only at the end of the argument in 15.1.5. It can be grasped better now: from $\Box(gCPp)$ it does not follow that $\Box p$. That means that although God's care by providence for a contingent event is necessary, it does not follow from that, that the event is necessary or occurs necessarily. Moreover it is already clear from chs. 12 and 13 that God's care by providence that p neither means that God wills that p nor that God causes that p. Since concerning actions of free will he permits that p and allows and entrusts creatures to cause that p. And in this case the very person who performs the action of free will is the cause for the obtaining of p.

15.4.6 (to 15.1.6)

Inwagen's problem has two components. The first is the claim that chance or chance-like events cannot be incorporated into a plan (particularly into God's providence) since a plan implies order and purpose (goal). That this first claim is wrong has been already shown in ch. 9 and particularly in section 9.4.5.

The second component of Inwagen's problem depends on a confusion concerning two different meanings of the expression "God's plan". It has been shown in section 10.4.2 how this problem can be solved: If God's providence and God's plan (as a part of it) is interpreted according to section 10.3.1 (definition Df 10.1) then also indeterministic states of affairs, like human free will decisions, can be incorporated into God's plan. Inwagen's problem comes up when he interprets (implicitly or in a hidden way) God's plan concerning an event e as God willing the occurrence of e or God causing the event e. However, this is a mistake: God's plan $\neq$ God's will as has been shown in chs. 12 and 13.

16 Whether God's providence is compatible with evil

16.1 Arguments Contra

16.1.1 First argument

Providence is the plan which leads things to their ends and goals. According to definitions Df 5.15 and Df 7.8, an end or goal is a highest value or a highest good. A highest value or highest good cannot be an evil.

Therefore: Providence is not compatible with evil.

16.1.2 Second argument

Providence guides things to some good goal. But some goals seem to be evils. For example, if an animal has the goal to kill another, then this is evil for the other and is not a good goal.

Therefore: Goals which are evil are not compatible with providence.

16.1.3 Third argument

According to ch. 10, everything that happens comes under God's providence. Since great evils like earthquakes and other natural disasters happen, they seem to come under God's providence also. But such evils cannot be the good goals or ends of God's providence.

Therefore: Providence is not compatible with evil.

16.1.4 Fourth argument

Providence guides things to some goal. Every goal is desired at least by something or somebody. Evil is not desired by anything or anybody.

Therefore: Providence is not compatible with evil.

16.1.5 Fifth argument

If an event belongs to God's providence, then God takes care of it. But if an event is an evil, then it seems that God does not take care of it. Therefore: An event which is an evil does not seem to belong to God's providence.

Thus evil does not seem compatible with God's providence.

16.1.6 Sixth argument

According to ch. 12 it holds that everything that comes under God's providence is either willed or permitted by God. From this it follows: If evil comes under God's providence, it is either willed or permitted by God. Yet if every evil is either willed or permitted by God, then God seems to be malevolent. But God is not malevolent.

Therefore: Evil does not come under God's providence. Or: Evil is incompatible with God's providence.

16.2 Arguments Pro

16.2.1 First argument

According to what has been justified in ch. 12, everything that comes under God's providence is either willed or permitted by God. Moral evil that occurs is never willed by God, but is permitted by God. Some other occurring evil may be willed by God as just punishment. Again other types of occurring evil may be permitted by God.

Therefore: Providence is not incompatible with evil.

16.2.2 Second argument

According to ch. 9 any event which occurs by chance is compatible with God's providence. Some evils occur by chance.

Therefore: All evils which occur by chance are compatible with God's providence.

16.3 Proposed Answer

The question whether providence is compatible with evil presupposes that there is evil. Although this is a most accessible and obvious fact, it has been denied by several people. If evil does not exist, the compatibility with anything (including providence) is a trivial matter. Therefore the first section of this chapter will be concerned with the question whether there is evil at all (16.3.1). The next section will deal with the relativity of evil in the sense that what is evil under one perspective is not so under another. Here a rough definition of three types of evil will help to give a first answer to the question of compatibility (16.3.2).

In order to discuss the question of compatibility of evil and providence, it will be necessary to give some more accurate definitions of the different types of evil (16.3.3). Only then shall we show the compatibility of God's providence with evil concerning the properties of providence listed in ch. 10 (16.3.4–16.3.8).

16.3.1 Is there evil at all?

(1) Evil does not seem to be real, because if something is real, it has an effect or in other words: Everything that is real produces (causes) some effect. On the other hand, lacks, deficits or privations do not seem to have effects. Yet according to the usual definition of evil, evil is a lack, deficit, or privation of some good.[1] Therefore evil does not seem to have an effect and consequently evil is not real.

(2) If the events called "evils" are unrealities or illusions and are correctly understood as nothingness – though they seem to be real to humans – then there are no evils. The belief system *Christian science* teaches that evils are unrealities and are correctly understood as nothingness:

> "If sin, sickness, and death were understood as nothingness, they would disappear" ... "the only reality of sin, sickness and death is the awful fact that unrealities seem real to human, erring belief until God strips off their disguise".[2]

Therefore there seem to be no evils.

Contrary to these two arguments, it is plain that there is evil.

1 Cf. the definitions in Aquinas (1995) 1,1 and Aquinas (1981) I, 48, 3.
2 Baker (1934) p.205 and 472. Mitchell (1971) p.93.

First, there is natural evil as a loss of natural good: Preserving life and health (for an appropriate period of time relative to the species) are great natural goods for every organism and loss of life or health (within this appropriate time) are great natural evils for every organism. Such a loss or deficit exists for several organisms. Therefore there is natural evil.

Secondly, there is moral evil. Killing innocent people is moral evil. In Hitler's war and Concentration Camps, about 6 million Jews, 7 million Poles and 24 million Russians were killed. Thus, Hitler's war and the Concentration Camps were great moral evils. Therefore there is moral evil.

As we have established this obvious fact, we shall now comment on the two arguments above.

ad (1) As claimed in (1), it is correct that a lack or deficit or privation as such does not have effects. However the thing or event or process which lacks something, i.e. which lacks some particular good, is real and has effects.

ad (2) The claim that evils like sin, sickness, pain and death are unrealities or illusions is similar to claims of the extreme skeptic or the extreme idealist as "there is no genuine knowledge", "there is no reliable sense perception" or "the world is my dream". All these views have several absurd properties in common, which have already been criticized in section 15.3.5.2 above (commentary to definition Df 15.16 (3)). The points made there also hold for the different types of evils as real facts. They are very well expressed in more general terms by the quote from Pascal.[3]

16.3.2 The "relativity" of evil

(1) One kind of evil is called "*metaphysical evil*". It consists of different degrees of imperfection and finitude.[4] Order and hierarchy of different degrees or imperfection and finitude are essential for the beauty and multitude of the

---

3 Pascal (1963) §268 (170): One needs to doubt, where necessary, to make sure where necessary, to submit where necessary. Who does not do so neglects the force of reason. There are some who offend against these three principles: who claim that everything is provable, because they do not understand what a proof is – or doubt everything, because they don't know where it is necessary to submit – or submit to everything, because they don't know where it is necessary to judge (author's translation).

4 Cf. the division of evils in Leibniz (1952) II, § 21.

world (universe) such that different degrees of imperfection and finitude essentially contribute to the beauty and multitude of the world (universe). If some (species of an) organism is less perfect than another one, it does not seem correct to call this fact an evil. Thus, that a horse does not have human intellect cannot be called an evil, though the horse is of course less perfect than man. On the other hand, if a particular horse has weak lungs, this can be called an evil, since it lacks something it should have (which is a peculiar property of its species).

(2) Another kind of evil consists of what we call *natural disasters*, like earthquakes, climate changes, … etc. and in consequence the extinction of certain species, the death of animals and humans and of cultural goods. Yet to judge such events as evils seems highly relative. Such catastrophes seem to be evils only with respect to a very particular point of view (of those animals or men killed). But they do not seem to be evils from a comprehensive point of view: neither are they evils for nature nor are they evils according to Darwin's theory or its improved successor theories. With respect to nature, they are particular parts contributing to the whole development of nature and with respect to the theory of evolution, they satisfy the process of selection and adaptation. However, the whole development of nature and selection and adaptation seems to be something good.

(3) Leibniz calls another kind of evil "*physical evil*"[5]. Leibniz describes this type of evil as pain, ache and agony. Sometimes causes of this kind of evil like diseases, monsters or freaks are also called physical evil. But first of all these evils appear to be evils only in a relative sense: what is evil for the mouse is good for the cat (who kills the mouse); pain, ache and agony are often part of a natural process in the course of overcoming a disease or regaining health. Secondly, the causes of these evils serve natural selection and adaptation, which is something good. Therefore, what serves something good can only be an evil in a relative sense.

(4) Punishment seems to be a further kind of evil. But punishment insofar it is just, cannot be evil, as just punishment is something good. As Thomas Aquinas says:

5 Ibid.

> "Punishment as such is just; and what is just is good; therefore punishment as such is something good".[6]

Therefore just punishment cannot be evil.

16.3.2.1 Three general types of evil

Df 16.1. An evil $E1$ is some lack, defect, absence, privation or deficit of some particular good, which ought to be present in a subject or organism.

Df 16.2. An evil $E2$ is some lack, defect, absence, privation or deficit which is acceptable to be absent in order to achieve another higher good.

In the first case ($E1$), the particular good ought to be present for different reasons: for example, in order to be a full member of the species (lacking sight is such an evil for animals or men) or in order to survive (food shortage or a lack of fresh air is such an evil) or in order to regain health or to preserve peace, or to receive education, to meet moral rules, ..., etc. In the second case ($E2$), the absence of the particular good is accepted in order to achieve another, higher good, which can be of different kinds: for example, the absence of being uninjured to regain health through an operation, or the absence of freedom in prison (for the murderer) in order to save the life of others ... etc.

From an ontological view, evils in the sense of $E1$ or $E2$ are states or events or processes of some organism or thing, but not organisms or things themselves. Evils in the sense of $E3$ (see below) however, can be things or organism.

Df 16.3. An evil $E3$ is a thing or organism or state or event which is a cause of an evil $E1$.

The respective cause may be a cause in the sense of a sufficient condition (assuming other conditions to be standard or normal) for producing $E1$ as an effect. The causal relation can even obey a dynamical law, such that the (state of the) effect is a definite function of the earlier state as the cause (recall condition D1 of section 4.3.1). But the causal relation can also be weaker in the sense of obeying statisti-

6 Aquinas (1995) 1,1, objection 18.

cal laws such that in most cases (or more likely) the cause produces the effect. In such a case, the cause may be a necessary condition or even neither sufficient nor necessary.

16.3.2.2 Commentary to the "relativity" of evil

ad (1) Concerning imperfection and finitude we have to distinguish a kind of imperfection which is necessary (a) because it is bound to the nature of a certain thing or organism from a kind of imperfection which is contingent (b) and not bound to its nature. Finally, we will deal with finitude (c).

(a) Imperfections which are necessary (bound to nature).

Those organisms for example, which – by their nature – cannot move (themselves) are relatively less perfect than those who can. Or those species of organisms which have a much simpler DNA are relatively less perfect than those which have a more complex one. But this is not a deficit of some particular good which *ought to be present* and therefore not an evil in the sense of $E1$. This can be substantiated in the following way: If there is no imperfection (in things or organisms) which is bound to nature, then there are no different degrees of (necessary) imperfection in the universe. If this is so, there are only things and organisms of one degree of perfection in the universe, distinguished only by contingent imperfections and consequently there is no such multitude and differentiation (which is necessary and given by nature). Indeed there is a multitude and differentiation in the universe which is usually accepted as a great good. Therefore there is imperfection which is necessary, because it is bound to the nature of certain organisms and things. And this kind of "imperfection", which in fact constitutes differentiation, is not only not incompatible with God's providence, but rather in accordance with his plan of a great multitude and differentiation in the universe.

Moreover, the kind of imperfection which is necessary because it is bound to nature cannot be understood as an evil in the sense of $E2$, although it contributes to achieve a higher good which is an ordered universe with great multitude and differentiation. This is so because the imperfection which is necessary because bound to the nature of things does not mean that there is anything absent concerning nature and consequently nothing concerning nature ought to be present. However certain imperfections which are necessary, may be called evils in a derived sense ($E3$) as far as they are causes for evils in the sense of $E1$; as for example certain imperfections in creatures are the cause of death or natural catastrophes are causes of many evils in the sense of $E1$.

(b) Imperfections that are contingent.

Not all things and organisms and not all states, events and processes obey dynamical laws, i.e. laws which do not have exceptions. On the other hand, if an ensemble of things or events obeys statistical laws (recall section 4.3.2), then the majority of the members of the ensemble behave in the same way, apart from few exceptions.

Such exceptions may be interpreted in different ways, depending on whether obeying most cases guarantees achieving a particular good which ought to be present (i) or whether being an exception guarantees achieving a particular good which is preferable to the one achieved by meeting the most cases (ii). In this latter case, exceptions are not imperfections but rather special perfections.

(i) In the first case, exceptions are failures in the sense of deviation from the general rule. Since these deviations do not necessarily happen (because the law permits them) they can be understood as contingent imperfections.

In this case, the contingent imperfection is a deficit of some particular good (achieved by behaving like most members of the ensemble) which ought to be present, i.e. an evil in the sense of $E1$. Examples: the state of crystals which deviate from the form of their respective crystalline system, the state animals which fail to produce offspring, the state of worker bees which fail to produce honey, … etc. Yet some of these examples may not only be seen as evils in the sense of $E1$ but also as evils in these sense of $E2$, i.e. as leading or even as means to achieve a higher good. Thus failing to produce offspring is first – seen from a "local" point of view – an evil with respect to the preservation of the (respective) species. But viewed in a larger context it may contribute to the balance of the population according to higher order principles and goals (goods).

(ii) In the second case, it is not that the exceptional behavior means that a particular good is absent which ought to be present. Therefore we cannot speak of an evil in the sense of $E1$ here. On the contrary, there are great particular goods which are achieved via such exceptions. Examples: The few seeds which successfully develop into a plant (in contradistinction to the millions which die), those mutations which lead to new differentiation among the species or exceptional genetic combinations which lead to a genius ... in general: exceptions which lead to particular goods via selection. In this second case therefore, the exceptions are not imperfections but rather perfections.

Are these contingent imperfections incompatible with God's providence as a teleological plan? This is not necessarily the case. Since there is no hindrance that contingent imperfections in the sense of (i) are local imperfections which can be incorporated into a network of global goal or in the case of (ii), the exceptions are rather perfections which satisfy respective goals.

(c) Concerning *finitude* in the universe, the question is whether that is an imperfection at all. Granted, *finitude* concerning the conceptual entities of mathematics (different types of numbers) would be a rather severe limitation. But concerning entities in space and time, *finitude* does not appear to be an imperfection.

First, it has to be stressed that the spatial and temporal *finitude* of the universe (and the things in it) is scientifically well confirmed: that the universe is spatially closed and finite follows from the Theory of General Relativity, which in turn is very well corroborated. Independently of that, if material bodies of finite extension are collected by adding one to the other, it can never become an infinite collection. However the universe consists of material bodies of finite extension and its extension is finite. (We do not refer to a mathematical continuum here, say between 0 and 1).

The finite age of the universe follows from both a theoretical and an experimental result: the theoretical result are the singularity theorems of Hawking and Penrose; they say that given the cosmological conditions of our universe, a singularity (or singularities) must exist.[7] The experimental result is the discovery of the cosmic background radiation by Penzias and Wilson[8] which is strong evidence for a finite age calculated as about 14.10^9 years, although such a calculation may be problematic[9]. Secondly, there are also consistent mathematical models of an everlasting universe (not finite in time) by Hawking (with imaginary time) and by Linde[10], but there is no experimental evidence for them.

The spatial finitude of the universe is neither an evil in the sense of $E1$ nor in the sense of $E3$, since it follows from laws and is therefore conditionally necessary. Therefore it cannot be a lack of something that should be there. The finitude in time does not follow from laws since laws are understood as time-translation invariant. Yet it both theoretically and experimentally follows form contingent conditions of the universe. Also, this finitude is neither an evil in the sense of $E1$ nor of $E3$. It is not a lack of some good since it can hardly be said that a universe infinite in time is a higher good relative to one which is finite in time. However, both the spatial and the temporal finitude could be considered as serving a higher good or goal (in the sense of $E2$).

From these considerations it is plain that the finiteness of the universe and of the things belonging to it cannot be incompatible with God's providence, since if he has created a finite universe with finite creatures, he has done this according to his teleological plan. Thus the finiteness of the universe and of the creatures are in accordance with his plan or providence. And if the finiteness serves a higher good or goal, then this must be a goal belonging to his plan viz. his providence.

ad (2) Natural disasters like earthquakes, climate changes, volcanic eruptions ... etc. cannot be called evils in the sense of $E1$. There is no lack or deficit of a particular good which were a necessary condition of the definiens of evil in the sense of $E1$. Some such disasters may be called evils in the sense of $E2$, if these events qualify as contributing to a higher good as

7 Hawking and Penrose (1970) and Penrose (1979)

8 Penzias and Wilson (1965)

9 Cf. Mittelstaedt (2008)

10 Hawking (1988), Linde (1990)

killing most members of a species and selecting some may lead to a group of fittest individuals. The theory of evolution stresses the natural evil in the world in the sense of $E2$:

> "A species perfectly adapted to its environment may be destroyed by a change in the latter if no hereditary variability is available in the hour of need. Evolutionary plasticity can be purchased only at the ruthlessly dear price of continuously sacrificing some individuals to death from unfavorable mutations."[11]

In general however, natural disasters can be called evils in the sense of $E3$, i.e. events causing evils in the sense of $E1$.

ad (3) An important answer concerning "*physical evil*" is already contained in (3): "*Physical evil*" is very often evil in the sense of $E2$ such that it is necessary for obtaining a higher good. A more complete answer will be postponed until some further types of evils have been clarified.

ad (4) Punishment, if it is just, is a necessary evil in the sense of definition Df 16.7 below. It is also an evil in the sense of $E2$, since it is accepted in order to achieve a higher good like penance, security of society, avoidance of repetition etc.

Further comments on (2), (3) and (4) will be given in sections 16.3.4 below.

16.3.2.3 *Privatio boni*?

From the definitions of the three general types of evil it should be clear that not every evil can be understood as *privatio boni*, i.e. as a lack or defect or privation of some particular good; although every lack or deficit or privation of some particular good can be understood as a particular evil. Especially evils in the sense of $E3$ cannot be interpreted as *privatio boni*: a virus or a terrorist is an evil in the sense of $E3$ but not in the sense of $E1$. Attacks on the interpretation of evil as *privatio boni* appear to be due to a neglect of differentiation between the three different types $E1$, $E2$ and $E3$ defined above:

> "It does however, seem very implausible to claim that pain and other suffering, bad desire, and wicked acts are just an absence of some good – pain is not just an absence of pleasure, and wicked acts are not just the non-occurrence of good acts."[12]

---

11 Dobzhansky (1937) p. 126f. Cf. Ruse (2001)

12 Swinburne (1998) p.32

There seems to be no hindrance to interpret some pain and suffering as $E1$, i.e. as a lack of the respective good state which is free of pain and suffering. Some other pain and suffering may be interpreted as $E2$, serving a higher good. Examples are the “biological costs” connected with every learning process *via trial and error*. The higher good achieved is adaption, inuring against illness and finally health and survival. Bad desires and wicked acts are mainly evils in the sense of $E3$, since they lead, especially on repetition, to bad habits and vices. Bad habits and vices are evils in the sense of $E1$ with reference to a good character (see section 16.3.3.4 below). Moreover, for the specific types of evils defined below, *privatio boni* is not used in the definiens.

16.3.3 Specific types of evil

As can be observed from definitions Df 16.1–Df 16.3 *evil* can only be defined relative to some good. Therefore different specific types of evil can only be defined with the help of respective types of good or value. We shall begin with basic evil (cf. section 7.3.3.1 above) and then proceed to other specific types of evil.

16.3.3.1 Basic evil

Df 16.4. A property or state or process (event) C of ls or a thing X of the environment of ls is a *primary evil* for ls iff avoiding C or X is necessary for ls to stay alive in its environment (including society).

Df 16.5. A property or state or process (event) C of ls or a thing X of the environment of ls is a *secondary evil* for ls iff avoiding C or X is necessary for ls to keep or regain health in the environment (including society) of ls

Df 16.6. A property or state or process (event) C of ls or a thing X of the environment of ls is a *basic evil* for ls iff C or X is either a primary or a secondary evil for ls.

16.3.3.2 Necessary evil

This type of evil is very widespread and can be found on all levels of living beings. The main point is that this evil is necessary to achieve a higher good. From this characterization it follows that this type of evil is an evil in the sense of $E2$. In some cases it can also be an evil in the sense of $E3$ (see the examples below).

Df 16.7. Let Y be a property or state or process (event) of ls or a thing belonging to the environment of ls. Then Y is a *necessary evil* iff

(1) Y is an evil in the sense of $E2$ or $E3$

(2) Y is not a *basic evil* or else it is a *basic evil* which contributes to avoiding a greater *basic evil*

(3) Y is not a *moral evil* (cf. Df 16.12, Df 16.13)

(4) Y is necessary for achieving or protecting a basic good (cf. Df 7.4)

Examples: Struggling for food is a necessary evil for staying alive (for animals and a great number of men). An operation for regaining health is a necessary evil. Prison is a necessary evil for a murderer if it is necessary for protecting further people from being killed by him. The death penalty cannot be a necessary evil according to Df 16.7, because it is itself a *basic evil* (but does not seem to avoid a *basic evil* greater than imprisonment). A drug with severe negative side effects or chemo-therapy can be a necessary evil in order to regain health.

16.3.3.3 Higher evil, legitimate and illegitimate

So far, the different types of evil were concerned with living beings in general (including humans). However, we speak of higher evil (legitimate or illegitimate) only w.r.t humans.

Df 16.8. Let Y be a property or state or process (event) or a thing belonging to the environment of some human person x. Then Y is a *higher evil* of x iff Y is the intentional object of an action of x which is an action of fear or of tending away which follows (at least one, but usually a series of) judgments of the human intellect of x about that object.

Higher evils can be legitimate or permitted or non-legitimate (illegitimate) or non-permitted.

Df 16.9. Higher evils are legitimate (illegitimate) iff they are objects (things) or events of legitimate (illegitimate) desires or wants.

Df 16.10. Legitimate (permitted) desire (want): X is a *legitimate desire* (want) of a human person x in circumstance c and living in society d iff X can be met in d

(1) without hindering the satisfaction of any basic good or need of any member of d and without doing basic evil to any of the members of d

(2) without endangering the integrity of any valuable subsystem of d much less that of d as a whole

Df 16.11. Illegitimate (non-permitted) desire (want): X is an *illegitimate desire* (want) of human person x in circumstance c and living in society d iff X does not satisfy conditions (1) and (2) of Df 16.10.

Every[13] legitimate evil is an evil in the sense of $E2$ which is clear from the definition. In addition, legitimate evils can sometimes – under certain circumstances and unintended – also be evils in the sense of $E3$, for example if the execution of school-attendance deprives the child from the ill mother who would need the child for help.

Examples of legitimate higher evil: The execution of school-attendance; bungling and botching of apprentices (beginners); justified punishment.

Note that circumstances can turn a legitimate desire (or want) (for example to go on holidays) into an illegitimate one if it is the duty to teach at that time. Or they can turn an illegitimate evil (deprive somebody of freedom) into a legitimate evil (prison) if this person has committed a crime.

There is illegitimate higher evil corresponding to higher values insofar these values are violated or hindered.

(1) Evil pertaining to mankind like lack of educational instruction and learning, war instead of peace, air and plant poisoning, … etc.

---

13 Df 16.10 is due to Bunge (1989) p.35, Def. 1.13

(2) Evil which violates personal values like hindrance of choosing one's profession.

(3) Evil which violates legitimate desires of religious people like hindrance or punishment for practicing their religion.

Every higher illegitimate evil is an evil in the sense of $E1$. Moreover it is usually also an evil in the sense of $E3$, since it causes further evil in the sense of $E1$.

16.3.3.4 Moral evil

Moral evil or sin can be defined as an action or as a disposition. The action or the disposition has always to be attributed to an individual man (woman). There is extensive agreement among moral scientists and theologians that moral evil (sin) cannot be attributed to collectives, i.e. groups or societies. The main reason is that a moral action is understood as a personal commission or omission which is voluntary or caused by free will. Understood as a disposition, it is a habit which develops and strengthens by repeated actions of the same type. If these actions are morally good, what they establish is virtue, if they are morally bad, they produce vice. On the other hand, if the virtue or vice is established as a habit, it causes or disposes his owner to realize a morally good or bad action. Thus moral evil as an action will be called *sin* as a disposition or habit will be called *vice*.

Df 16.12. Moral Evil as an Action (Sin): Let Y be a state or process (event). Then Y is a moral evil as an action (sin) iff Y is a free voluntary action of commission (omission) which is forbidden (obligatory) by

(1) the promulgated ethical (moral) standards of some human society or

(2) the *Human Rights* which are based on an international agreement of many societies w.r.t. ethical (moral) standards

(3) the law of God or

(4) a combination of these three

A sin as an action of commission means *doing what one should not do*. A sin as an action of omission means *not doing what one should do*. "Doing what one should not do" can happen through a word, through deed or through desire. Respectively, "not doing what one should do" can happen through omission of a word, deed or desire.

Every moral evil as an action (sin) is an evil in the sense of $E1$, i.e. a lack or privation of some particular good, which ought to be present (as a morally correct action) according to one of the above four conditions. In addition, every moral evil as an action (sin) is also an evil in the sense of $E3$, since it contributes to produce a vice.

Df 16.13. Moral Evil as a Disposition or Habit (Vice): Let Y be a state or property. Then Y is a moral evil as a disposition or habit (vice) iff Y is a trait of character that disposes the owner to commit a sin (moral evil as an action).

Every moral evil as a habit (vice) is an evil in the sense of $E1$, i.e. a lack or privation of some particular good which ought to be present (as a good habit, i.e. virtue) according to human standards or according to *Human Rights* or according to the law of God or according to all of these. In addition, every moral evil as a habit (vice) is also an evil in the sense of $E3$, since it is a causal factor for producing sin.

16.3.4 Is providence compatible with the specific types of evil?

First, it should be emphasized that the gist of chapter 16 is a question of compatibility and in this sense it is that we understand the problem of theodicy: As the question whether the existence of evil in all its different forms is compatible with God's providence and with God's goodness. We agree with Swinburne that the traditional problem of theodicy is a problem of *compatibility*, but not a question of God's actual reasons for allowing evil to occur. This might be close to what Plantinga calls a "defence". Platinga's concern in his Plantinga (1974) is the *compatibility* or *consistency* of the two premises

(1) God is omniscient, omnipotent and wholly good and

(2) There is evil.[14]

Before we go into detail concerning specific types of evil, we will consider some questions of compatibility, which equally concern all the different types of evil defined in section 16.3.3. Such general questions are concerned with the first three conditions (a)–(c) of the definition of providence Df 10.1.

---

14 Cf. Swinburne (1998) p.15 and Plantinga (1974) chs. 3-10

Condition (a) of the definition of providence Df 10.1 says that any state of affairs which belongs to God's providence belongs to God's creation and vice versa. Since any (specific) type of evil, insofar as it is the case, is a fact or a state of affairs of the universe, it follows that in this sense – as a fact of creation – it belongs to God's providence. Therefore there cannot be any incompatibility of any (specific) type of evil with God's providence in the sense of condition (a) of providence. This kind of compatibility also goes beyond the types of evils defined in 16.3.3. It simply means that two facts which are represented by two true propositions cannot be incompatible. Therefore it follows that those metaphysical evils which are realized, further those natural disasters which are realized and the "physical evil" which is realized also belong to God's providence as occurring facts.

Condition (b) says that both omnitemporal (everlasting) states of affairs and states of affairs which last only for a limited time belong to God's providence. There are evils which are omnitemporal like some metaphysical evil (cf. 16.3.2.2 above) and evils which only last for some time, like natural catastrophes, "physical evil" and the specific types of evil. Insofar they are facts and everlasting or last only for some time, they belong to God's providence according to condition (b). Therefore there cannot be any incompatibility between God's providence w.r.t. condition (b) and any kind of factual evil. Condition (c) says that every state of affairs which belongs to God's providence and therefore also belongs to his creation is known to God. Consequently, any evil which occurs (is a fact) in the universe (in creation) is known to God. W.r.t. condition (b) we also have to say that God knows all the evils which are everlasting, for example metaphysical evil, and those which occur at a certain time t. Since we assume that God is omniscient, he can also have a method to know all evils occurring in future times.[15]

Therefore: Since every state of affairs that belongs to God's providence is known to God and what is known to him is true and every fact concerning evil also represents a true proposition, there cannot be any incompatibility between states of affairs belonging to his providence and states of affairs about evil in the world, because true propositions or obtaining facts cannot contradict each other.

15 The problem of omniscience concerning contingent future events like free will decisions is quite complicated and has a long history. For a historical study cf. Craig (1988) and Craig (1991). For a systematic study cf. Weingartner (2008a) ch.11.

16.3.5 God's providence is not incompatible with moral evil

This and the following sections will be concerned with the specific types of evil defined in section 16.3.3. But here and subsequently, these types of evil will be compared with properties (d), (e) and (f) of providence, elaborated in ch. 10. We shall begin with moral evil and illegitimate evil, since the proof for the compatibility is rather simple here. Then we shall proceed to the more complicated cases.

(1) According to condition (d) of definition Df 10.1, everything (every state of affairs that happens) which belongs to God's providence is either willed or permitted by God. Yet moral evil cannot be willed by God; it is merely permitted by him. This can be proved as follows:

   (a) First, every occurring moral evil is a fact (an obtaining state of affairs). Therefore it is compatible with his providence in the sense of conditions (a), (b) and (c) of Df 10.1, i.e. it belongs to his creation, it occurs at a certain time and it is known by God.

   (b) That moral evil cannot be willed by God can be shown as follows:

   Assume that moral evil is willed by God. Then, since God causes by his will and everything that he wills concerning creation, he causes, it follows that moral evil is caused by God. Yet this is absurd, since first, it is inconsistent with God's own rules (for example the Ten Commandments) and secondly, it is inconsistent with men's free will and free will decision (cf. 15.3.5). Therefore moral evil is not willed but consequently permitted by God. What is permitted by God's providence cannot be incompatible with his providence.

   Therefore: Moral evil is compatible with God's providence in the sense of condition (d) of Df 10.1.

(2) According to condition (e) of Df 10.1, everything that belongs to God's providence is either caused by God or by creatures. Yet moral evil cannot be caused by God. Thus it must be caused by creatures. That moral evil cannot be caused by God has been justified in (b) above: Since it would be inconsistent with God's moral commandments and also with men's free will and free will decision. What is not caused (not produced) by God's providence cannot be incompatible with his providence. Therefore: Moral evil is compatible with God's providence in the sense of condition (e) of Df 10.1.

(3) According to condition (f) of Df 10.1, everything that belongs to God's providence is directed to some goal or integrated into a network of goals. Although

God neither wills nor causes moral evil, he can integrate the action and the effects of moral evil into a network of good goals, such that some good is produced form that moral evil. As Augustine says:

> "Almighty God would in no wise permit evil to exist in His works, unless he were so almighty and so good as to produce good even from evil".[16]

This is possible in more than one way: the agent (sinner) may repent; he may learn from his mistake and from its morally bad consequences; others may help to repair the bad consequences. According to Christian understanding, God can forgive a morally bad action (sin) and he can also remove all bad consequences of it in the mind and body of the agent. But the fact of having committed a morally bad action (sin) cannot be removed from the agent, since it would be contradictory that an action occurs (occurred) at time t and that it does not occur (did not occur) at time t.[17]

It follows from what has been said that even moral evil can be integrated into a network of good goals. Therefore moral evil is compatible with God's providence in the sense of condition (f) of Df 10.1.

(4) Illegitimate higher evil is illegitimate relative to what illegitimate human desires in a certain society are. And what is legitimate and illegitimate has to be established by man, since man is endowed with intellect and will to solve these problems. In other words, it can be assumed that God does not will to directly interfere in such matters, i.e. he neither wills nor causes illegitimate higher evil, but permits it to be caused by human creatures. Furthermore God can integrate illegitimate higher evil into a network of good goals as it has been stated in Df 10.1 above. Thus he may permit persecution of Christians in order to not hinder the human freedom of the persecutor on the one hand and to strengthen faith on the other. From this it follows that illegitimate higher evil is not incompatible with God's providence.

16.3.6 God's providence is not incompatible with legitimate higher evil

(1) Just punishment
Just punishment as a past or future fact belongs to God's providence according to Df 10.1, condition (b). According to condition (d), God wills or permits

---

16 Augustine (1887) II
17 Cf. Aquinas (1981) I, 25,5 ad 3

just punishment. The punishment ordained by the Last Judgment is certainly willed by God. The just punishment decreed by a judge is at least permitted by God. Unjust punishment ordained by an unjust judge is permitted by God insofar as he does not take away the ability of making free will decisions from man (the judge). However, unjust punishment is illegitimate (higher) evil and moral evil. Although God neither causes nor wills it, he can integrate it into a network of good goals in the sense of 16.3.5 (3) and (4).

(2) Hume's premise

Hume's premise – if God is able to avoid evil but is not willing to avoid it, then God is malevolent – is a frequently used premise in arguments against God's goodness and providence. It is even claimed as a universal principle for anyone who is able to avoid evil. However it is easily refuted by many counterexamples. We shall provide four types of counterexamples:

a) Just punishment as a fact is a refutation of Hume's accepted premise that generally: If God is able to avoid evil but does not will to avoid it, then God is malevolent.[18] A judge might be able to avoid the evil of just punishment for the criminal (by acquittal), but does not will to avoid just punishment. Yet according to Hume this judge is malevolent. This is of course absurd. On the contrary, we have to say that this judge is just and he would be unjust if he gave acquittal to the criminal.

b) Take necessary evil, an operation for regaining health, as an example. It would be foolish to say that those who can avoid evil but do not avoid it are malevolent (cf. 16.3.7 below).

c) God has endowed man with free will (recall ch. 15). Many free will decisions lead to great evil for the deciding individual and for communities as well as societies. God would be inconsistent and imperfect if he prevented such evils and took away man's free will.[19]

d) Moreover, to avoid every evil w.r.t. living systems would annihilate any kind of learning by trial and error and all kinds of adaption, since they are necessarily connected – via errors and improvements – with *biological costs* (cf. 16.3.7).

---

18 Hume (1977) p.198. Hume's argument is a logical fallacy even independent of the wrong premise. Cf. Weingartner (2003) p.127 ff. and below (5).

19 Cf. Plantinga's *Free Will Defence* inPlantinga (1971) and section 16.3.8 (2) below.

Such counterexamples could be continued. They show that the following universal premise which Hume uses is false: For every evil x and for every person a it holds: If person a is able to avoid evil x and person a does not will to avoid evil x, then person a is malevolent.

(3) Particularizations of Hume's Premise
However, we may ask the question whether the following particularizations of the above statement are true:

a) For every person a there is at least *some* (or other) evil x such that it holds: If person a is able to avoid evil x and person a does not will to avoid evil x, then person a is malevolent.

This statement is certainly true. We can find several types of evil for which this holds, provided that certain conditions are satisfied. Thus, to hurt or injure another person without necessity is malevolent. But we have to stress the "without necessity", since the surgeon needs to do this in order to achieve a higher goal, i.e. health. Similarly, to not avoid denting another's car without necessity is malevolent. Yet sometimes this may be necessary to avoid a greater accident as for example to avoid killing a person. Further, to lie to a friend without necessity is malevolent. But a physician might do so, in order not to take away a cancer patient's hope. In all three cases the actions are integrated into a network of good goals and can be justified only under such conditions.

Observe however that the following particularization is also a true statement:

b) For every person a there is at least some (or other) evil x such that it holds: If person a is able to avoid x, and person a wills and causes to avoid x then person a is immoral (or unjust).

Think of the example of the unjust judge in section (2) above.

From this consideration of the two particularizations, it is evident that for some evils that could be avoided it is not good if they are avoided, whereas for some others that could be avoided it is good that they are avoided.

(4) Application to God
If the first particularization a) of Hume's premise is applied to God, then it seems to be that he is malevolent by being able to avoid evil but not willing to do so. If the second particularization b) is applied to God, then allowing certain types of evil, such as just punishment, takes away the charge of being malevolent. This leads to considering some general conditions which show

that God needs to permit some evil (see also (2) above). Swinburne has formulated such conditions:

> "Since all things are possible for an omnipotent being, except the logically impossible, the theist's defense is then that, compatibly with his perfect goodness, God may allow a bad state E to occur, caused either by himself or some other agent, if (and only if):
>
> (a) God has the right to allow E to occur.
>
> (b) Allowing E (or a state as bad or worse) to occur is the only morally permissible way in which God can bring about a logically necessary condition of a good G.
>
> (c) God does everything else logically possible to bring about G.
>
> (d) The expected value of allowing E, given (c), is positive."[20]

(5) Hume's argument from evil
Hume tries to prove that God is either not omnipotent or God wills evil:

> "Is he willing to prevent evil, but not able? then is he impotent. Is he able but not willing? then is he malevolent. Is he both able and willing? whence then is evil."[21]

Hume assumes certainly in addition the following two true premises, the first of which is already stated in his question at the end: There is evil. And: Everyone who is malevolent (i.e. willing the bad) wills evil. Then Hume's argument can be stated more accurately in the following way:

(1) If God wills that evil does not occur (W) but is not able to make it that evil does not occur ($\neg A$) then God is not omnipotent ($\neg O$).

(2) If God is able to make it that evil does not occur (A) but does not will that evil does not occur ($\neg W$), then God is malevolent (M), i.e. God wills evil to occur.

(3) If God is able to make it that evil does not occur (A) and wills that evil does not occur (W), then there is no evil ($\neg E$).

(4) But there is evil (E).

(5) Therefore God is either not omnipotent ($\neg O$) or God is malevolent (M). And consequently

(6) God is either not omnipotent ($\neg O$) or God wills evil (WE).

In symbolic form the argument runs as follows:

---

20 Swinburne (1998) p.14
21 Hume (1977) p.198.

(1) $(W \land \neg A) \rightarrow \neg O$

(2) $(A \land \neg W) \rightarrow M$

(3) $(A \land W) \rightarrow \neg E$

(4) E

(5) $\neg O \lor M$ additional assumption: $M \rightarrow WE$

(6) $\neg O \lor WE$

Concerning any argument we have to ask two questions: Is the argument logically valid? Are the premises true? Concerning the second we have shown already in (2) above that the second premise is not true; since it is stated as a universal premise there are many counterexamples. From this it follows already that the conclusions i.e. (5) and (6) are not proved by this argument.

However independently of that also the first question has to be answered in the negative, which means: the argument is not logically valid, i.e. it is a logical fallacy. This can be shown by a simple truth-value assignment which shows the possibility that all premises get the value true and the conclusion gets the value false. By such a possible assignment an argument can be shown to be invalid:

$(W\land\neg A)\rightarrow\neg O;(A\land\neg W)\rightarrow M;(A\land W)\rightarrow\neg E;E.\because.\neg O\lor M$

F FWF T FW F FWF T F FF F TFT T FWF F

In a similar way one can easily show that neither one of the following statements follows from Hume's 4 premises above: $\neg O$, M, W, $\neg W$, A, $\neg A$, $W \lor A$, $\neg A \lor W$. Moreover conclusion (6) does not follow either from the 4 premises, even if premise (5) contains the additional assumption: $M \rightarrow WE$ (if God is malevolent then God wills evil). Hume praised his argument as certain and infallible: "there are no inferences more certain and infallible than these."[22] He was mistaken; this argument is a fallacy.

Logic tells us that any invalid argument can be turned into a valid one either by adding certain premises or by weakening its conclusion or by both. Such an argument has been attributed to Epicure. In the terminology above it runs as follows, where (1E) is Epicure's premise corresponding to (1) of Hume's premises:

22 Hume (1977) p.198.

(1E) = (1) and (but) God is omnipotent

(2E) = (2) and (but) God is not malevolent

(3E) = (3)

(4E) If God is not able to cause it that evil does not occur and if God does not will that evil does not occur, then he cannot be called God. (4E) is the additional premise

(5E) The weakened conclusion is a fourfold disjunction: Either God is not omnipotent or God is malevolent or there is no evil or one cannot call him God.

This argument is logically valid, whereas Hume's amputation of it is logically invalid (a fallacy). But for the conclusion being proved by an argument it is not sufficient that the argument is valid. We have to ask whether all the premises are true. And here we have already seen that the second premise cannot be true (see 16.3.6 (2) above). Therefore the conclusion is not proved.

16.3.7 Is God's providence compatible with *necessary evil*?

The universe consists of a huge number of *necessary evil* (recall definition Df 16.7) in order to achieve a huge amount of basic good on all levels of living systems. The evolutionary process of selection and adaptation, for example, makes it necessary that many sperm and egg cells and individuals die and that some species even die out. In a similar way, children's diseases, the struggle for food and shelter, fighting for life … etc. are necessary evils. Therefore if God wills and causes a universe in which achieving basic goods and avoiding basic evils can be gained by a learning process of how to overcome *necessary evil*, then he wills (causes) necessary evil conditionally: i.e. under the condition that he wills that the respective organism (including men) achieve basic goods and avoid basic evils by some process of learning he wills conditionally that necessary evil occur. Such necessary evil is very well described in modern biology:

> "The Christian defense does not take the fact of evil as just a coincidental given, but rather as a real presence in life: there, horrible, meaningless, depressing, defeating, challenging …"
>
> "Natural selection has costs – physical pain – but these are costs that must be paid. And this applies also if you think that a scientific solution must be found to account for the appearance of humans, and if you think that arms races offer the most convincing explanation.

> The pain and violence which results from there is simply an inevitable tariff for achieving the desired end."[23]

Observe further that every symbiosis and every cooperation requires costs in the sense of necessary evil. This is shown in detail by the evolution of symbiosis and cooperation.[24]

One should also remember the huge number of interdependencies necessary for the extraordinary *fine-tuning* of the cosmos. Such interdependencies underlie all biological processes and prescribe many necessary evils for achieving basic goods (values) and higher goods (values). Consider the following example:

> Imagine what kinds of wholesale changes would be needed to pain-proof various processes. Fire could no longer burn, for fear that children and others might get trapped in smoke-filled apartments. But if fire did not burn, how could I warm myself through the Canadian winter and how cook my food and so much more? One change by God would require another and another and another, until everything had been altered. And could this be possible? Where would it end and where could it end in a satisfactory manner?[25]

> In particular, the introduction of different natural laws affecting human beings in order to prevent the frequent instances of natural evil would entail the alteration of human beings themselves.[26]

Thus if God wills the realization of these goods, he also conditionally wills or at least permits the necessary means even if these means are sometimes necessary evils. In this sense, necessary evils are compatible with God's providence according to ch. 10 Df 10.1 (d) and chs. 12 and 14.

16.3.8 Is God's providence compatible with evil that is beyond human control?

(1) Partially controllable evil
Living organisms in general and mankind, societies and individual people suffer from evil of different sorts in such a way that

(i) the respective evil is apparently not punishment, because the person to whom the evil happens is not guilty

---

23 Ruse (2001) p.134 and 137. Recall the quotation by Dobzhansky, note 11.
24 Cf. Maynard-Smith and Szathmary (1999) chs. 11 and 16.2
25 Ruse (2001) p.135
26 Reichenbach (1982) p.111

(ii) the respective evil is not caused by other human beings (as in case of war) or only very partially and indirectly caused by human beings

(iii) the respective evil is not completely beyond human control but beyond control of the society in which it occurs. Examples: hunger and disease.

This kind of evil can be at least partially solved by mankind, but certainly not by individuals or single societies; the problem can only be solved if all (or a great part) of the civilized societies (countries) work together and spend a considerable part of their budget on it (instead of spending it on armament); and if in addition people in poor countries are being educated to solve some part of the problem more and more by themselves.

Also with respect to this kind of evil, one could argue that God might tolerate this kind of evil conditionally insofar as he wills that both those societies in which the evil occurs and those which have learned to avoid such evil, will improve by a process of developing their human and moral values and new means and techniques.

In this sense this kind of evil which is at least partially controllable by humans is – as the necessary evils of section 16.3.7 above – not incompatible with God's providence. But it seems to me that while this argumentation is not incorrect, it is insufficient as an explanation for this kind of evil. Some complementation will therefore be given in 16.3.9 below.

(2) Uncontrollable evil
Living organisms in general and mankind, societies and individual people, suffer from evil for which it holds that

(i) the respective evil is apparently not punishment, because the person to whom the evil happens is not guilty

(ii) the respective evil is not caused by other human beings (as in case of war)

(iii) the respective evil is beyond control. Examples: natural disasters like earthquakes, mine disasters, certain diseases ... etc.

For this kind of evil it holds that man (and mankind) is not responsible for and it and also there is hardly an argument for waiting until man could learn to control or to avoid such evil. Neither is there a necessity to leave room for a free decision of men since by (ii) it is assumed that this kind of evil is not even partially or indirectly caused by men. Thus it seems inevitable to say first that God wills (and causes) such kind of evil and secondly, that if he is benevolent, he should will (cause) that such evil will not occur. Although the fatalistic thesis: "If p is the case then God wills (causes) that p is the case" is not true for all states of affairs p (cf. ch. 12) here we face the weaker thesis: If p is the case and if p is not caused by man, then God wills (causes) that p is the case.

However, from the thesis of ch. 10 that every occurring states of affairs comes under God's providence together with the thesis of ch. 13 that everything that comes under God's providence is either caused by God or caused by creatures, the following weaker thesis follows: Every occurring state of affairs is either caused by God or caused by creatures. Thus if there are other creatures than humans, these kinds of occurring evil need not be caused by God. Consequently, the above weaker thesis "If p is the case and if p is not caused by men, then God wills (causes) that p is the case" need not be true. And it is not true provided that we accept that other creatures may cause that kind of evil. For the reference of "other creatures" there are two possibilities: other creatures belonging to our universe or other creatures not belonging to our universe.

Plantinga takes the latter possibility to solve the problem of theodicy: In order to liberate God from causing (even indirectly or conditionally) any evil, he charges all evil to creatures with intellect and free will, either human or non-human. In this case all evils are consciously willed and caused by these creatures and God cannot interfere or hinder them, since he has endowed them with intellect and free will. In this sense Plantinga states: "All the evil in Kronos is broadly moral evil."[27] Since God does not will or cause moral evil in any sense[28], all evil must be caused by immoral actions of human or non-human creatures; and if not by humans then by other morally bad intelligent creatures like Satan.

This defense or argument for theodicy seems to be problematic and its premise appears improbable, for the following reason: since God's will applies to very event which occurs, in the sense that he either wills or permits that it occurs, it would follow that God wills that Satan causes such evil or God does not will that such evil occurs but permits Satan to cause it. The first possibility would not save God from causing evil and would claim that God causes evil "through" Satan (which seems further incompatible with statements from the Bible). The second possibility (probably Plantinga's position) also seems very improbable because of the following reason: if God does not will such evil to occur but permits Satan to cause it,

---

27 Plantinga (1974) p.59. See also Plantinga (1971) part III. This statement forms the gist of Plantinga's "Free Will Defense" and of chs. 1-10 of part I of his book: God, Freedom, and Evil.
28 Cf. Aquinas (1981) I, 19,9

then this means that God has given Satan the great power to cause all uncontrollable evil, which seems rather improbable. In his "Free Will Defense", Plantinga has given several arguments in this direction. In my opinion, this kind of defense is important for every theodicy even if it gives too much power and domain to Satan and the fallen angels. But from a more general point of view the "Free Will Defense" is concerned with only one part of theodicy, the part on the side of creatures. The other part, God's side, is not discussed, which is that God is *not all-willing* and *not all-causing* (cf. ch. 12). Without that fact one can hardly defend the non-interference of God with his will successfully, especially in the case of moral evil and other kinds of evil for which man is (at least partially) responsible.

Therefore we take the other option for a possible explanation: other creatures belonging to our universe. This amounts to the medieval doctrine of the so-called *secondary causes*. In Thomas Aquinas' words:

> "Therefore to some effects He has attached necessary causes, that cannot fail; but to others defectible and contingent causes, from which arise contingent effects. Hence it is not because the proximate causes are contingent that the effects willed by God happen contingently, but because God has prepared contingent causes for them, it being His will that they should happen contingently."[29]

In modern terms these are causes with respect to which God tolerates chance, randomness, branching, exceptions, failure, imperfection, and contingency. This is connected to the thesis that God not only accepts but wills the contribution also of imperfect creatures as cooperators of the happenings and development in the universe (recall the example of the master builder in section 14.3.7 (2)). With respect to what has been said in ch. 4, this kind of causation cannot be described by dynamical laws, but must be understood through statistical laws which permit chance, degrees of freedom, exceptions, failures (relative to the average), ... etc.

With the help of the explanation by secondary causes, we may say that God's providence is compatible with evil that is beyond human control, since he wills the contribution of imperfect creatures in his creation just as the master builder also incorporates bungling and botching of beginners in his plan. However this explanation though justified w.r.t several uncontrollable evils does not seem to be entirely sufficient for the great amount of that sort of evil. Therefore we shall give three further possible explanations in the next section.

---

29 Aquinas (1981) I, 19,8

16.3.9 Three further possible explanations

(1) The status of men in this world

According to the first explanation, the status of men in this world is not a final one. It is the status of pilgrimage in order to reach a final state (of happiness) or in other words, the state of men in this world is a state of probation or of crucial test in order to become worthy of the final state (of happiness). If this is true, (human) life in this world without suffering would be a strange thing since the test would not be crucial but very weak. More precisely, such a life would be a kind of counterexample which would prove that the above theory on the status of men in this world was not true. Because this theory, which all five major religions accept, assumes that happiness without any suffering is a possible state after this life, but not a possible state in this life. Irenaeus stresses this explanation and John Hick elaborates on it in detail.[30]

This explanation does not give an answer to the degree of weight (heaviness) of suffering. Therefore one may say that it still does not explain why heavy outrage, harm, sorrow and grief happen to the innocent and why heavy suffering is distributed in an unequal way. This shows that the above theory cannot be interpreted in the following way: "There is a certain amount of suffering which corresponds to the status of man in this world". "This degree of suffering is the one which is just with respect to the person's status; what is less than this degree and especially what is more than this degree is unjust and

---

30 Hick (1977), part III. This explanation and also the two subsequent ones ((2) and (3)) are not available to individuals who do not believe in another life after this life and in most cases also not for non-theists (I say in "most cases" since in religions such as Hinduism or Buddhism some or the other of the three explanations might be reasonable without believing in a personal God). Therefore it is generally not correct to say that "the point, however, of the argument from evil is to present premises that both theist and non-theist can agree to so that it can be shown whether or not the argument in fact succeeds" (Weisberger (1999), p.25). However, Weisberger is correct concerning such arguments of which one can show solely by logical means that they are fallacious. Of these there are in fact many (including that of Hume) as the answer to the objections of ch. 7 in Weingartner (2003) and section 16.3.6 (5) of this chapter show. This criterion by Weisberger is also sound w.r.t. a second class of arguments. These are valid arguments which use only empirically well-established scientific results as premises. To these belong the results of biology and evolutionary theory about the necessity of physical evil and pain. But all other arguments, which are valid and use philosophical or religious premises, are not such that both theists and non-theists can agree to them. Therefore Weisberger's criterion can only be accepted in a rather limited sense.

cannot happen" ... etc. A partial answer to this question may be the second explanation (2) which applies specifically to Christian religion.

(2) Guilt and suffering
It is an essential doctrine of the New Testament that guilt, sin and debt are neither necessary nor sufficient conditions for suffering. That is, the following statements do not hold generally:

(i) If someone suffers, then he is guilty (in some way or other).

(ii) If someone is guilty, then he suffers (or will suffer or should suffer).

The first (i) is not true generally, since some (if not many) suffer, although they are innocent; Christ is the greatest example for this. Remember that according to the New Testament (Joh. 9), the apostles were sure that (i) must hold. Therefore they asked Jesus when meeting the blind man: "Who has sinned, he himself or his parents?". Jesus answered: neither of them. The drastic example of the Old Testament on the other hand, for someone who suffers immensely but is not guilty (at least not in the beginning) is Job. And since Job firmly believed that (i) is universally true, he found himself in a completely paradoxical situation.

The second (ii) is not true generally since for some, guilt and punishment are remitted. Again Christ, who saved man from guilt and sin and from its consequences of suffering (after this life), is the greatest example. Remember that according to the New Testament (Joh. 8), the Phariseans were certain that principle (ii) must hold. Therefore, when they accused the woman of adultery, they said that Moses permitted to throw stones at her. But Christ neither condemned nor sentenced her.

Concerning (i), an important aspect is that someone innocent can suffer for someone's guilt or crime, either on his or her own accord or by way of force. Criminal politicians, who provoke war, plunge many innocent into misery. Red Cross and charity helpers or firemen suffer by choice, for both innocent and criminal alike.

How can someone innocent suffer for someone else? The simplest explanation and the strongest motive for such behavior is love. This is also the explanation the New Testament gives for Christ's suffering.

Concerning (ii), an important aspect is that someone innocent can remit someone else's guilt or debt or (just) punishment. The simplest explanation and the strongest motive for such behavior is also love. This is the explanation the New Testament gives for God's mercy.

According to Plantinga, all evil from which *innocent* people suffer – since it can hardly be caused by other human beings – must be due to Satan and his bad angels. There are many biographies of saints who suffered from incurable diseases, but why should all these have been caused by Satan and his bad angels? A much simpler explanation is that such evil, e.g. an incurable disease, is caused by other non-human creatures of the universe: by bacteria, viruses, bodily weakness, a weak immune system … etc. Generally: by imperfect and failing *secondary causes*. Moreover, the Passion of Christ is theologically not entirely explicable by saying that it was caused by the Jews of Jerusalem and by Satan, who might have influenced the Jews. More importantly, it was the free will decision of Christ according to the plan of God to suffer for mankind.

(3) Evil as a means against failing the ultimate goal
According to all five major religions, the ultimate goal of mankind (a final state of happiness) is not of this world (does not lie in this world), but can be earned in this world by appropriate way of life together with the help (grace) of God. God's explicit help through giving grace is certainly the doctrine of the Old and the New Testament. According to the three Abraham religions, faith (religious belief) is also one important necessary condition – as a contribution from man's side – for reaching the ultimate goal. Whereas being without sin or without guilt is not a necessary condition, because it is a condition which cannot be fulfilled in any case by any human being; otherwise Christ, who came to save men from sin, would be a liar.

Thus unbelief is a most serious danger to reaching the ultimate goal. If God, who offers the ultimate goal (final state of happiness) to every man, is almighty and a God of love, it seems that he could change the unbelief into belief. But this is not so, for then he would interfere with man's free will and his own will would be inconsistent having created man with free will. This becomes clear from the following consideration: Religious belief (and also scientific belief) in contradistinction to knowledge and proof, is always incomplete with respect to the justifying reasons; as long as it is belief (be it religious or scientific), this gap can never be closed by adding additional reasons in such a way as to gain knowledge. In science, belief can be replaced by knowledge with the help of a proof or a repeated experimental result.[31] Religious belief can be replaced by knowledge in eternal life. Therefore belief needs the assent (consent) of free will as a necessary component. Consequently, no human person will be forced by anyone (not even God) to believe

31 Cf. Weingartner (1994)

or not believe in a religious way. What else then could God do in order to rouse man (shake him into action) from his unbelieving without interfering with his free will? One possibility is to send him evil in order to "open his eyes". Evil of any kind, not caused by man or partially caused by man, may lead to purification[32] and may even at the same time have the positive consequence of giving man the opportunity to work out a part of his guilt.

16.4 Answer to the Objections

16.4.1 (to 16.1.1)

All evil which is a respective necessary means for reaching a goal is compatible with that goal. Thus all evil in the sense of $E2$ (Df 16.2) is a lack or defect, which is accepted for achieving a higher good or goal. Thus it is correct that the evil as evil cannot be a goal, but it can be a necessary means for achieving a goal.

Therefore providence can be a plan which leads things to their goals even if the way to reach that goal may be full of hindrances and evils functioning as necessary conditions.

16.4.2 (to 16.1.2)

As is evident from section 16.3.2, evil can be relative, such that what is evil for one can be good or even a goal for the other. However, we know from Df 5.15 and Df 7.8 that also goals are usually not absolute: they are states of a maximum or optimum relative to the earlier (or in general: other) states of the respective development. And therefore states which are less good or not yet at the maximum (or optimum) level are *permitted* by God's providence, either in order to achieve a higher good or to be at least integrated into a network of goals.

Therefore providence is not incompatible with relative goals that are relative evils.

32 Cf. the passage of Gregorius: "The evils that press on us in this world force us to go to God" (Migne (1887) 76,360).

16.4.3 (to 16.1.3)

The answer to this objection should be clear from section 16.3.8: The universe and especially the earth is full of *secondary causes*, which are imperfect and contingent and sometimes fail to perform their task. Since God has endowed his creatures with the ability to take part in the execution of his plan according to his providence. But God can integrate such local imperfect behavior into a global network of good goals.

16.4.4 (to 16.1.4) Good accompanied by evil

The objection that evil as such (as evil) is not desired by anything or anybody is correct. But evil may be conditionally accepted or even conditionally desired, if it is a necessary condition for achieving a basic good or a higher good. In this case, accepting, suffering and surmounting evil leads to a goal. This process however is not only compatible, but in agreement with providence.

Observe further that good and evil can be desired at the same time: Although evil is the opposite of good in general (unspecifically), it does not follow from that that a particular evil is the opposite (lack, absence) of a particular good; since it does not hold that every particular evil is the opposite of any particular good. Thus an operation which is an evil for the person A is not the opposite (lack) of (the state of) health of the person A, which is the good goal to be achieved. But it is the opposite of another good, namely of the state of being uninjured of that person A. If therefore a particular evil E is the opposite, i.e. the lack or absence of a particular good G, then G and E cannot be willed at the same time. On the other hand, if the particular evil E^* is the opposite (lack, absence) of another particular good G^* and therefore not the opposite (lack, absence) of G, then it is possible that G and E^* can be willed (desired) at the same time. Thus health (as the goal) and an operation (as a necessary condition) may be willed (desired) by the same person at the same time. In this case, good and evil are willed (desired) at the same time, even if the evil is willed (desired) only conditionally.

In connection with this, it is important to realize that in many, if not in all cases of achieving a good, this process is accompanied by evil or by several evils. There is an important principle which aptly describes this situation: *That* good which is accompanied by a certain evil is more desired than *that other* good which is cancelled by this evil. Thomas Aquinas was clearly aware of this principle:

"Never therefore would evil be sought after, not even accidentally, unless the good that accompanies the evil were more desired than the good of which the evil is the privation."[33]

(1) The general principle: good accompanied by evil
The general principle concerning good accompanied by evil (GAE) can be stated in the following precise form:

$$\text{GAE: } \forall p, q, r[(E(p) \wedge Priv(p, r) \wedge G(r) \wedge Conn(p, q) \wedge G(q) \wedge p \neq q \neq r) \rightarrow ((aWq \wedge aPref(q, r)) \rightarrow aWAp)]$$

Here 'p', 'q', 'r' are propositional variables representing states of affairs; '$Priv(p, r)$' means that p is the privation or cancellation of r, '$Conn(p, q)$' that p is necessarily connected with q in such a way that p is at least a necessary condition for q. '$aPref(q, r)$' means that a prefers q to r, and '$aWAp$' means that a accidentally wills that p.

In natural language: If an evil p is the privation of a good r and if the evil p is a necessary means for obtaining a good q, which is wanted to obtain (occur) by person a and good q is preferred to good r by a, then a accidentally (conditionally) wills that p obtains.

The above principle has some similarity to the so called "Practical Syllogism" of v.Wright, although the above is not a syllogism, but a factually true sentence in the sense of a law which holds either strictly (without exception) or statistically (with some exceptions). In fact, the so called "Practical Syllogism" is not logically valid as a syllogism, but can be turned into a general premise (which is factually true): If a wants that p obtains and a knows that q is a necessary condition for p then a wants q (or sets him- or herself to bring about q). But this consequent (then: ...) is not a conclusion which would logically follow from the two antecedent sentences. However given the factually true if – then – statement plus an instantiation of the antecedent, the respective instantiation of the consequent follows (by modus ponens) logically.[34]

Thomas Aquinas's principle however is much more sophisticated than the "Practical Syllogism": it explicitly speaks of the good r, which is cancelled by accepting the (necessary) evil p and of the preference of (the goal) q over r.

---

33 Aquinas (1981) I, 19,9

34 Cf. Weingartner (1984) ch.5 and Tuomela (1977). However I do not agree with Tuomela's revision of von Wright's Practical Syllogism, which Tuomela presents on pages 177, 178 of Tuomela (1977). This version still does not have a logically valid form. Only the different version in Tuomela (1977) p.180, where Tuomela adds a general premise – like the one mentioned above – is acceptable as a logically valid argument.

Thus the evil p is only conditionally and accidentally wanted (or willed): under the condition that it is necessary to achieve the goal (the higher good) and that the goal is preferred to that good which is cancelled by the (occurrence of the) evil.

(2) Applications of the principle
The evil of lying (to the judge) is accidentally and conditionally willed, i.e. under the condition that the liar desires to make the judge believe that he is innocent and that he prefers that to the not-committing a lie (being innocent concerning lying, i.e. being honest) such that he only accidentally wills to lie. Also, the example of an operation again applies: The operation is willed accidentally and conditionally, i.e. under the condition that it is a necessary condition for retaining health and that the good of (retaining) health is preferred to the good (of being unhurt) which is erased by the operation. In a similar way, all necessary evil (cf. 16.3.3.2) obeys this principle.

Consider as a further group of examples those of making mistakes during a process of learning. It is an experienced fact that some mistakes are made in every learning process; since learning is a process of trial and error and learning without error is, realistically speaking, either impossible or extremely improbable. Such errors or mistakes are evils and they are necessary in order to improve, which is possible by learning from one's own mistakes and from the mistakes of others. Thus the mother who wills (as a goal) that her daughter learns to cook, conditionally wills (or wills as a means) that the daughter tries cooking herself while taking into account that the daughter will make mistakes. Similarly, the teacher in the physical laboratory wills (as a goal) that his students learn to carry out physical experiments and he conditionally wills (as a means) that they (learn to) operate or (to) use the physical instruments properly, in order to make measurements. As the mother, the teacher also knows (can predict with high probability) that the students will make mistakes. In a similar way, the master allows for bungling and botching of his apprentices.

In all these cases the goal (to improve by a process of learning) is preferred to the respective good which is cancelled by making mistakes which are a part of the necessary means (as a process of trial of error) which are willed conditionally. In a similar way, God's providence cares for the global and superior goal, permitting failures concerning local goals and in this way is compatible with necessary evil as means for realizing higher goals.

16.4.5 (to 16.1.5)

According to ch. 10, every occurring event comes under God's providence; consequently, every occurring evil comes under God's providence, since every evil is an event. Still, from this it does not follow that God takes care of all evil in the same sense. Of some evils caused by creatures, God takes care as the master builder takes care of his apprentices, leading them to improvement; of others by using them as a means to reach some local or global goals. Moral evils caused by humans presuppose the ability of free will and free will decision. Since this ability was given to man by God via his creation, it must come under his providence and consequently be compatible with his providence. In this sense, God's care refers equally to humans, but in another sense, there might be a difference as explained by Thomas Aquinas:

> "God however, extends His providence over the just in a certain more excellent way than over the wicked; inasmuch as He prevents anything happening which would impede their final salvation ... (cf. Rom. 8,28). But from the fact that He does not restrain the wicked from the evil of sin, He is said to abandon them: not that he altogether withdraws His providence from them."[35]

Again in another sense, God's care is different with respect to humans and animals:

> "Since a rational creature has, through its free will, control over its actions, ... it is subject of divine providence in an especial manner, so that something is imputed to it as a fault, or as a merit; and there is given it accordingly something by way of punishment or reward. In this way the Apostle withdraws oxen from the care of God: not, however, that individual irrational creatures escape the care of divine providence; as was the opinion of the Rabbi Moses (Moses Maimonides)."[36]

16.4.6 (to 16.1.6)

It is correct that *that* evil which comes under God's providence is either willed or permitted by God. But from this it does not follow that all evil is either willed or permitted by God. Since providence is concerned with creation, it only follows that evils *occurring* in creation (in the universe) – may they be past, present or future (relative to our time reference) – are either willed or permitted by God. But

35 Aquinas (1981) I, 22,2 ad 4.
36 Ibid. Ad 5.

there is a great amount of evil conceivable which is neither willed nor permitted by God: a disease which would cause all mankind to die out, to take away free will from mankind, to take away rationality from mankind or to erase salvation through Christ ... This list could be continued indefinitely. Therefore it is not true that all evil is either willed or permitted by God. But it is true that all occurring evil is either willed or permitted by God. And thus the antecedens of the third premise of 16.1.6: "But if all evil ... " is false and so the premise is trivially true such that the consequence can be false too, as it in fact is. In symbolic language the premises are these:

1. $[(\forall p)[Prov(p) \rightarrow (gWp \vee gPp)]$
   ... where 'p' is a propositional variable representing states of affairs, $Prov(p)$ is used as in ch. 1 and gWp and gPp as in ch. 12. Since all evil can be interpreted as a state of affairs premise, 1. also holds for all evils:
2. $[(\forall e)[Prov(e) \rightarrow (gWe \vee gPe)]$
3. $(\forall e)(gWe \vee gPe) \rightarrow MVg$ ... MV for 'malevolent'
4. $\neg MVg$

Since from 3. and 4. it follows by *modus tollens* that $(\exists e)(\neg gWe \wedge \neg gPe)$ -- i.e. for some evil, God neither wills it nor permits it – it further follows w.r.t 2. and 1. only that some evil does not belong to God's providence. This is true and also evident from the above list of examples. On the other hand, nothing follows for evil which is in fact occurring. Therefore nothing hinders that all occurring evil comes under God's providence and consequently such evil is not incompatible with God's providence.

Bibliography

Th. Aquinas. *De Veritate. Engl.Transl.: The Disputed Questions on Truth, Vol. I-III.* H. Regnery Company, Chicago, 1954.

Th. Aquinas. *Summa Theologica.* Christian Classics, Westminster, Maryland, 1981.

Th. Aquinas. *On Evil (De Malo).* Univ. of Notre Dame Press, Notre Dame, 1995.

W. Arber. Genetic Variation: Molecular Mechanisms and Impact on Microbial Evolution. *FEMS Microbiology Reviews*, 24:p.1–7, 2000.

Aristotle. Nichomachean Ethics. In J. Barnes, editor, *The Complete Works of Aristotle. Revised Oxford Translation, Vol.1.* Princeton, 1985.

A. Aspect et al. Experimental Tests of Bell's Inequalities using Time-varying Analysers. *Phys. Rev. Lett*, 49:pp. 1804–1807, 1982.

Augustine. Enchiridon de Fide Spe et Charitate. In J.P. Migne, editor, *Patrologia, Ser.Lat.* Paris, 1887.

F. Ayala. Teleological Explanation in Evolutionary Biology. *Philosophy of Science*, 37:p.1–15, 1970.

F. Ayala. The Mechanism of Evolution. *Scientific American*, 239, 1978.

F. Ayala. Intelligent Design: The Original Version. In J.S. Wilkins, editor, *Intelligent Design and Religion as a Natural Phenomenon, Vol.V*, pages pp.361–384. Ashgate, London, 2010.

J.A. Baird and D.A. Baldwin. Making Sense of Human Behavior. Action Parsing and Intentional Inference. In B.F. Malle, L.J. Moses, and D.A. Baldwin, editors, *Intentions and Intentionality. Foundatioons of Social Cognition MA*, pages pp.193–206. The MIT Press, Cambridge Mass, 2001.

E.M. Baker. *Science and Health with Key to the Scriptures.* Authorized Edition, 1934.

J. Bargh and M. Ferguson. Beyond Behaviorism. *Psychological Bulletin*, 126:p.925–945, 2000.

J.D. Barrow and F.J. Tipler. *The Anthropic Cosmological Principle.* Oxford Univ. Press, Oxford, 1986.

Basilius. Hexaemeron. In J.P. Migne, editor, *Patrologia, Ser.Graeca.* Paris, 1886.

J. Bell. On the Einstein Podolski Rosen Paradox. *Physics*, I:p.195–200, 1964.

J. Bell. On the Problems of Hidden Variables in Quantum Mechanics. *Reviews of Modern Physics*, 38:p.447–452, 1966.

J. Bell. *Bertlmann's Socks and the Nature of Reality. Reprinted in: Bell (1987) p. 139-158.* Cambridge University Press, Cambridge, 1981.

J. Bell. *Speakable and Unspeakable in Quantum Mechanics.* Cambridge University Press, Cambridge, 1987.

M.R. Bennett and P.M.S. Hacker. *Philosophical Foundations of Neuroscience.* Blackwell, Oxford, 2003.

E.E. Boesch. *Symbolic Action Theory and Cultural Psychology.* Springer, Berlin, 1991.

D. Bohm. A Suggested Interpretation of the Quantum Theory in Terms of "Hidden Variables". Part I and II. *Physical Review*, 85:p.166–193, 1952.

V. Braitenberg. *Vehicles.* Cambridge Univ. Press, Cambridge, 1984.

R.N. Brandon. *Adaption and Environment.* Princeton Univ. Press, Princeton, 1990.

Th. Breuer. The Impossibility of Accurate State Self-Measurements. *Philosophy of Science*, 62: pp. 197–214, 1995.

Th. Breuer. Subjective Decoherence in Quantum Measurements. *Synthese*, 107:pp. 1–17, 1996.

M. Bunge. *The Furniture of the World (=Treatise on Basic Philosophy Vol III)*. Reidel, Dordrecht, 1977.

M. Bunge. *A World of Systems (=Treatise on Basic Philosophy Vol IV)*. Reidel, Dordrecht, 1979.

M. Bunge. *The Good and the Right (= Treatise on Basic Philosophy, Vol VIII)*. Reidel, Dordrecht, 1989.

G. Casati and B.V. Chirikov. The Legacy of Chaos in Quantum Mechanics. In G. Casati and B.V. Chirikov, editors, *Quantum Chaos: Between Order and Disorder*. Cambridge Univ. Press, Cambridge, 1995a.

G. Casati and B.V. Chirikov. *Quantum Chaos: Between Order and Disorder*. Cambridge Univ. Press, Cambridge, 1995b.

G. Chaitin. On the Length of Programs for Computing Finite Binary Sequences. *Journal of the ACM*, 13(4):pp.547–569, 1966.

G. Chaitin. *Information, Randomness and Incompleteness; Papers on Algorithmic Information Theory*. World Scientific Publ. Comp, 1987.

B.V. Chirikov. Natural Laws and Human Prediction. In P. Weingartner and G. Schurz, editors, *Law and Prediction in the Light of Chaos Research. Lecture Notes in Physics 473*, pages p.10–33. Springer, Berlin, 1996.

B.V. Chirikov. Linear and Nonlinear Dynamical Chaos. *Open Systems and Information Dynamics*, 4:p.241–280, 1997.

J.F. Clauser et al. Proposed Experiment to Test Local Hidden-Variable Theories. *Phys.Rev.Lett*, 23:p. 880f, 1969.

J.H. Conway and S. Kochen. The Strong Free Will Theorem. *Notices of the American Mathematical Society*, 56,2:p.226–232, 2009.

W.L. Craig. *The Problem of Divine Foreknowledge and Future Contigents from Aristotle to Suarez*. Brill, Leiden, 1988.

W.L. Craig. *Divine Foreknowledge and Human Freedom*. Brill, Leiden, 1991.

G. Csibra, S. Bíró, O. Koós, and G. Gergely. One-Year-Old Infants use Teleological Tepresentations of Actions Productively. *Cognitive Science*, 27:111–133, 2003.

P.C.W. Davis. *The Accidental Universe*. Cambridge Univ. Press, Cambridge, 1982.

R. Dawkins. *Climbing Mount Improbable*. Vicking, London, 1996.

E. de Schutter. Computational Neuroscience: More Math is Needed to Understand the Human Brain. In B. Engquist and W. Schmid, editors, *Mathematics Unlimited – 2001 and Beyond, Vol I*, pages p.381–391. Springer, Heidelberg, 2001.

M.J. Denton. *Nature's Destiny. How the Laws of Biology Reveal Purpose in the Universe*. The Free Press, New York, 1998.

T. Dobzhansky, F.J. Ayala, G.L. Stebbins, and J.W. Valentine. *Evolution*. Freeman, S. Francisco, 1977.

Th. Dobzhansky. *Genetics and the Origin of Species*. Columbia Univ. Press, New York, 1937.

Th. Dobzhansky. On some Fundamental Concepts of Darwinian Biology. *Evol. Biol*, 2,1, 1968.

J. Eccles. A Unitary Hypothesis of Mind-Brain Interaction in the Cerebral Cortex. *Proceedings of the Royal Society, London*, B1990 240:p.433–451, 1990.

J. Eccles. *How the Self Controls its Brain*. Springer, Berlin, 1994.

P. Ehrenfest. In what Way does it Become Manifest in the Fundamental Laws of Physics that Space has Three Dimensions. *Proceedings of the Amsterdam Academy*, 20:p.200f, 1917.

P. Ehrenfest. Welche Rolle spielt die Dreidimensionalitaet des Raumes in den Grundgesetzen der Physik? *Annalen der Physik*, 61:p.440f, 1920.

M: Eigen and P. Schuster. *The Hypercycle. A Principle of Natural Self-Organisation*. Springer, Berlin, 1979.

A. Einstein. Kosmologische Betrachtungen zur allgemeinen Relativitätstheorie. *Königliche Preussische Akademie der Wissenschaften (Berlin) Sitzungsberichte*, I:p.142–152, 1917.

A. Einstein, B. Podolsky, and N. Rosen. Can the Quantum-Mechanical Description of Physical Reality be Considered Complete. *Phys.Rev*, 47:pp. 777–780, 1935.

H.J. Fahr. Zum Wachstum kosmischer Strukturen. Aspekte und Ideen zur Strukturierung des Universums. In K. Decker, editor, *Wachstum als Problem. Modelle und Regulation*, pages p.7–51. Alber, Freiburg, 1997.

B. Falkenburg. *Mythos Determinismus. Wieviel erklärt uns die Hirnforschung?* Springer Spektrum, Heidelberg, 2012.

R.P. Feynman. *Six Not so Easy Pieces. Einstein's Relativity, Symmetry and Space-Time*. Perseus Books, Cambridge, Mass, 1997.

S.J. Freedman et al. Experimental Test of Local Hidden-Variable Theories. *Phys. Rev. Lett*, 28: 938–941, 1972.

D.J. Futuyma. *Evolutionary Biology*. Sinauer Associates, Massachusetts, 1986.

D.J. Futuyma. *Evolutionsbiologie*. Birkhaeuser, Basel, 1990.

P.T. Geach. *Providence and Evil*. Cambridge Univ. Press, Cambridge, 1977.

G. Geraci. A Molecular Mechanism for the Evolution of Eukaryotes. In J. Mosterin, editor, *Intern. Conf. on Philosphy of Science. Univ. De Vigo*, pages p.59–73. 1996.

K. Gödel. *MAX PHIL X (posthumous works prepared for publishing by G. Crocco and E.M. Engelen.)*.

K. Gödel. Die Vollständigkeit der Axiome des logischen Funktionenkalküls. *Monatshefte für Mathematik und Physik*, 37:p.349–360, 1930.

K. Gödel. Über formal unentscheidbare Sätze der Principia Mathematica und verwandter Systeme. *Monatshefte für Mathematik und Physik*, 38:p.173–198, 1931.

K. Gödel. An Example of a New Type of Cosmological Solution of Einstein's Field Equations of Gravitation. Reviews of Modern Physics, 21, 1949, p.447-450. Reprinted in:. In S. Feferman, editor, *K. Gödel, Collected Works. Vol.II*. Oxford Univ. Press, Oxford, 1990a.

K. Gödel. Rotating Universes in General Relativity Theory. Proceedings of the Intern. Congress of Mathematicians 1950. American Math. Society, Vol.I, p.175-181 Reprinted in:. In S. Feferman, editor, *K. Gödel, Collected Works. Vol.II*. Oxford Univ. Press, Oxford, 1990b.

J. Hadamard. *Lectures on Cauchy's problem in linear partial differential equations*. Yale Univ. Press, New Haven, 1923.

H. Haken. *Synergetics. An Introduction*. Springer, Berlin, 1983.

H. Haken. *Advanced Synergetics*. Springer, Berlin, 1987.

H. Haken. *Information and Self-Organisation. A Macroscopic Approach to Complex Systems*. Springer, Berlin, 1988.

H. Haken. *Synergetik*. Springer, Berlin, 1990.

H. Haken and A. Wunderlin. *Die Selbststrukturierung der Materie*. Vieweg, Braunschweig, 1991.

H. Haken, A. Wunderlin, and S. Yigitbasi. On the Foundations of Synergetics. In P. Weingartner and G. Schurz, editors, *Law and Prediction in the Light of Chaos Research. Lecture Notes in Physics 473*, pages p.243–279. Springer, Berlin, 1996.

J.B.S. Haldane. *Possible Worlds*. Chatto & Windus, London, 1930.

J.B.S. Haldane. *The Inequality of Man*. Penguin Books, Harmondsworth, 1937.

J.J. Halliwell. Quantum Cosmology and Time Asymmetry. In J.J. Halliwell et al., editor, *Physical Origins of Time Assymetry*, pages pp.369–389. Cambridge Univ. Press, Cambridge, 1994.

J.K. Hamlin, K. Wynn, and P. Bloom. Social evaluation by preverbal infants. *Nature*, Vol. 450 Issue 7168 – 11/15/2007:557–559, 2007.

S. Haring. *Probleme mit Identitätsaussagen im Kindergartenalter. Diploma Thesis.* University of Salzburg, Department of Psychology, Salzburg, 2013.

S. Haring and P. Weingartner. On the Conceptual Clarification of Human Environment, Action Space and Quality of Life. In M.G. Weiss and H. Greif, editors, *Ethics – Society – Politics. Papers of the 35th International Wittgenstein Symposium 2012*, pages 345–347. Kirchberg, 2012.

S. Haring and P. Weingartner. Children's Understanding of Identity. In D. Camhy, editor, *Cognition, Emotion, Communication. Proceedings of the International Conference on Philosophy for Children*. Ontos/de Gruyter, Berlin, 2014a.

S. Haring and P. Weingartner. Environment, Action Space and Quality of Life. An Attempt for Conceptual Clarification. In J.V. Beziau and D. Krause, editors, *Essays in Honour of Patrick Suppes' 90th birthday*. College Publications, Tributes Series, 2014b.

J.B. Hartle and S.W. Hawking. Wave Function of the Universe. *Physical Review*, D28:p.2960–2975, 1983.

S.W. Hawking. *A Brief History of Time*. London, Bantam, 1988.

S.W. Hawking and G.F.R. Ellis. *The Large Scale Structure of Space-Time*. Cambridge University Press, Cambridge, 1973.

S.W. Hawking and W. Israel. *General Relativity: An Einstein Centennary Survey*. Cambridge University Press, Cambridge, 1979.

S.W. Hawking and R. Penrose. The singularities of gravitational collapse and cosmology. *Proceedings of the Royal Society London*, A314:p.529–548, 1970.

M. Heller. Can the Universe Explain Itself? In W. Löffler and P. Weingartner, editors, *Knowledge and Belief. Proceedings of the 26th International Wittgenstein-Symposium*, pages p.316–328. öbv&hpt, Vienna, 2004.

H. Helmholtz. Über die Tatsachen, welche der Geometrie zugrunde liegen. *Göttinger gelehrte Nachrichten*, 1868.

J. Hick. *Evil and the God of Love*. Macmillan Press, London, 1977.

F. Hoyle and Ch. Wickramasinghe. *Evolution from Space*. Simon and Schuster, New York, 1981.

D.L. Hull. *Philosophy of Biological Science*. Prentice Hall, Englewood Cliffs, 1974.

D. Hume. *Dialogues Concerning Natural Religion. Ed. N.K. Smith*. Bobbs-Merrill, Indianapolis, 1977.

J. Huxley. *Evolution. The Modern Synthesis*. Allen and Unwin, London, 1974.

P.v. Inwagen. *God, Knowledge and Mystery*. Cornell Univ. Press, Ithaca and London, 1995.

E. Jablonka and M.J. Lamb. *Evolution in Four Dimensions*. MIT Press, Cambridge Mass, 2005.

M. Jammer. *The Philosophy of Quantum Mechanics*. Wiley, New York, 1974.

M. Jammer. *Concepts of Simultaneity*. John Hopkins U.P, Baltimore, 2006.

R. Junker and S. Scherer. *Evolution. Ein kritisches Lehrbuch*. Weyel, Giessen, 1998.

I. Kant. *Kritik der reinen Vernunft, Hartknoch, Riga. Engl. Transl.: Critique of Pure Reason, 1787*. McMillan, London, 1929.

St.A. Kauffman. *The Origins of Order. Self-Organization and Selection in Evolution*. Oxford Univ. Press, Oxford, 1993.

St.A. Kauffman. *At Home in the Universe*. Oxford Univ. Press, Oxford, 1995.

St.A. Kauffman. *Investigations*. Oxford University Press, Oxford, 2000.

St.A. Kauffman. Prolegomenon to a General Biology. In W.A. Dembski and M. Ruse, editors, *Debating Design: From Darwin to DNA*. Cambridge Universtiy Press, Cambridge, 2004.

St.A. Kauffman. *Reinventing the Sacred: A New View of Science, Reason, and Religion.* Basic Books, New York, 2008.

T.S. Kemp. *The Origin and Evolution of Mammals.* Oxford Univ. Press, Oxford, 2005.

A.N. Kolmogorov. On Tables of Random Numbers. *Sankhya: The Indian Journal of Statistics,* Series A 25:pp.369–376, 1963.

A.N. Kolmogorov. Three Approaches to the Quantitative Definition of Information. *Problemy Peredaci Informacii,* 1:pp.4–7, 1965.

B.O. Küppers. *Information and the Origin of Life.* The MIT-Press, Cambridge, Mass, 1990.

U. Kutschera. *Evolutionsbiologie.* Eugen Ulmer, Stutgart, 2008.

P.G. Kwiat et al. High-Visibiliy Interference in a Bell-Inequality Experiment for Energy and Time. *Phys. Rev. Lett,* 75:4337, 1995.

P. Laplace. *Essay philosophique sur les probabilities. Courcier, Paris, Engl. Transl.: A philosophical essay on probabilities, 1814.* Dover, New York, 1951.

J. Laskar. Large Scale Chaos in the Solar System. *Astronomy and Astrophysics,* 287:L9–L12, 1994.

K.V. Laurikainen. *Beyond the Atom.* Springer, Heidelberg, 1988.

G.W. Leibniz. *Die philosophischen Schriften von G.W. Leibniz. Ed. by C.I. Gerhardt, 7 vols.* Berlin, 1875–1890.

G.W. Leibniz. *Theodicy. Essays on the Goodness of God, the Freedom of Man and the Origin of Evil. Transl. by E.M. Huggard.* Edinburgh and London, 1952.

G.W. Leibniz. *Opuscules et fragments inedits de Leibniz, ed. L. Couturat. Presses Universitaires de France. 1903 Reprint: Olms, Hildesheim.* Paris, 1961.

R.C. Lewontin. The Units of Selection. *Annual Review of Ecology and Systematics,* 1:p.1–18, 1970.

B. Libet. Do We Have Free Will? In R. Kane, editor, *The Oxford Handbook of Free Will,* pages p.551–564. Oxford UP, Oxford, 2002.

B. Libet. *Mind Time. Wie das Gehirn Bewusstsein produziert.* Suhrkamp, Frankfurt, 2005.

A. Linde. *Inflation and Quantum Cosmology.* Academic Press, 1990.

W. Löffler and P. Weingartner. *Knowledge and Belief.* öbv&hpt, Vienna, 2004.

C.O. Lovejoy. *Life in the Universe. (edited by Billingham, J.).* MIT Press, Cambridge Mass, 1981.

M. Mahner and M. Bunge. *Philosophische Grundlagen der Biologie.* Springer, Berlin, 2000.

F.W. Maitland. Elizabethan Gleanings. In F.W. Maitland, editor, *Collected Papers, Vol. 3,* pages p.157–165. London, 1911.

J. Maynard-Smith. *Evolution and the Theory of Games.* Cambridge Univ. Press, Cambridge, 1982.

J. Maynard-Smith and E. Szathmary. *The Major Transitions in Evolution.* Oxford Univ. Press, Oxford, 1999.

E. Mayr. *Systematics and the Origin of Species.* Columbia Univ. Press, New York, 1942.

E. Mayr. *Das ist Biologie.* Spektrum, Heidelberg, 1998.

N.A. Meltzoff and R. Brooks. “Like Me” as a Building Block for Understanding Other Minds. Bodily Acts, Attention and Intention. In B.F. Malle, L.J. Moses, and D.A. Baldwin, editors, *Intentions and Intentionality. Foundatioons of Social Cognition MA,* pages pp.171–191. The MIT Press, Cambridge Mass, 2001.

A. Meyer. Porträt, Interview. *Spektrum,* 2010.

A. Meyer et al. Monophyletic origin of Lake Viktoria Cichlid Fishes Suggested by Mitochondrial DNA-Sequences. *Nature,* 355 (1990):p.352f, 1990.

J.P. Migne. *Patrologia, Ser.Lat.* Paris, 1887.

B. Mitchell. *The Philosophy of Religion.* Oxford Univ. Press, Oxford, 1971.

P. Mittaelstaedt. *The Interpretation of Quantum Mechanics and the Measurement Process.* Cambridge University Press, Cambridge, 1998.

P. Mittelstaedt. Concepts of Time in Physics and Cosmology. In E. Agazzi, editor, *Time in the Different Scientific Approaches*, pages p.113–141. Epistemologia 14, 2008.

P. Mittelstaedt. On the meaning of the constant “c” in modern physics. *Journal of General Philosophy of Science*, 2009.

P. Mittelstaedt and P. Weingartner. *Laws of Nature*. Springer, Berlin, 2005.

J.L. Monod. *Chance and Necessity: An essay on the natural philosophy of modern biology (engl. translation)*. Knopf, New York, 1972.

J.L. Monod. On the Molecular Theory of Evolution. In R. Harré, editor, *Problems of Scientific Revolution. Progress and Obstacles to Progress in Science*. Oxford, 1975.

Moses Maimonides. *Guide of the Perplexed. French Translation: Le guide des egares, traite de theologie et de philosophie. 3 Vols*. Paris, 1856–66.

E. Nagel. *The Structure of Science*. Routledge, 1971.

G. Nicolis and I:. Prigogine. *Die Erforschung des Komplexen*. Piper, Munich, 1987.

M.A. Nowak. *Evolutionary Dynamics*. Harvard Univ. Press, Cambridge Mass, 2006.

K.H. Onishi and R. Baillargeon. Do 15-month-old infants understand false beliefs? *Science*, 308: 255–258, 2005.

B. Pascal. *Pensées. In: Oevres Complétes*. Editions du Seuil, Paris, 1963.

R. Penrose. Singularities and Time-Asymmetry. In S.W. Hawking and W. Israel, editors, *General Relativity: An Einstein Centennary Survey*, pages pp. 581–638. Cambridge University Press, Cambridge, 1979.

R. Penrose. *The Road to Reality*. A. Knopf, New York, 2005.

A.A. Penzias and R.W. Wilson. Measurement of Excess Antenna Temperature at 4080 Mc/s. *Astrophysical Journal*, 142:p. 419, 1965.

J. Perner. *Understanding the Representational Mind*. MIT Press, Cambridge, Mass., 1991.

Johannes. Philoponos. *De aeternitate mundi: contra Proclum. Engl. Transl. by M.Share: Against Proclus. On the Eternity of the World*. Duckworth, London, 2004.

A. Plantinga. The Free Will Defence. In B. Mitchell, editor, *The Philosophy of Religion*, pages p.105–120. Oxford Univ. Press, Oxford, 1971.

A. Plantinga. *God, Freedom and Evil*. Erdmans Publ. Comp, Michigan, 1974.

K.S. Pollard. Der feine Unterschied. *Spektrum der Wissenschaft (Scientific American)*, 7:p.56–62, 2009.

K. R. Popper. Indeterminism in Quantum Physics and in Classical Physics. *British Journal for the Philosophy of Science*, 1:p.117–133 (part I) and 173–195 (part II), 1950.

K.R. Popper. *The Logic of Scientific Discovery*. Hutchinson, London, 1959.

K.R. Popper. *Of Clouds and Clocks. In: Popper: Objective Knowledge*. pp. 206–255, Oxford, 1965.

K.R. Popper and J. Eccles. *The Self and its Brain*. Springer, Berlin, 1985.

I. Prigogine. *From Being to Becoming*. Freeman, San Francisco, 1977.

I. Prigogine. Time, Chaos and the Laws of Nature. In P. Weingartner and G. Schurz, editors, *Law and Prediction in the Light of Chaos Research. Lecture Notes in Physics 473*, pages p.3–9. Springer, Berlin, 1996.

I. Prigogine and I. Stengers. *Time, Chaos and the Quantum. Towards the Resolution of the Time Paradox*. Munich, 1993.

W. Prinz. Der Mensch ist nicht frei. In Ch. Geyer, editor, *Hirnforschung und Willensfreiheit*, pages p.20–26. Suhrkamp, Frankfurt, 2004.

M. Rees. *Our Cosmic Habitat*. Princeton Univ. Press, Princeton, 2001.

M. Rees. Numerical Coincidences and ‘Tuning’ in Cosmology. *Astrophysics and Space Time*, 285: p.375–388, 2003.

B.R. Reichenbach. *Evil and a Good God.* Fordham Univ. Press, New York, 1982.

I. Reznikoff. A Logical Proof of the Free-Will Theorem. *Arxiv: 1008.3661v1 [quant-ph]*, 21 Aug: p.1–3, 2010.

B. Riemann. *Uber die Hypothesen welche der Geometrie zugrunde liegen, In: Abhandlungen der Königlichen Gesellschaft der Wissenschaften zu Göttingen, 1867.* Suhrkamp Verlag, Frankufrt/M, 1854.

G. Roth. *Fühlen, Denken, Handeln.* Suhrkamp, Frankfurt, 2001.

G. Roth. Worüber wir Hirnforscher reden – und in welcher Weise? In Ch. Geyer, editor, *Hirnforschung und Willensfreiheit.* Suhrkamp, Frankfurt, 2004.

D. Ruelle. Deterministic Chaos: The Science and the Fiction. *Proceedings of the Royal Society London*, A 427:p.241–248, 1990.

M. Ruse. *Can a Darwinian be a Christian? The Relationship between Science and Religion.* Cambridge University Press, Cambridge, 2001.

W. Salzburger and A. Meyer. The species flocks of East African cichlid fishes: recent advances in molecular phylogenetics and population genetics. *Naturwissenschaften*, 91:p.277–290, 2004.

D. Schluter. Evidence for ecological specification and its alternative. *Science*, 323:p.737–741, 2009.

E. Schrödinger. *Was ist ein Naturgesetz?* Oldenburg, München, 1961.

G. Schurz. *The Is-Ought Problem. An Investigation in Philosophical Logic.* Kluver, Dordrecht, 1997.

H.G. Schuster. *Deterministic Chaos.* VCH, Weinheim, 1989.

P. Schuster. From Belief to Facts in Evolutionary Theory. In W. Löffler and P. Weingartner, editors, *Knowledge and Belief*, pages p.353–363. öbv&hpt, Vienna, 2004.

P. Schuster. Evolution und Design. Versuch einer Bestandsaufnahme der Evolutionstheorie. In S.O. Horn and S. Wiedehofer, ed., *Schöpfung und Evolution*, p.25–56. St. Ulrich, Augsburg, 2007.

P. Schuster. Free Will, Information, Quantum Mechanics, and Biology. *Complexity*, 15,1:p.8–10, 2009.

G.G. Simpson. *The Meaning of Evolution.* Yale UP, Connecticut, 1949.

W. Singer. Verschaltungen legen uns fest: Wir sollten aufhören von Freiheit zu sprechen. In Ch. Geyer, editor, *Hirnforschung und Willensfreiheit*, pages p.30–65. Suhrkamp, Frankfurt, 2004.

J.M. Sobel et al. The biology of speciation. *Evolution*, 64:p.295–315, 2010.

F.J.K. Soontiens. Evolution: Teleology or Chance? *Journal for General Philosophy of Science*, 22: p.133–141, 1991.

E.J. Squires. The Unique World of the Everett-Version of Quantum Theory. *Foundations of Physics Letters*, 1 (1988):p.13–20, 1988.

H.P. Stapp. Quantum Propensities and the Brain-Mind Connection. *Foundations of Physics*, 21: p. 1451–1477, 1991.

H.P. Stapp. *Mind Matter and Quantum Mechanics.* Springer, Berlin, 1993.

G.L. Stebbins. *From DNA to Man.* Freeman, 1982.

W. Stegmüller. *Hauptströmungen der Gegenwartsphilosophie Vol II.* Kröner, Stuttgart, 1975.

P. Suppes. *Representation and Invariance of Scientific Structures.* CSLI, Stanford, 2002.

L. Susskind. *The Cosmic Landscape: String Theory and the Illusion of Intelligent Design.* Back Bay Books, New York, 2006.

R. Swinburne. *The Existence of God.* Clarendon Press, Oxford, 1991.

R. Swinburne. *Providence and the Problem of Evil.* Clarendon Press, Oxford, 1998.

R. Swinburne. God as the Simplest Explanation of the Universe. In A. O'Hear, editor, *Philosophy and Religion*, pages p.3–24. Cambridge Univ. Press, Cambridge, 2011.

M. Tomasello, M. Carpenter, J. Call, T. Behne, and H. Moll. Understanding and sharing intentions. The origin of cultural cognition. *Behavioral and Brain Sciences*, 28:675–735, 2005.

R. Tuomela. *Human Action and its Explanation.* Reidel, Dordrecht, 1977.

A. Vilenkin. Creation of Universes from Nothing. *Physics Letters*, 117B:pp. 25–28, 1982.

S. Walter. Wie frei sind wir eigentlich – empirisch? *Philosophia Naturalis*, 46:p. 8–35, 2009.

G. Weihs et al. Violation of Bell's Inequality under Strict Einstein Locality Conditions. *Phys. Rev. Lett*, 81:pp. 5039–5043, 1998.

St. Weinberg. Towards the Final Laws of Physics. In St. Weinberg, editor, *Elementary Particles and the Laws of Phyiscs. The 1986 Dirac Memorial Lectures*, pages pp.61–110. Cambridge U.P, Cambridge, 1987.

P. Weingartner. *Wissenschaftstheorie II,1. Grundlagenprobleme der Logik und Mathematik.* Frommann-Holzboog, Stuttgart-Bad Cannstatt, 1976.

P. Weingartner. Analogy among Systems. *Dialectica*, 33:355–378, 1979.

P. Weingartner. A System of Rational Belief, Knowledge and Assumption. *Grazer Philosophische Studien*, 12/13 (1981):143–165, 1981.

P. Weingartner. Conditions of Rationality for the Concepts Belief, Knowledge and Assumption. *Dialectica*, 36 (1982):243–263, 1982.

P. Weingartner. The Ideal of Mathematization of All Sciences and of "More Geometrico" in Descartes and Leibniz. In W.R. Shea, editor, *Nature Mathematized*, pages pp. 151–195. Dordrecht, Holland, 1983a.

P. Weingartner. Auf welchen Prinzipien beruht die Naturrechtslehre? In D. Mayer-Maly and P.M. Simons, editors, *Das Naturrechtsdenken heute und morgen. Gedächtnisschrift für René Marcic*, pages 517–544. Duncker & Humblot, Berlin, 1983b.

P. Weingartner. On the Introduction of Teleological Arguments into Scientific Discourse. *La Science Face aux Attentes de l'Homme Contemporain. Colloque de l'Académie Internationale de Philosophie des Sciences, Sevilla 1983. Archives de l'Institut International des Sciences Théoriques*, 26. Bruxelles 1984:196–218, 1984.

P. Weingartner. *Scientific and Religious Belief. Philosophical Studies Series 59.* Dordrecht, Kluwer, 1994.

P. Weingartner. Under what Transformations are Laws Invariant? In P. Weingartner and G. Schurz, editors, *Law and Prediction in the Light of Chaos Research. Lecture Notes in Physics 473*, pages pp.47–88. Springer, Berlin, 1996.

P. Weingartner. Can the Laws of Nature (of Physics) be Complete? In M.L. Dalla Chiara et al., editor, *Logic and Scientific Method*, pages p.429–446. Kluwer, Dordrecht, 1997.

P. Weingartner. Are Statistical Laws Genuine Laws? A Concern of Poincaré and Boltzmann. *Philosophia Scientiae*, 3(2) 1998/99:pp.215–236, 1998.

P. Weingartner. *Evil. Different Kinds of Evil in the Light of a Modern Theodicy.* Peter Lang, Frankfurt, 2003.

P. Weingartner. *Omniscience. From a Logical Point of View.* Heusenstamm, Ontos, 2008a.

P. Weingartner. The Places of Value in Science. In E. Agazzi and F. Minazzi, editors, *Science and Ethics. The Axiological Contexts of Science*, pages 141–154. Peter Lang, Bruxelles, 2008b.

P. Weingartner. Time-Reversibility and Time-Irreversibility of Laws of Nature. In E. Agazzi, editor, *Time in the Different Scientific Approaches*, pages 207–220. Epistemologia 14, 2008, 2008c.

P. Weingartner. Kinds of Chance and Randomness. In St. Borrmann and G. Rager, editors, *Kosmologie, Evolution, und Evolutionäre Anthropologie*, pages 223–254. Alber, Freiburg, 2009a.

P. Weingartner. Matrix Based Logic for Application in Physics. *The Review of Symbolic Logic*, 2 (2009):132–163, 2009b.

P. Weingartner. Basic Logic for Application in Physics and its Intuitionistic Alternative. *Foundations of Physics*, 40:1578–1596, 2010a.

P. Weingartner. The Concept of Chance in the Theory of Evolution. In E. Agazzi and F. Minazzi, editors, *Evolutionism and Religion*, pages 49–75. Mimesis, Milano, 2010b.

P. Weingartner. *God's Existence. Can it be Proven? A Logical Commentary on the Five Ways of Thomas Aquinas*. Ontos, Frankfurt, 2010c.

P. Weingartner and S. Haring. On the Compatibility of Evil and Freedom. In G. Crocco and E.M. Engelen, editors, *Goedelian Studies on the Max-Phil Notebooks, Vol.1*. Presses Universitaires de Provence, Aix en Provence, 2014.

P. Weingartner and G. Schurz. *Law and Prediction in the Light of Chaos Research. Lecture Notes in Physics 473*. Springer, Berlin, 1996.

A.M. Weisberger. *Suffering Belief. Evil and Anglo-American Defence of Theism*. Peter Lang, New York, 1999.

H. Weyl. *Space, Time and Matter*. Dover, New York, 1922.

J.A. Wheeler. On Recognizing 'Law without Law'. *American Journal of Physics*, 51:pp.398–404, 1983.

W. Wickler and U. Seibt. *Das Prinzip Eigennutz*. München, 1987.

E.P. Wigner. *Symmetries and Reflections. Scientific Essays of Eugene P. Wigner, ed. by Moore, W.J. and Scriven, M.* Indiana Univ. Press, Bloomington, 1967.

E.P. Wigner. *Philosophical Reflections and Synthesis*. Springer, Berlin, 1995.

H. Wimmer and J. Perner. Beliefs about beliefs: Representation and constraining function of wrong beliefs in young children's understanding of deception. *Cognition*, 13:pp.103–128, 1983.

L. Wittgenstein. *Tractatus Logico Philosophicus, Schriften 1*. Suhrkamp, Frankfurt/M, 1960.

H.P. Yockey. A Calculation of the Probability of Spontaneous Biogenesis by Information Theory. *Journal of Theoretical Biology*, 67, 1977.

L. Zagzebski. Foreknowledge and Human Freedom. In Ph.L. Quinn and Ch. Taliaferro, editors, *A Companion to Philosophy of Religon*. Blackwell, Oxford, 1997.

List of definitions

Df 1.1. The state of affairs p belongs to God's Providence (abbreviated as $Prov(p)$) iff p belongs to God's plan ($PL(p)$) or p belongs to God's execution of his plan ($EC(p)$).
In symbols: $Prov(p) \leftrightarrow (PL(p) \vee EC(p))$ (2)

Df 1.2. The state of affairs p belongs to God's plan (abbreviated as $PL(p)$) iff p belongs to the state of affairs which describe the order in change and in the development of things (abbreviated as $Ord(p)$ i.e. their order) and p belongs to the states of affairs which describe the directedness of the things towards their ends (abbreviated as $TO(p)$ i.e. their teleological order).
In symbols: $PL(p) \leftrightarrow (Ord(p) \wedge TO(p))$ (2)

Df 1.3. $p \in Tg's(Prov) \leftrightarrow p \in Tg's(Pl) \vee p \in Tg's(EC)$ (4)

Df 1.4. $p \in Tg's(Pl) \leftrightarrow p \in T(Ord) \wedge p \in T(TO)$ (4)

Df 3.1. A thing or event e belongs to God's providence iff

a) e belongs to creation

b) e happens at some time

c) God has complete knowledge about e

d) God wills that e happens or he permits that e happens

e) God causes that e happens or he entrusts creatures to cause that e happens

f) God directs e towards a goal or he subordinates e under a goal or he entrusts creatures to direct (or subordinate) e towards (under) a goal. (14)

Df 5.1. $Comp(s) =_{df}$ the set of the parts of s. (32)

Df 5.2. $Env(s) =_{df}$ those things y (which are not parts of s) such that

(a) s or some part z of s acts causally on y or

(b) y acts causally on s or on some part z of s (32)

Df 5.3. $Struct(s) =_{df}$ those relations R (R can be two-place, ... , n-place) such that

(i) R are linkage or non-linkage relations

(ii) R hold internally among the parts of s

(iii) R hold externally between the parts of s on the one hand and the things of the environment on the other. (33)

Df 5.4. A thing or system has Ord_1 (or is in order-state$_1$) iff it has structure (Df 5.3). (36)

Df 5.5. A thing or system has Ord_2 (or is in order-state$_2$) iff it has a structure (Ord_1) and some of its internal or external relations obey special mathematical (arithmetical or geometrical) relations. (36)

Df 5.6. s_1 is a subsystem of s_2 ($Subs(s_1, s_2)$) iff

(i) $Comp(s_1) \subseteq Comp(s_2)$

(ii) $Env(s_2) \subseteq Env(s_1)$

(iii) $Struct(s_1) \subseteq Struct(s_2)$ (37)

Df 5.7. A thing or system s_1 has Ord_3 iff

(i) s_1 has Ord_2

(ii) There is an s_2 such that $Subs(s_1, s_2)$ or $Aggr(s_1) \neq Aggr(s_2)$ and $AtComp(s_1) = AtComp(s_2)$

(iii) s_1 is an open system

(iv) $Ent(s_1) \ll Ent(s_2)$ (37)

Df 5.8. B is a *process* of system s iff B is a transition from state $S_1(t_1)$ of s to $S_2(t_2)$ of s; where $t_2 > t_1$. (39)

Df 5.9. B is a *process of becoming* of system s iff

a) B is a process of s

b) s in state $S_2(t_2)$ (denoted by s_2) has Ord_3 relative to s in state $S_1(t_1)$ (denoted by s_1). (39)

Df 5.10. TO is a *teleological order* of a process B of system s iff

a) B is a process of becoming of a non-living system nls

b) the final state $S_g(t_g)$ of higher order of nls is a relative goal w.r.t. other states of lower order of nls from which it developed or to which it is compared. (41)

Df 5.11. A property or process C of a nls or a thing X of the environment of nls is a *primary value* for nls iff meeting C or X is necessary to increase order of nls relative to its environment. (42)

Df 5.12. A property or process C of nls or a thing X of the environment of nls is a *secondary value* for nls iff meeting C or X is necessary to keep or regain a certain level of order relative to its environment. (42)

Df 5.13. A primary or secondary value of nls is called a *basic value* of nls. (42)

Df 5.14. B is a *higher value* of nls iff

(a) B is a process of becoming of nls

(b) B is a basic value of nls (Df 5.13)

(c) B contributes to the continuation of the history of nls or B contributes to the conservation of nls and its basic values (42)

Df 5.15. X is a *relative goal* of a nls iff

(a) X is a state of $S(t)$ of a process B of becoming of nls

(b) B is a basic value or a higher value of nls (Df 5.14)

(c) X has a level of order such that

   (i) it is the highest level of order L_m relative to other states of B

   (ii) L_m is compatible with laws of nature, fundamental constants, and contingent initial conditions. (42)

Df 6.1. The state of affairs p is arithmetically random (algorithmically random) iff p is not ruled (decided) by any law of arithmetic (by any algorithm or computer program). (51)

Df 6.2. The state of affairs p is geometrically contingent iff p is dependent on the existence of rigid bodies, which are freely movable in space. (51)

Df 6.3. A law is naturally necessary iff it is invariant under a change of initial conditions. (52)

Df 6.4. p is not naturally necessary (or: empirically random or accidental) w.r.t. dynamical laws iff p can change without changing any (fundamental) dynamical law.

(53)

Df 6.5. Assume p to be an individual state, event or process. Then p is statistically random (statistically accidental) iff p can change without changing any (fundamental) statistical law. Similarly, one may define *thermodynamically random* and *quantumstatistically random.* (55)

Df 6.6. The Kolmogorov Complexity KC of the sequence $sq =_{df}$ the minimal length of a code cd such that cd can reproduce sq. (56)

Df 6.7. A sequence sq is G-random iff the minimal length of any code or algorithm cd, such that cd can reproduce sq, is not shorter than sq itself. (57)

Df 6.8. A thing or system s is random w.r.t. Ord_2 iff s does not have Ord_2 in the sense that its internal or external relations do not include special arithmetical or geometrical relations. (58)

Df 6.9. A thing or system s_1 is random w.r.t. both Ord_3 and system s_2 iff conditions (i)–(iii) of Df 5.7 are satisfied, condition (iv) of Df 5.7 is not satisfied. This means that s_1 does not have much lower entropy than s_2 (s_1 may have even higher entropy than s_2). (59)

Df 6.10. A process B from $S_1(t_1)$ to $S_2(t_2)$ of system s is random iff there is no entropy decrease but only an entropy increase from $S_1(t_1)$ to $S_2(t_2)$ w.r.t. the whole system s. In such a case there is no becoming from $S_1(t_1)$ to $S_2(t_2)$ w.r.t. the whole system s according to Df 5.9 (section 5.3.4). (59)

Df 6.11. A process B of system s is random w.r.t. teleological order iff either

(1) B is not a process of becoming of s or

(2) it is not the case that the final state $S_2(t_2)$ of higher order of s is a relative goal w.r.t. the initial state $S_1(t_1)$ of lower order of s from which it developed

(3) both (1) and (2) are the case. (60)

Df 7.1. ls is a living system (biosystem) iff the following conditions are satisfied:

(i) ls consists of chemical and biochemical subsystems (cf. Df 5.6, section 5.3.3) containing water, proteins, nucleic acids, carbon hydrates and fats where the parts of ls are in interaction and the border of ls is a flexible and semipermeable biomembrane

(ii) ls possesses metabolism

(iii) ls possesses self-regulation

(iv) ls possesses a genetic subsystem (DNA-structure) which controls propagation if available

(v) ls possesses adaption concerning some changes of the environment (of ls). (64)

Df 7.2. A property or process C of ls or a thing X of the environment of ls is a *primary good* (primary value) (or primary need) for ls iff meeting C or X is necessary for ls to stay alive in its environment. (66)

Df 7.3. A property or process C of ls or a thing X of the environment of ls is a *secondary good* (or secondary need or value) for ls iff meeting C or X is necessary to keep or regain health in the environment (including society) of ls. (66)

Df 7.4. A property or process C of ls or a thing X of the environment of ls is a *basic good* (basic value) for ls iff C or X is either a primary or a secondary good (value) for ls. (66)

Df 7.5. A *basic evil* of ls is a lack of a basic good for ls (i.e. is a lack of a primary or of a secondary good for ls).

Or in the terminology of the above definitions: A basic evil of ls is a property (state, process) C of ls or a thing X of its environment iff avoiding C or X is necessary for ls to stay alive or keep (regain) health in the environment of ls. (67)

Df 7.6. Assume C to be a property or a process of an eukaryotic compound ls (i.e. of an individual organism). Then C is *species-valuable* to ls iff possessing or having access to C contributes to the continuation of the species-history of ls or contributes to the conservation of the species of ls. Otherwise C is either neutral of harmful to ls. (69)

Df 7.7. Process C of ls possesses higher-level teleological order (HTO) iff

(a) C is a becoming of ls (Df 5.9, section 5.3.4)

(b) the final state $S_2(t_2)$ of higher order of ls is a relative goal w.r.t. the initial state $S_1(t_1)$ of lower order of ls, in the sense that

(i) $S_2(t_2)$ is closer to the basic good (value) of ls (Df 7.4) than $S_1(t_1)$ or

(ii) $S_2(t_2)$ is closer to the continuation of species-history of ls (Df 7.6) than $S_1(t_1)$. (69)

Df 7.8. X is relative goal of a ls iff

(a) X is a state $s(t)$ of a process C of becoming of ls

(b) C is a basic goal (value) of ls or C is a HTO of ls

(c) X has a level of order such that

(i) it is the highest level of order L_m relative to other states of C

(ii) L_m is compatible with laws of nature, fundamental constants and contingent initial conditions (69)

Df 7.9. A property (event, process) C is a *higher human value* iff C is the intentional object of a higher human desire which follows a series of judgements of the human intellect about that object. (70)

Df 7.10. X is a *legitimate higher human desire* of person b, living in society d iff X can be met in d

(a) without hindering the satisfaction of any basic good (value) of any member of d and without doing basic evil to any members of d

(b) without endangering the integrity of any valuable subsystem of d much less of d as a whole. (70)

Df 7.11. A property (event, process) C is a *legitimate* higher human value iff

(a) C is a higher human value and

(b) C is the intentional object of a legitimate higher human desire (70)

Df 7.12. $Actionspace(x) =_{df}$ those things y (which are not parts of x) such that x or some part z of x acts on y. (72)

Df 7.13. *Projected Action Space(x)* $=_{df}$ those things y (which are not part of x) such that x believes that x or a part z of x acts on y. (72)

Df 7.14. *Projected Teleological Order (x)*$=_{df}$ those things y (which are not part of x) such that x, when acting on y, believes that the things y are ordered in a relation of means and goals. (73)

Df 8.1. A biological sequence (specifically the DNA) is random iff it has no structure.

A consideration of the definition Df 5.3 of structure and of the following facts shows that the DNA is not random in the sense of Df 8.1. The facts are as follows:

a) It is a double strand helix.

b) It has 4 subunits with linkage-relations; special nucleotides (phosphate, ribose, GCTA).

c) It has geometric perfection: guarantees the right degree of stability: 5 hydrogen bonds with bond lengths at the energy maximum.

d) The rolled up ball or cluster is not arbitrary: it obeys laws of energy distribution.

e) It possesses metastability: it stabilizes its own structure. (80)

Df 8.2. Let p be the state or event of a mutation of the DNA of a living system ls. Then p is mutationally random iff the probability of p does not depend on the usefulness of p for ls. (85)

Df 8.3. Living system ls_2 is less random than living system $ls_1 =_{df}$

(i) ls_1 and ls_2 have structure (Df 5.3, section 5.3)

(ii) ls_2 can build new structures and stabilize them (if this offers any selection advantage) – more efficiently than ls_1

(iii) ls_2 can change its shape (if this offers any selection advantage) – more efficiently than ls_1

(iv) ls_2 can store and transmit (by self-reproduction) more information than ls_1

...

(v) $Ent(ls_2) < Ent(ls_1)$.
The number of microstates, which can realize ls_2 is much smaller than the number of microstates which can realize ls_1. (86)

Df 8.4. Let p be a state of affairs describing some condition like (1)–(5) above or some other condition concerning genetic frequencies. Then p is HW-random iff a change of p does not change the Hardy-Weinberg equilibrium (where 'HW' stands for 'Hardy-Weinberg'). (87)

Df 8.5. A process B of a living system ls is random iff

(1) it does not satisfy definition Df 7.4 or

(2) it does not satisfy definition Df 7.6, i.e. it neither contributes to the continuation of the species-history of ls nor to the conservation of the species of ls or

(3) it does not satisfy condition (b) of definition Df 7.7 for higher-level teleological order. (87)

Df 9.1. Two things or systems which are not human thoughts are compatible iff they coexist, i.e. iff both exist in reality. (96)

Df 9.2. Two properties (or events or processes) P_1 and P_2 are incompatible w.r.t. the thing or system x iff x possesses P_1 implies not: x possesses P_2; In other words: iff possessing P_1 precludes possessing P_2.That is iff: $\forall x(P_1 x \rightarrow \neg P_2 x)$ (97)

Df 9.3. Two properties (or events or processes) P_1 and P_2 are compatible w.r.t. the thing or system x iff they are not incompatible. That is iff $\exists x(P_1x \wedge P_2x)$. (97)

Df 9.4. Two predicates (or two concepts) C_1 and C_2 are incompatible iff their extensions exclude each other. (98)

Df 9.5. Two predicates (or two concepts) C_1 and C_2 are compatible iff their extensions do not exclude each other; i.e. iff their extensions have at least one common element: $\exists x(x \in Ext(C_1) \wedge x \in Ext(C_2))$. This condition may be written in PL1 also in this form: $\exists x(C_1x \wedge C_2x)$. (98)

Df 9.6. Two propositions p and q are compatible iff p does not contradict q and there is no consequence of p which contradicts any consequence of q and vice versa. (98)

Df 9.7. Two states of affairs are compatible iff the propositions which represent them are compatible. (98)

Df 9.8. Two human thoughts are compatible iff the propositions which represent them are compatible. (98)

Df 10.1. The proposition p (representing a state of affairs) belongs to the theorems of God's providence iff the following conditions (a)–(f) are satisfied:

(a) p belongs to the theorems concerning creation and to the theorems concerning the universe.

(b) p is the case at all times t (omnitemporal) or at some time(s); where t is a time relative to a reference system of the universe and where some specific t may be past, present or future relative to that reference system.

(c) God knows that p is the case

(d) God wills that p is the case or God permits that p is the case.

(e) God causes that p is the case or God entrusts creatures to cause that p is the case

(f) God directs p towards some goal or integrates p into a network of goals. (108)

Df 10.2. $p \in Tg's(Prov)$ iff

(a) $p \in T(CR)$ and $p \in T(U)$, where $T(U) \subset T(CR)$

(b) $(\forall t)p_t$ or $(\exists t)p_t$, where t is as above

(c) gKp

(d) $gWp \vee gPp$

(e) $gCp \vee gEtr(crCp)$

(f) $(\exists x)(Goal(x) \wedge gDir(p/x)) \vee (\exists y)(NGoal(y) \wedge gInt(p/y))$ (109)

Df 11.1.
$p \in T(U) \leftrightarrow p \in T\text{-}Law(U) \vee p \in T\text{-}Const(U) \vee p \in T\text{-}State(U) \vee p \in T\text{-}Init(U) \vee p \in T\text{-}Event(U)$

$p \in T\text{-}Law(U)$ ... p belongs to the law-theorems of U

$p \in T\text{-}Const(U)$ ... p belongs to the theorems about the value of fundamental constants of U

$p \in T\text{-}State(U)$ ... p belongs to the theorems describing states of U

$p \in T\text{-}Init(U)$ ... p belongs to the theorems describing initial conditions of U

$p \in T\text{-}Event(U)$ ... p belongs to the theorems describing events or processes of U. (121)

Df 12.1. $gPp \leftrightarrow \neg gW\neg p$

1. $\neg gPp \rightarrow gW\neg p$ from Df 12.1
2. $gWp \rightarrow p$ God's will is always fulfilled (cf. 12.3.3)

3. $gW\neg p \rightarrow \neg p$ from 2. $\neg p/p$

4. p fact (established in chs. 4.,5.,7.)

5. $\neg gW\neg p$ from 1. and 4. by M.T.

6. gPp from 5. and 1. (131)

Df 13.1. 0-1 selection (Env, ls) = those interactions between ls and $Env(ls)$ which have a causal influence on the continuation of the existence of ls in relation to $Env(ls)$. (146)

Df 13.2. Let A(POP) be the aggregate (not set) of a population POP of differently adapted living systems (ls) of the same species with shared environment (Env). Further let N be the set of descendants of the ls of A(POP). Then: POP-selection = those interactions between the ls of A(POP) and their $Env(ls)$ which lead to a sorting (grading) of the descendants of the ls of A(POP), or in other words to a reduction of POP to a part of it. (146)

Df 13.3. D is a *development* of living system ls iff

(a) D is a process of becoming of ls (Df 5.9) and

(b) D is not directly or exclusively produced by the environment $Env(ls)$ of ls. (147)

Df 13.4. Like Df 13.3 where "living system ls" is replaced by "system s". (148)

Df 13.5. E is an *evolution* of living system ls iff

(a) E is a development of ls (Df 13.3) and

(b) either

  (i) there is a species A and A' such that ls belongs to species A at t_1 and to a variation A' of species A at t_2 or

  (ii) there is a species A and B such that ls belongs to species A at t_1 and to species B at t_2 (149)

Df 13.6. E is a POP-*evolution* of a population (POP) of different adapted living systems ls of the same species A in the same environment $Env(ls)$ iff

(a) E is a development of all ls belonging to POP

(b) there is a 0-1 selection (Df 13.1) of all ls belonging to POP

(c) there is a POP-selection (Df 13.2) of all ls belonging to POP

(d) there is an evolution (Df 13.5) of some of the ls belonging to POP (149)

Df 13.7. Property P of ls is *hereditary* iff ls possesses P in state $S_o(t_o)$ of ls (154)

Df 13.8. Property Q of ls is *non-hereditary* iff

(a) ls does not possess Q in state $S_o(t_o)$ of ls

(b) ls possesses Q in some state $S_1(t_1)$ of ls where $t_1 > t_o$. (154)

Df 13.9. Let Q be a *non-hereditary* property of ls and $S_o(t_o)$ be the state of the origin of ls. Then: Property Q of ls is *hereditarily dependent* iff

(a) ls possesses Q in some state $S_1(t_1)$, where $t_1 > t_o$.

(b) Q is the result of a process of development (Df 13.3) where the initial state in the process of becoming is the state of origin of the living system (154)

Df 13.10. Property Q is an *only-acquired* property of ls iff ls possesses Q at some $t_1 > t_o$ (i.e. after the state of the origin of ls) and Q is neither *hereditary* nor *hereditarily dependent*. (154)

Df 13.11. Property Q is an *acquired* property of ls iff

(a) ls possesses Q in some state $S_2(t_2)$ where $t_2 > t_1 > t_o$

(b) Q is the result of a process of development with the initial state $S_1(t_1)$ when ls possesses property P

(c) P is *hereditarily dependent* (155)

Df 14.1. A biological process B of ls is teleological (or possesses teleological order) iff

(a) B supports life or health + life of ls or a society of ls or

(b) B contributes to the continuation of the species-history of ls or to the conservation of the species of ls. (177)

Df 14.2. A non-biological process C is teleological (or possesses teleological order) iff

(a) C is a process of becoming (Df 5.9)

(b) the final state of C is a relative goal w.r.t. its initial state (Df 5.10) (178)

Df 14.3. A non-living system is teleological (or possesses teleological order) iff some of its processes are teleological (possess teleological order) according to definition Df 14.2. (178)

Df 14.4. A living system ls is integrated into a network of goals iff

(a) there is some teleological process Tl of ls

(b) there is some extrinsic goal Gl outside ls such that Tl contributes to the realization of Gl

(c) Gl is interrelated to other extrinsic goals outside ls (180)

Df 14.5. A non-living system nls is integrated into a network of goals iff

(a) there is some teleological process or property p of nls

(b) there is some goal Gl outside nls such that p contributes to the realization of Gl

(c) Gl is interrelated to other extrinsic goals outside nls. (184)

Df 14.6. p can be integrated into a network of goals iff

(a) p represents a state of affairs in this world (universe)

(b) p is true

(c) p is the conclusion of a *teleological explanation* (185)

Df 15.1. A physical, chemical, biological or psychological system with states $S_i(t_i)$ obeying a dynamical law L is *deterministic* (det_1) iff the following three conditions are satisfied:

(a) For any (future) state $S_2(t_2), t_2 > t_0$, there is a (past) state $S_1(t_1), t_1 < t_0$, such that from the proposition describing $S_1(t_1)$ plus the law of nature L (in the form of a differential equation) the proposition describing $S_2(t_2)$ is derivable.

(b) For any (past) state $S_1(t_1), t_1 < t_0$, there is a future state $S_2(t_2), t_2 > t_0$, such that from the proposition describing $S_2(t_2)$ plus the law of nature L (in the form of a differential equation) the proposition describing $S_1(t_1)$ is derivable.

(c) The dynamical law is understood in such a way that it satisfies conditions D1, D2 and D4 (in some cases also D3) of ch. 4. (203)

Df 15.2. *Determinism* (Det_1) is the doctrine that a certain physical, chemical, biological or psychological system (or in general: any system, the whole universe) is deterministic according to Df 15.1. Df 15.2 expresses the global determinism described by Laplace in ch.2 of his Essai philosophique sur les probabilités of 1814. Laplace assumed (wrongly) that D4 is always satisfied. (203)

Df 15.3. An event (or state) e is *determined* iff e is a later state $S_2(t_2)$ of a physical, chemical, biological or psychological system which is a definite function of earlier states $S_i(t_i)$ of that system (according to Df 15.1). (204)

Df 15.4. A physical, chemical, biological or psychological system is *deterministic* (det_2) iff the same initial (or past) states lead with the same dynamical law to the same successor (or future) states. (204)

Df 15.5. *Determinism* (Det_2) is the doctrine that a certain physical, chemical or biological system (or in general any system, also the whole universe) is deterministic (det_2) according to Df 15.4. (204)

Df 15.6. A physical, chemical, biological or psychological system is *indeterministic* ($indet_1$) iff it satisfies the conditions S1, S2, S3 and S4 of ch.4. (205)

Df 15.7. An event or state e is *undetermined* iff e is a later state $S_2(t_2)$ of a physical (chemical, biological or psychological) system which is not a definite function of earlier states $S_i(t_i)$ of that system. (205)

Df 15.8. *Indeterminism* ($Indet_1$) is the doctrine that a certain physical, chemical, biological or psychological system (or in general any system, also the whole universe) is indeterministic ($indet_1$) according to definition Df 15.6. (205)

Df 15.9. An event or state e is *undetermined* ($indet_2$) iff e is not strictly predictable, i.e. with probability = 1, but only with a lower degree of probability. (205)

Df 15.10. $FP(x, d)$ iff there is no serious restriction (as for example illness) for x in the range d of bodily capacity and actual performance. (217)

Df 15.11. $FPs(x, d)$ iff there is no serious restriction (as for example mental illness) for x in the range d of psychic (mental) capacity and actual performance. (217)

Df 15.12. $CPe(x, d)$ iff CPe is a restriction or constraint of the physical (bodily) capacity or of the respective actual performance of x in d, caused by the environment of x and contrary to the inclination of x in d. (217)

Df 15.13. $CPi(x, d)$ iff CPi is a restriction or constraint of the physical (bodily) capacity or of the respective actual performance of x in d, caused by bodily defects of x and contrary to the inclination of x in d. (217)

Df 15.14. $Cpse(x, d)$ iff $Cpse$ is a restriction or constraint of the psychic (mental) capacity or of the respective actual performance of x in d, caused by the environment of x and contrary to the inclination of x in d. (217)

Df 15.15. $CPsi(x, d)$ iff $CPsi$ is a restriction or constraint of the psychic (mental) capacity or of the respective actual performance of x in d, caused by mental defects of x and contrary to the inclination of x in d. (218)

Df 15.16. $FW(x, p, d)$ iff the following conditions are satisfied:

(1)

- (1a) $FPs(x, d)$
- (1b) Not: $CPse(x, d)$ and not: $CPsi(x, d)$

(2)

- (2a) $xCanWp$
- (2b) Both $xCanW\neg p$ and $xCan\neg Wp$ hold, provided that the state of affairs p is not the realization of:
  - (i) a basic good (value) (cf. Df 7.4) or
  - (ii) the state of ultimate happiness

(3) If the state of affairs p is a goal for x then: $xCanWp$ and $xCanRealize\,p$

(4) If p is a goal for x and if there are means $q_1 \ldots q_n$ which support the realization of p, then for some q_i: $xCanWq_i$ and $xCanRealize\,q_i$

(5) If p is forbidden or if p is permitted (or obligatory) then: $xCanWp$ and $xCanRealize\,p$

(6) If xWp and $xRealizes\,p$, then x causes that p (is the case) and x knows that x causes that p

(7) The (complex) state of affairs (xWp and $xRealizes\,p$) at t is not a definite function of an earlier state of affairs at $t < t_o$ (218)

Df 15.17. $FWD(x, p, d)$ iff

(1) $FW(x, p, d)$

(2) x uses deliberation and planning with the help of reason. This includes:

  (i) Council about goals

  (ii) Council about the means for reaching the respective goal

  (iii) Council about moral goodness or badness of means and goals

(3) x knows that x has responsibility for *his (her)* actions and decisions; x knows that – especially in connection with the evidence x has about the fact that the decision was in *his (her)* power – that it was *he (she)* who caused the action.

(223)

Df 16.1. An evil $E1$ is some lack, defect, absence, privation or deficit of some particular good, which ought to be present in a subject or organism. (241)

Df 16.2. An evil $E2$ is some lack, defect, absence, privation or deficit which is acceptable to be absent in order to achieve another higher good. (241)

Df 16.3. An evil $E3$ is a thing or organism or state or event which is a cause of an evil $E1$. (241)

Df 16.4. A property or state or process (event) C of ls or a thing X of the environment of ls is a *primary evil* for ls iff avoiding C or X is necessary for ls to stay alive in its environment (including society). (247)

Df 16.5. A property or state or process (event) C of ls or a thing X of the environment of ls is a *secondary evil* for ls iff avoiding C or X is necessary for ls to keep or regain health in the environment (including society) of ls (247)

Df 16.6. A property or state or process (event) C of ls or a thing X of the environment of ls is a *basic evil* for ls iff C or X is either a primary or a secondary evil for ls. (247)

Df 16.7. Let Y be a property or state or process (event) of ls or a thing belonging to the environment of ls. Then Y is a *necessary evil* iff

(1) Y is an evil in the sense of $E2$ or $E3$

(2) Y is not a *basic evil* or else it is a *basic evil* which contributes to avoiding a greater *basic evil*

(3) Y is not a *moral evil* (cf. Df 16.12, Df 16.13)

(4) Y is necessary for achieving or protecting a basic good (cf. Df 7.4) (248)

Df 16.8. Let Y be a property or state or process (event) or a thing belonging to the environment of some human person x. Then Y is a *higher evil* of x iff Y is the intentional object of an action of x which is an action of fear or of tending away which follows (at least one, but usually a series of) judgments of the human intellect of x about that object. (248)

Df 16.9. Higher evils are legitimate (illegitimate) iff they are objects (things) or events of legitimate (illegitimate) desires or wants. (249)

Df 16.10. Legitimate (permitted) desire (want): X is a *legitimate desire* (want) of a human person x in circumstance c and living in society d iff X can be met in d

(1) without hindering the satisfaction of any basic good or need of any member of d and without doing basic evil to any of the members of d

(2) without endangering the integrity of any valuable subsystem of d much less that of d as a whole (249)

Df 16.11. Illegitimate (non-permitted) desire (want): X is an *illegitimate desire* (want) of human person x in circumstance c and living in society d iff X does not satisfy conditions (1) and (2) of Df 16.10. (249)

Df 16.12. Moral Evil as an Action (Sin): Let Y be a state or process (event). Then Y is a moral evil as an action (sin) iff Y is a free voluntary action of commission (omission) which is forbidden (obligatory) by

(1) the promulgated ethical (moral) standards of some human society or

(2) the *Human Rights* which are based on an international agreement of many societies w.r.t. ethical (moral) standards

(3) the law of God or

(4) a combination of these three (250)

Df 16.13. Moral Evil as a Disposition or Habit (Vice): Let Y be a state or property. Then Y is a moral evil as a disposition or habit (vice) iff Y is a trait of character that disposes the owner to commit a sin (moral evil as an action). (251)

List of theorems

T 6.3. *There is chance and randomness in things (systems) in the sense that they do not possess Ord_2 or that they do not possess Ord_3 or that they have no processes of* becoming *(cf. 6.3.6).* (60)

T 6.4. *There is chance and randomness in things (systems) in the sense that some of their processes do not possess teleological order (cf. 6.3.7).* (60)

T 7.1. *All living systems possess teleological order (cf. 7.3.2).* (74)

T 7.2. *All living systems possess basic goods or values (cf. 7.3.3).* (74)

T 7.3. *All living systems possess higher-level teleological order and relative goals (cf. 7.3.5).* (74)

T 8.1. *The DNA-sequence is not random in the sense that it has no structure. On the contrary it has many very sophisticated structural features (cf. 8.3.1).* (89)

T 8.2. *The so-called "chance hypothesis" (cf. 8.3.2) is not a possible scientific explanation for the emergence of life or of the DNA.* (90)

T 8.3. *Mutation is random concerning the* mutation-rate *and concerning its usefulness for the ls, but it is not random in many other aspects (cf. 8.3.3).* (90)

T 8.4. *There may be relative randomness of high-level ls in the sense that ls_1 is more random than ls_2, but never in an absolute sense (cf. 8.3.4).* (90)

T 8.5. *Every ls has also several properties or processes, which are random in the sense that they are neither basic goods, nor valuable for the conservation and continuation of the species, nor possessing higher-level teleological order.* (90)

T 9.1. *God's providence is compatible with any kind of order which is realized in the universe. This is true for different types of compatibility defined as coexistence, non-exclusion of properties or predicates, non-contradiction of propositions or states of affairs.* (102)

T 9.2. *God's providence is compatible with any kind of chance which is realized in the universe. This holds for different types of compatibility defined as coexistence, non-exclusion of properties or predicates, non-contradicting propositions or states of affairs.* (103)

T 10.1. *Everything that happens comes under God's providence.* (114)

T 10.2. *Everything that happens in creation (in the universe) belongs to God's providence.* (114)

T 10.3. *Everything that happens omnitemporally and everything that happens at some time (where time is the time of a reference system of our universe) belongs to God's providence.* (114)

T 11.1. *Everything that comes under God's providence is known by God.* (126)

T 11.2. *Since the universe belongs to God's providence, everything about the Universe – its laws, constants, states, initial conditions, events – is known by God.* (126)

T 11.3. *Since the universe belongs to God's providence, everything that happens in the universe – be it past, present or future (relative to some reference system of the universe) – is known by God.* (126)

T 12.1. *Everything that comes under God's providence is either willed or permitted by God.* (136)

T 12.2. *God wills and permits order and teleological order in the universe.* (136)

T 12.3. *God wills and permits chance and randomness in the universe.* (136)

T 12.4. *God is neither all-willing nor all-causing.* (136)

T 12.5. *God's will is always fulfilled.* (136)

T 12.6. *For every state of affairs of the universe it holds: God wills or permits it.* (136)

T 12.7. *For every occurring immoral human action of free will it holds: God neither wills that it does nor that it does not occur; God merely permits its occurrence (see 12.4.1 below).* (137)

T 13.1. *Not everything belonging to the universe including the universe itself can be caused by creatures, i.e. by things belonging to the universe.* (164)

T 13.2. *The question whether the universe has a finite age or is everlasting is independent of the question whether it has a cause.* (164)

T 13.3. *A universe finite in time is scientifically confirmed to a greater extent (cosmic background radiation, Standard Big Bang Theory) than an everlasting one (13.4.3).* (164)

T 13.4. *The universe cannot contain its own cause as a singularity (13.4.4).* (164)

T 13.5. *The universe cannot be self-contained in the sense of containing its intelligent observer or its intelligent cause (13.4.4).* (165)

T 13.6. *God is needed as a cause and explanation of the fundamental laws of nature, of the fundamental constants of nature of the space time (3+1) dimension and of the extremely precise fine tuning and coincidences.* (165)

T 13.7. *God is needed as a cause and explanation for the creation of creatures which have the ability to contribute to the development of the universe.* (165)

T 14.1. *Every living system ls is teleological, although not every process of a ls is teleological. (14.3.1)* (195)

T 14.2. *Every non-living system nls is teleological in the weaker sense that nls possesses some process (or property) of teleological order; even though not every non-biological (non-living) process is teleological (14.3.2)* (195)

T 14.3. *All living systems can be integrated into a network of goals extrinsic to the living system: some in a stronger sense, some others in a weaker sense (14.3.3).* (195)

T 14.4. *All non-living systems can be integrated into a network of goals extrinsic to the non-living system either directly and locally or indirectly and globally (14.3.4).* (195)

T 14.5. *It seems very likely that all obtaining states of affairs can be integrated into a network of goals if not locally than globally (14.3.5). The reasons for Theorem 14.5 are given in 14.3.7.* (195)

T 15.1. *The same initial (or past) states lead with the same dynamical law to the same successor (or future) states.* (203)

T 15.2. *There are several physical, chemical, biological or psychological systems which are deterministic (Df 15.1).* (231)

T 15.3. *There are several physical, chemical, biological or psychological systems which are indeterministic. (Df 15.6)* (231)

T 15.4. *Both determined and undetermined events and processes can occur in one and the same physical, chemical, biological or psychological system. Since most such systems are usually mixed and neither purely deterministic nor purely indeterministic.* (231)

T 15.5. *Determinism, causality and predictability do not necessarily go together; see the confusions in 15.3.2.* (231)

T 15.6. Neuronal Determinism *is untenable since:*

(i) *it neglects a great part of modern physics*

(ii) *it is inconsistent with the quantum mechanical basis of the molecular structure of the brain*

(iii) *it is incompatible with the interaction of electromagnetic radiation, with electron transport, with proton transfer through tunneling, all occurring in the brain, since none of them obey exclusively dynamical deterministic laws.* (231)

T 15.7. *Free will of human persons presupposes that there is no serious restriction (for example illness) for the person – with the exception of being only bodily handicapped – in both his/her bodily capacity and actual performance and psychic (mental) capacity and actual performance.* (231)

T 15.8. *There is* free will *of human persons in the sense of Df 15.16.* (231)

T 15.9. *There is* free will decision *of human persons in the sense of Df 15.17.* (232)

T 15.10. *Man's* free will *and* free will decision *are compatible with nature's order and God's providence and with the following components of the latter: with his knowledge, with his permission, with his or creatures' causation, with his integration of them into a network of goals.* (232)

List of names

List of subjects